The Intelligence Loop

A New Model for Growth and How We Get Smarter Together

Robin D. Green

INTELLIGENCE LOOP LLC
Austin | Nashville | New York

Cover design by Robin and René Green

ISBN 979-8-234-13080-8 (Paperback)
ISBN 979-8-234-06091-4 (e-book)

Intelligence Loop LLC
Austin, Texas
www.robindgreen.com

The Intelligence Loop

"The future doesn't belong to organizations with the most powerful machines. It will belong to the most collaborative humans."

Robin Green

Table of Contents

Introduction

Artificial intelligence is not replacing humanity. It's redefining it. This is because of one simple truth: even with the largest chip arrays and abundant power sources, at its core AI remains little more than an elaborate probability calculator requiring original query to perform.

In simpler language, AI can do nothing without human consciousness.

That truth sat at the back of my mind through a career spent in enterprise technology, through rooms where multi-million-dollar platform decisions were made, through conversations with CMOs and CDOs who were simultaneously excited and terrified by what they were being asked to deploy.

I've watched organizations spend fortunes on AI infrastructure and then struggle to explain what they got for it. I've watched others, with less capital and fewer resources, move faster and more confidently because they had figured out the one thing the technology could not provide on its own: purpose.

That gap – between what AI can compute and what humans must decide – is the central subject of this book.

Across virtually every industry and segment of society, AI is reshaping how we create, connect, and grow. Amidst the disruption lies an extraordinary opportunity: to build a future where technology extends human capability rather than replaces it. The organizations and individuals who understand this, who choose deliberate collaboration over passive automation, will define the next decade. Those who mistake the tool for the strategy will spend years recovering from the confusion.

In The Intelligence Loop, we explore the intersection of technology and humanity with clarity, purpose, and optimism. Through data, real-world examples, and human stories, we reveal how AI is reshaping not only business strategy but the very nature of creativity and leadership. The book is structured across eight chapters, supported by over 100 meticulously researched case studies. It begins with the technological transformation of markets, moves through the redefinition of work, creativity, leadership, ethics, and purpose, and culminates in a call to co-create a future built on collaboration rather than competition.

This is not a book about algorithms or prompt engineering. It's a book about us: our values, our imagination, and our shared destiny with the intelligent systems we have created. The central truth is simple but important: the future will not belong to the smartest bots and most clever prompts, but to the most collaborative humans.

The Core Argument

Stripped from the hype, AI is a technology of extraordinary sophistication. It can synthesize patterns from vast datasets, generate plausible text, accelerate research, and surface insights that no single human could find alone. But it cannot initiate a thought without a human query. It cannot decide what matters without human values to guide it. It cannot lead, inspire, or take moral responsibility. Every meaningful thing AI accomplishes begins with – and must remain accountable to – a human being.

That's not a limitation to be engineered away. It's the architecture of collaboration.

The distinction matters more than it might appear at first glance. When we frame AI as a replacement technology, we set up a zero-sum competition – one in which every advance for the machine registers as a loss for the human. That framing generates fear, resistance, and defensive behavior in organizations. It produces the kinds of decisions that create the worst outcomes: either organizations resist AI adoption entirely, protecting legacy processes at the cost of competitive relevance, or they adopt it indiscriminately, eliminating the human judgment and oversight that makes AI applications trustworthy and durable.

When we frame AI as a collaboration technology – as a genuinely new kind of partner that expands what human beings can do – something different becomes possible. Organizations start asking better questions. Not "how many roles can we eliminate?" but "what would our people accomplish if machines handled everything routine?" Not "how do we keep humans out of the loop?" but "where in this process is human judgment irreplaceable, and how do we make sure it's there?"

That question isn't hypothetical anymore. It's playing out on public streets, in real time, with billion-dollar consequences.

Waymo, the Alphabet-owned robotaxi company, has logged well over 100 million fully autonomous miles. By most safety measures, its vehicles outperform human drivers. In 2025, the company delivered 14 million trips. By early 2026, it was running 500,000 paid rides a week across ten American cities. By any reasonable definition, this is AI working.

And then December 20, 2025 arrived.

A substation fire knocked out power to roughly 130,000 San Francisco customers. Traffic lights went dark across the city.

Waymo's vehicles are programmed to treat a dead signal as a four-way stop, exactly what human drivers are taught to do. But the system also routes edge-case decisions, situations the vehicle isn't certain how to handle, to a team of remote human supervisors for confirmation before proceeding. Under normal conditions, that works. The December blackout wasn't normal conditions. With hundreds of intersections going dark simultaneously, confirmation requests flooded the human support pipeline all at once. The team couldn't keep up.

So, the cars did the only thing they could: they waited. Videos spread quickly of Waymo vehicles sitting motionless in busy intersections, hazard lights blinking, blocking buses and cross traffic, while human-driven cars navigated around them. San Francisco's District 5 Supervisor called for a formal hearing. Waymo paused service citywide.

The problem, as MIT robotics professor emeritus Rodney Brooks explained to the San Francisco Standard that week, wasn't a flaw in the AI. It was an edge case: something the engineers hadn't fully anticipated at that scale. "You think you have a bunch of problems solved," Brooks said, "and then there's an edge case, something you hadn't considered."

Less than five months later, on April 20, 2026, an unoccupied Waymo in San Antonio detected standing floodwater on a roadway and drove in anyway, eventually being swept into Salado Creek. There were no passengers and no injuries. But within ten days, Waymo had filed a voluntary recall with the National Highway Traffic Safety Administration covering 3,791 vehicles, its entire active fleet.

Waymo's response to both incidents followed the same pattern: pause, involve humans in the assessment, update the software, and refine the system for what it had just learned. That's not a public relations strategy. It's an operating model. The company has built human oversight directly into how its vehicles function, not as a fallback when things go wrong, but as a designed feature of a system that knows what it doesn't know.

There's a reason Waymo keeps humans in the loop. The AI handles the expected. The humans handle the rest. Every organization navigating AI adoption will eventually arrive at the same structural question, and the answer will define what kind of organization it becomes.

Those questions lead to very different organizations. And the evidence is accumulating that they lead to better-performing ones.

Research by Accenture found that organizations investing in AI-human collaboration saw significantly higher revenue growth and actually expanded their workforces, while those pursuing automation-for-automation's-sake didn't enjoy the same benefits. MIT's Center for Collective Intelligence found that the most impactful applications of AI aren't the ones that replace human judgment, but the ones that combine AI's processing speed and pattern recognition with human creativity and contextual understanding in iterative, generative loops. The firms getting the most from AI aren't the ones deploying it most aggressively. They're the ones deploying it most thoughtfully.

Why Now?

Every era of technological change feels urgent to the people living through it, and we should be appropriately skeptical of our own tendency to declare the present moment uniquely consequential. But there are specific characteristics of the current AI wave that genuinely do make it different from what came before – and that make the quality of our thinking about it unusually important.

The first is speed of adoption. The Industrial Revolution took decades to move from invention to broad economic impact. The internet took roughly a generation. Generative AI went from laboratory curiosity to widespread enterprise deployment in less than three years. That compression doesn't give individuals, organizations, or societies time to adapt organically. The usual mechanisms of adjustment – workforce retraining, regulatory frameworks, cultural norms about appropriate use – are running years behind the technology itself. The gap between what AI can do and what we've figured out it should do is wide, and it's where most of the risk lives.

The second is breadth of application. Previous waves of automation affected specific sectors and specific types of work – manufacturing qualitatively different. It touches knowledge work across virtually every domain: legal analysis, medical diagnosis, financial modeling, creative production, strategic planning. There is almost no professional field that isn't being asked to reconsider what it does and why. That universality means the workforce questions this technology raises aren't sector-specific disruptions. They're civilizational ones.

The third is the proximity to what makes us human. When machines replaced physical labor, no identity crises emerged over what made human beings special – we still had our minds. When machines replaced routine cognitive labor, we still had creativity and judgment. Now machines are generating language, producing art, composing music, and offering analysis that can be difficult to distinguish from expert human work. That proximity to the distinctly human domains of thought and expression creates a different kind of anxiety – one that isn't really about job security, even when it presents as such. It's about meaning. And meaning is harder to reassign than a job title.

We face an inflection point that doesn't announce itself gently. In the span of three years, AI moved from curiosity to consequence. Boards of directors who had never said the word "algorithm" are now approving nine-figure AI infrastructure budgets. Universities are banning tools their graduates will be required to use on their first day of work. Workers who spent careers building expertise are watching entry-level roles disappear, not through layoffs, but through subtle hiring freezes as organizations discover AI can handle the intake before a human ever touches it.

Gallup polling released in 2026 found that Gen Z excitement about AI dropped fourteen points in a single year. Hopefulness fell nine points. Anger rose nine. And the data point that matters most: daily AI users showed the biggest drops in sentiment of all. The more they engage with the technology, the worse they feel about it.

This is not a technology problem. It's a leadership failure. The cultural dialogue around AI is currently dominated by two voices: the cheerleaders who promise a frictionless future of abundance and the "doomers" who warn of civilizational collapse. Both camps have audiences. Neither is particularly useful to someone who has to show up Monday morning and figure out what to do with their team, their organization, and their career.

This book is written for that person.

The urgency is not abstract. The decisions being made right now – about how AI is adopted, who benefits, what work is preserved, what values are encoded, and who holds the judgment that guides all of it – will compound for decades. The organizations and leaders who get this right in the next three years will set the terms for everyone who follows. Those who get it wrong will create the fragile, costly implementations that someone else will spend years untangling.

The window for thoughtful action is open. It won't stay open indefinitely.

What You'll Find Here

The Intelligence Loop is organized around a central journey. We begin with the great historical shift underway – the speed and scale of AI's arrival – and what it's actually changing about the economics of growth. We move through the transformation of organizations, examining how the companies that thrive are not automating their people but augmenting them. We explore what it means to retain a human edge when machines can replicate so many of our competencies. And we arrive at the harder questions of ethics, leadership, and purpose that technology forces us to confront.

Throughout, I've drawn on research from leading institutions, conversations with practitioners, and a career's worth of watching what actually happens when technology meets human behavior at scale. I've been rigorous about the evidence and honest about the uncertainty. Where case studies illustrate a principle, I've noted whether they're drawn from documented events or are composites designed to represent patterns I've observed repeatedly across organizations and industries.

My background is in data and technology. Most recently I spent ten years in advertising and marketing – an industry sitting at the precise intersection of data and human emotion, efficiency and creativity, measurement and meaning. If there is any field feeling the pressure of AI most directly, and learning to navigate its consequences most thoughtfully, it's ours.

The advertising industry evolved from understanding how human beings think and feel, and on using that understanding to create work that moves people. AI can now replicate many of the technical executions of that work. It cannot replicate the understanding that makes the work worth doing.

Navigating that distinction – knowing which parts to delegate and which parts to protect – is a daily challenge in our industry, and one I've been living for several years.

I write from that vantage point, but the questions this book addresses reach far beyond any single industry. Every organization that serves human beings, which is all of them, is confronting some version of the same fundamental question: how do we use technology that can do more and more of what we once did ourselves, without losing the humanity that made what we did valuable in the first place?

A Word About Humility

I want to be direct about something before we go further: I don't have all the answers. Neither does anyone else.

The honest truth about AI is that we're in a period of genuine uncertainty. The technology is moving faster than our ability to study its effects. The economic models for how it will reshape labor markets are contested. The ethical frameworks for governing its use are still being built. The cultural norms about what's appropriate and what's not are forming in real time, messily and unevenly across different industries and geographies.

Anyone writing a book like this one in this moment faces a choice: pretend to more certainty than the evidence supports or acknowledge the uncertainty and try to be useful anyway. I've chosen the second path, which means you'll find some sections of this book where I offer frameworks and principles rather than prescriptions, and where I'm candid about what we don't yet know.

What I'm confident about is this: the questions matter. The way an organization frames its relationship to AI – as a threat to be managed, a cost to be reduced, a tool to be deployed, or a collaborator to be engaged – informs the kind of organization it becomes and the kind of value it creates. Getting that framing right is not a technical question. It's a leadership question. And leadership questions are exactly what I've spent twenty-plus years thinking about.

The Advertising Industry as a Laboratory

Let me spend a moment on an industry with which I'm intimately familiar as it's where I spent the past ten years of my career. Advertising offers a useful lens for the broader themes of this book, and was one of the first mass adopters in the AI transformation in ways that have produced both genuinely instructive successes and genuinely instructive failures.

Advertising is, at its core, the business of human attention. It exists to move people: to create connections between ideas and emotions, between products and values, between brands and the communities they serve. The measure of good advertising is not based on the purely technical. It's always anchored in human experience: Does this reach someone? Does it move them? Does it speak to something real?

For much of the 20th century, advertising operated much like an art form practiced with craft, intuition, and a fair amount of educated guessing. Research existed, but inevitably slow, expensive, and often captured stated preferences rather than actual behavior. The gap between what people said they would do and what they actually did became a constant source of frustration for anyone trying to understand audiences at scale.

Digital technology changed that in the 2000s and 2010s by making behavior observable. Every click, every share, every pause and scroll became data. For the first time, advertisers could see what their audiences actually did rather than what they said they would do. This provided genuine insight. Yet, in retrospect, technology created a new set of problems the industry is still working through.

The problem: behavioral data, while more reliable than stated preference data, turned out to be a seductive but partial lens. It told you what people did, but it had very little to say about why. It told you which creative executions drove clicks, but it couldn't tell you whether those clicks built genuine brand affinity or simply exploiting momentary curiosity. It told you which targeting parameters correlated with conversions, but it couldn't tell you whether the experience it optimized toward created genuine value to the people having it.

AI amplifies both the power and the limitations of this behavioral focus. The optimization systems now governing most digital advertising can process behavioral signals at a scale and speed no human team could match. They can personalize messaging to an extraordinary degree, reaching specific individuals with content calibrated to their demonstrated preferences at precisely the moment they're most receptive to it.

They can also optimize for things that look like value but aren't – engagement metrics that drive clicks without building trust; personalization so precise it crosses into the uncanny and creates discomfort rather than connection; targeting so narrow it reinforces filter bubbles rather than expanding perspectives.

Balancing these tensions – using AI's extraordinary power to understand and reach audiences while preserving the human qualities that make the work worth doing and the relationships worth having – is the daily challenge of modern marketing leadership. It's a microcosm of the broader challenge this book addresses.

The failures are instructive. When campaigns generated by AI systems without adequate human creative judgment land poorly – when they feel soulless, tone-deaf, or disconnected from genuine human experience – the damage is real and sometimes difficult to repair. The audience hasn't just failed to respond. They've actively formed a negative impression that colors future encounters with the brand. The efficiency logic that justified the AI-generated approach turns out to have been false economy.

The successes are equally instructive. When AI is used to understand audiences more deeply – to surface insights about what matters to people, what concerns them, what they're hoping for – and when those insights are given to human creative teams who have the skill and the latitude to translate them into genuinely resonant work, the results can be extraordinary. The combination of machine-depth understanding and human creative expression produces work that neither could produce alone.

That's the laboratory lesson. And I believe it generalizes well beyond advertising and marketing to every domain where organizations are figuring out how to work alongside intelligent machines.

In full disclosure

This book was not written by AI. The thoughts, voice, insights, phrasing, and overall thesis are entirely the creation of me – Robin D. Green – based on a career lived in technology enablement and deep experience working with industry professionals on driving AI adoption.

The Intelligence Loop was finished with significant AI assistance. Not as a shortcut, but as a method and a demonstration of the book's thesis. I run a multi-agent AI operating system built on OpenClaw. My research agents handle a substantial portion of the deep research, verification, and synthesis work: cross-referencing market data, drafting and revising at a speed no single author could match alone. *Syn* is the name of my primary agent utilizing Sonnet, Claude Opus, and Haiku with additional support from Grok and Perplexity.

In parallel, I've added a Hermes Agent stack built on Llama 3, Nous Research for orchestration, and Claude Code agents. This is integrated with an Obsidian vault and Discord. This stack serves as (in the current vernacular) my "second brain."

My process is to work with those agents to pull research data, produce recommended usage drafts, then challenge those drafts aggressively against my own industry and operational knowledge, refining toward a final version that is accurate, honest, and truly collaborative. This is not incidental to the book. It is the book.

The same convergence of AI and domain expertise that produced these pages is shaping the adoption curve of AI across all industries right now. The technology is available to everyone. What is not available to everyone is the hard-won understanding of how decisions actually get made inside organizations, what leaders actually fear and want, and where the gap between a vendor's promise and an enterprise's reality actually lives.

You can't automate that understanding. It has to be earned.

Practitioners who have earned it – and who learn to work at the intersection of that earned knowledge and the new capabilities AI provides – will define the world in 2030.

This book is for all of them.

Robin Green
Austin, Texas 2026

Acknowledgments

Every book like this is built on conversations that happened years before a word was written, with colleagues who pushed back on easy answers, with clients who trusted me with real problems, and with people inside organizations trying to do the right thing under genuine pressure.

To my family and friends, who heard more about artificial intelligence at dinner tables and over cocktails than anyone should have to endure: thank you for your patience, and for asking the questions that kept reminding me who this is really for.

A special word of gratitude to my loving wife René and my daughter Danielle for their patience and calm guidance when my instincts and sense of urgency sometimes tried to get the best of me!

To the researchers, practitioners, and leaders whose work I've drawn on throughout these pages: your honesty about what AI can and can't do has been more useful than enthusiasm.

A special shout-out to my friend and brother in the cause Dave Hendricks for opening doors to platform capabilities no 7-prompt text on X or LinkedIn could ever provide.

And to readers, employees, and anxious observers everywhere who are skeptical of both the hype and the fear, this book is for you.

Chapter 1

The Great Shift: Why AI Changed the Rules of Growth

Part I – The Tipping Point

Great shifts in history rarely announce themselves with fanfare. They begin quietly, in the corners of conversation, in prototypes on lab benches, in questions that start challenging boardrooms and classrooms alike.

And then, all at once, they're everywhere.

That's how what some have called The Intelligence Age began.

Artificial intelligence lived in academic papers and science fiction for decades. Then, suddenly, it crossed the line from theory to ubiquity, not as a distant dream but as a force reshaping daily life. Within just a few years, the world went from asking if AI could work to asking how fast it would change everything we know.

When you think about it, this moment feels oddly familiar. Humanity has stood at this crossroads before.

- At the dawn of the Industrial Revolution, machines multiplied **muscle**.
- At the rise of the Digital Revolution, computers multiplied **memory**.
- Now, in this Intelligence Revolution, AI multiplies ***meaning***. And meaning changes everything.

This time, the speed of transformation is breathtaking. In the 19th century, it took half a century for industrialization to span continents. In the 20th, it took two decades for computing to become mainstream. In the 21st, it took less than five years for AI to touch every industry, every profession, and nearly every person with an Internet connection.

PwC recently estimated the global economic contribution of AI could exceed $15.7 trillion by 2030. But this isn't just about money, it's about **momentum**.

The pace of change has outstripped the **pace of comprehension**.

AI didn't just accelerate productivity; it rewrote the very grammar of growth. It changed the verbs of business. "Produce" becomes *"predict,"* "manage" is replaced by *"model,"* and "control" is redefined as *"collaborate."*

Just as importantly, it changed the nouns of success, from "market share" to "mindshare," from "output" to "insight."

This isn't just a story about technology. It's a story about what it means to be human in a world where intelligence itself becomes a shared resource.

A Shift Hidden in Plain Sight

At any marketing or innovation conference ten years ago, you would have heard the same refrain: "Data is the new oil."

It was catchy, but it missed something crucial.

Oil is extracted, refined, and consumed. Once it's used, it's gone. Data, however, behaves more like sunlight, endlessly renewable, illuminating everything it touches when channeled with purpose.

Until recently, we lacked the proper lenses to turn that sunlight into clarity. We had more data than we could interpret, more information than we could apply, and more complexity than our brains could process.

That's where AI entered the frame.

First generation AI automated tasks: emails, logistics, recommendations, keywords. Then it started anticipating behavior, accelerating learning, and personalizing experiences in ways no spreadsheet ever could.

It was as though the world had built a nervous system with sensors and signals everywhere, constantly learning, constantly adapting.

This wasn't the birth of a new machine. It was the birth of a new relationship.

The Great Compression

Human progress rarely moves in a straight line. It unfolds in cycles of expansion and compression. Expansion creates room to explore, to build, to scale. Compression, by contrast, removes slack. It forces decisions, accelerates trade-offs, and exposes what actually matters. What feels chaotic in the moment often proves catalytic in hindsight.

The early 2020s were one of those compressive moments. The pandemic collapsed a decade of digital adoption into a single year. Practices once facing cultural resistance or budget restrictions, remote work, telehealth, e-commerce, digital-first marketing, were no longer operational options; they became strategic necessities.

Organizations didn't gradually transition. They leapt. Infrastructure that was "on the roadmap" suddenly had to be fully functional by Monday morning. Companies with offices in multiple countries where all employees dutifully trudged to cubicles in high rise buildings to tens of thousands of home offices, overnight.

In that same window, AI moved from being a backroom experiment to a boardroom mandate. AI stopped being framed as an experiment and started being discussed as capability. When borders closed, data opened. When physical proximity paused, intelligent connection accelerated.

Decision-making increasingly relied on models rather than meetings, on insight rather than intuition alone.

The numbers reflect how quickly the ground shifted. In 2021, less than one in ten companies used AI meaningfully across their operations. By 2025, according to PwC, that number had surpassed 60% and continues climbing. Adoption wasn't uniform, but momentum was unmistakable. Leadership began asking not whether AI was being explored, but how it was being governed, scaled, and aligned with business goals.

AI became not just a technological advantage but a cultural one, a symbol of adaptability, learning, and evolution. AI became valuable not because it replaced effort, but because it surfaced relationships humans couldn't see unaided. In that sense, AI evolved from a technological advantage into a cultural signal. It marked organizations willing to learn continuously rather than rely on static playbooks.

It wasn't enough to automate; organizations needed to understand.

The Great Compression accelerated timelines, collapsed assumptions, and forced a reckoning with how value is created in a connected world. The shift was subtle but seismic: we stopped asking,

"What can machines do?" and started asking, "What can we do with machines?"

What emerged wasn't just faster digital adoption, but a new growth geometry, one where intelligence compounds, learning loops tighten, and collaboration between humans and machines becomes the defining force of the next era.

The New Equation of Growth

For centuries, growth was linear. You added more people, more factories, more output, and you got more results. It was a simple equation: effort equals reward.

But the AI era broke that equation. Growth is no longer proportional to input. Smarter insights produce outsized results that raw effort can't match.

Consider:

- A small startup with a well-trained AI model can outperform a Fortune 100 company with ten times the resources.
- A nonprofit with the right data strategy can reach more people than a government department.
- A single creator can now produce, distribute, and monetize content globally, powered by algorithms acting like personal production teams.

AI democratizes capacity. It compresses scale. It levels the playing field, but only for those willing to learn faster than they fear.

This is the new currency of growth: learning velocity.

It's not who knows the most; it's who learns the fastest and adapts with the greatest purpose.

From Control to Curiosity

The traditional mindset of business leadership, control, efficiency, predictability, evolved during an age of scarcity and stability. Capital was limited, distribution was constrained, and information moved slowly. Control wasn't a flaw; it was a survival strategy.

The adoption of AI reverses those conditions. We now operate in abundance. Data, content, channels, choice are all coupled with persistent volatility. Markets change faster than planning cycles. Cultural signals emerge and fade before organizations can formalize a response. In this environment, control simply can't scale gracefully.

In abundance, control becomes more challenging. Curiosity becomes essential. Leaders who thrive today aren't the ones demanding certainty, but those embracing ambiguity with humility. They don't just make decisions; they design learning environments. They ask less, "Did we follow the process or plan?" and more, "What did we discover?"

Nowhere is this shift more visible than in advertising and marketing, disciplines where data and human emotion intersect most directly.

Every impression, click, pause, and share becomes a measurable signal. AI systems ingest these signals at scale, identifying patterns no individual could track alone. Yet behind every data point is a human moment, curiosity sparked, trust tested, identity affirmed, or meaning questioned.

Numbers may describe behavior, but they can't fully explain motivation.

AI can measure sentiment, but only humans can feel it. AI can generate copy, but only humans can make it mean something.

Leaders who work in this landscape well resist the temptation to outsource thinking to machines or instinct to dashboards. Instead, they use intelligence as a mirror, a way to see more clearly what humans are responding to and why.

The future of leadership isn't found in perfect answers, it's found in better questions. It won't be defined by perfect directives delivered from the top; it will be defined by the quality of inquiry fostered throughout the organization.

The Shift's Emotional Core

Behind every technological revolution is a human revolution. Tools change first. People change next. Meaning changes last.

The steam engine freed our bodies. The Internet freed our access.

AI holds the promise of freeing our attention. Not by doing more for us, but by allowing us to focus on what matters most. That promise comes with a condition: we must learn to reclaim our attention faster than AI accelerates everything competing for it.

The irony is that while AI expands capability, it also exposes **vulnerability**. We now confront our own cognitive biases, our ethical blind spots, our dependency on systems we don't fully understand. The discomfort isn't a side effect; it's the signal that something fundamental is changing.

This tension between capability and anxiety is what makes this era so deeply human. The same technology that can design life-saving drugs can also spread misinformation. The same algorithm that can predict hurricanes can also reinforce prejudice.

AI hasn't arrived as hero or villain. It serves as a **multiplier**. In this paradox, we rediscover something timeless: technology magnifies *intent*. It doesn't define who we are; it amplifies what we *choose to be*. If intent is thoughtful, progress compounds.

That realization marks the true tipping point. Not when machines became intelligent, but when humanity was asked to become wiser. The future of AI won't be determined solely by what it can do, but by what we decide how it should be used. Just as importantly, what we choose to protect.

A New Kind of Growth Story

Think of a global brand like Unilever.

For decades, Unilever built success through scale, efficiency, and distribution. But in 2023 and 2024, the company increasingly turned to AI to understand not just what consumers were buying, but why they were moved to act. Their "Desire at Scale" initiative used AI to analyze social signals and consumer sentiment across dozens of markets and languages in real time, enabling campaigns to be shaped around genuine emotional resonance rather than assumed messaging.

The results were instructive. Dove's "Change the Compliment" campaign, built using AI to identify which messages were connecting most deeply with its audience, achieved 700 million impressions and 94% positive sentiment within its first 30 days across 25 markets. The campaign moved faster than traditional production would have allowed, but more importantly, it moved people.

What Unilever found wasn't just marketing data. It was meaning data.

That growth wasn't only economic. It was ethical. It proved that alignment with genuine human sentiment can outperform automation of assumed sentiment. And it suggests a larger principle for the intelligent age: the brands that will endure aren't the loudest, but the most truthful.

This is the essence of the new growth story: one written not in quarterly earnings, but in long-term trust.

The Invitation to Rethink

Every revolution gives humanity a chance to rethink something fundamental. A moment where humanity is asked to pause and reconsider what it truly values.

In the Industrial Age, we redefined labor and productivity. In the Digital Age, we redefined communication and access. In the Intelligence Age, we are being asked to redefine value itself.

What if growth is no longer about accumulating more, but about becoming more capable, more aware, more human?

What if the purpose of technology isn't to replace our capacity, but to enhance and magnify it, to reveal creativity, judgment, and empathy that were previously constrained by scale, process, and speed?

That's the invitation AI places before us. To measure success not only by what we build, automate, or optimize, but by who we choose to become while doing so.

And that's where this book's argument truly begins.

Part II: The Death of Linear Growth

Every age of progress begins with a story about growth, and every story eventually becomes outdated.

During the 20th century, business leaders believed progress was a straight line: more effort produced more output, which produced more profit. Growth was mechanical, measurable, and mostly predictable.

But the straight line has bent, and today's growth curves look more like waves, rising, compounding, colliding, and occasionally crashing into one another. AI didn't create this turbulence; it exposed it.

The Limits of Linear Thinking

For generations, the world's economies ran on a simple rule: produce more, earn more. Factories scaled by adding workers. Marketing scaled by adding media. Innovation scaled by adding departments. Then digital disruption rewrote the math.

When **Netflix** replaced late-fees with algorithms, it didn't just out-market Blockbuster; it abolished scarcity as the growth engine. In the early 2000s, Blockbuster generated hundreds of millions annually from late fees, a penalty-based revenue model that trained customers to feel punished for engagement. Netflix inverted the equation by using recommendation algorithms and subscription pricing to remove friction, proving that predictive personalization could outperform punitive economics and scale trust faster than storefront expansion ever could.

When **Airbnb** connected unused bedrooms to global travelers, it grew without owning a single hotel. What began in 2008 as a way for its founders to rent out air mattresses during a design conference evolved into a marketplace that reframed idle personal space as global hospitality infrastructure. By digitizing trust through reviews, identity verification, and two-sided reputation systems, Airbnb demonstrated how distributed human assets, not centralized capital, could become the largest lodging network in the world.

When **Spotify** turned listening habits into dynamic playlists, it proved that data, not distribution, could create loyalty. In an era when music ownership once defined fandom, Spotify shifted value toward continuous discovery, using machine-learning models to anticipate taste before listeners could articulate it themselves. The platform's success showed that emotional resonance could be engineered through pattern recognition, turning passive consumption into an evolving relationship between listener, artist, and algorithm.

In each case, growth detached from linear inputs.

The world learned that exponential outcomes emerge not from doing more, but from learning faster, and applying that learning in real time.

Linear growth assumes yesterday's success guarantees tomorrow's. Exponential growth understands that yesterday's logic is tomorrow's liability.

Case Study 1: The Pivot of Netflix

Netflix's rise is more than a business success story; it is a parable of adaptive intelligence. Around 2007, as streaming was still experimental, the company faced a clear strategic fork: continue optimizing its dominant DVD rental business or commit fully to a digital future.

Rather than relying on traditional spreadsheets, Netflix deployed predictive algorithms that sensed viewer desires before they were explicitly expressed. The system mapped not just what people watched, but nuanced patterns of comfort, curiosity, and community. By 2013, this intelligence directly informed the commissioning of House of Cards – one of the earliest major original series greenlit primarily through data.

It was not an AI miracle. It was human insight multiplied by machine precision. Netflix's evolution from distributor to discovery engine illustrates the enduring growth pattern of our age: sense > respond > refine > repeat. That cycle now powers progress in healthcare diagnostics, retail personalization, climate modeling, and beyond.

The Cost of Predictability

Predictability was once the gold standard of corporate excellence. The ability to forecast demand, optimize supply chains, and eliminate variance was what separated well-run organizations from chaotic ones. and it has become a liability.

When every competitor has access to the same predictive tools, predictive accuracy stops being a differentiator. What remains is an organization trained to follow patterns rather than respond when the patterns break. And they always break eventually.

The most resilient organizations today treat their strategies as working hypotheses rather than settled answers. When things go wrong, they treat the failure as information rather than a reputational threat. This requires a different kind of leadership, not the leader who sees around corners, but the one who builds teams capable of navigating when the forecast turns out to be wrong.

A 2025 Harvard Business Review study of high-performing organizations found that teams practicing what researchers called "learning-based leadership" achieved markedly higher long-term revenue growth than those focused solely on operational efficiency. Efficiency optimizes the present. Learning compounds the future.

From Industrial Chains to Intelligent Loops

For most of the industrial era, organizations were designed like chains. Raw material entered one end, labor and machinery transformed it in the middle, and finished goods exited the other.

The chain metaphor wasn't accidental, it reflected a worldview rooted in mechanical certainty. If each link performed its task consistently, the outcome would be predictable. Efficiency was achieved by tightening each link, minimizing slack, and ensuring nothing deviated from plan. It was a brilliant model for a world defined by physical production and relatively stable demand.

Artificial intelligence changes that architecture. Instead of straight lines, modern systems increasingly resemble loops: data flows in, insights are generated, decisions are made, and those decisions immediately produce new data that feeds the next cycle.

The shift may appear subtle on a whiteboard, arrows curving back instead of pointing forward, but in practice it's revolutionary. Chains deliver outputs. Loops cultivate resilience and reinforcement. A chain is optimized for repetition; a loop is optimized for learning.

The practical difference becomes clear during moments of disruption. In a chain-based system, a broken link halts progress. In a loop-based system, a disruption becomes new information informing and reshaping the next move. The organization doesn't simply recover; it evolves.

What once required quarterly reviews and retrospective analysis now happens continuously, often invisibly, in the background of daily operations.

A vivid example emerged during the global shipping disruptions of the early 2020s, when multinational companies were forced to confront the fragility of linear logistics.

Unilever's development of an Adaptive Supply Network illustrated what an intelligent loop looks like in motion. Rather than anchoring decisions to monthly or even weekly forecasts, the company deployed AI systems that ingested live streams of information, port congestion metrics, trucking availability, customs delays, fuel prices, and even localized weather patterns. Decisions about routing, inventory allocation, and production timing were no longer static plans drafted in advance; they became dynamic responses recalculated hour by hour.

What made the system powerful wasn't merely its speed, but its memory. Each decision produced an outcome, and each outcome became training data for the next cycle. The network began to behave less like a pipeline and more like an organism, sensing, adjusting, and improving through continuous feedback. Efficiency didn't disappear; it was redefined.

The organization became simultaneously leaner and more flexible, cutting waste while increasing responsiveness to local demand. In Unilever's case, measurable reductions in excess inventory and transportation inefficiencies were paired with faster replenishment times in key markets. The same infrastructure that once optimized cost alone began optimizing adaptability.

This transition marks a broader philosophical shift. Industrial chains were built on the assumption that stability was the norm and disruption the exception. Intelligent loops are built on the opposite premise: change is constant, and advantage comes from learning faster than circumstances evolve. The linear supply chain, once the pinnacle of operational excellence, begins looking like a relic when compared to a system that improves itself with every cycle.

The language of "loops" also carries an important human implication. These systems aren't autonomous replacements for people; they are amplifiers of human judgment. A loop still requires direction, interpretation, and ethical boundaries. What changes is the cadence. Instead of relying on periodic reports to trigger action, leaders interact with a living stream of insight.

Decision-making becomes less about issuing commands and more about guiding momentum.

In this sense, the death of the linear chain isn't a loss of order but the birth of a new kind of stability, one rooted in adaptability rather than rigidity. Chains were strong until they snapped. Loops bend, learn, and continue. Resilience today is no longer a structural feature bolted onto the side of an organization; it's a behavior embedded in how the system thinks.

The Human Learning Loop

What happens inside organizations is mirrored inside the people who work in them. For most of the twentieth century, the ideal career moved in a straight line: education at the start, steady employment in the middle, retirement at the end. Expertise was something you accumulated once and then spent.

That model no longer fits. Learning is no longer a phase, it's the ongoing condition of staying relevant. People now move through cycles of acquiring skills, discarding outdated assumptions, and rebuilding knowledge in response to new tools and new realities.

AI accelerates this shift by acting as a real-time training partner. It can surface patterns in how people absorb information, flag gaps a human mentor might miss, and provide feedback that previously took weeks to arrive. The relationship is collaborative. A mentor with intelligent tools can focus on nuance and judgment while the system handles repetition and data analysis.

The practical implications show up across professions. A marketing analyst can run experiments in minutes that used to take months. A surgeon can rehearse edge cases in simulation. A teacher adapt based on real-time engagement rather than waiting for end-of-term results. In each case, the machine gives human expertise more to work with.

The Collapse of Scale for Scale's Sake

The human loop naturally leads to a more profound organizational reality: if individuals now succeed by learning faster rather than accumulating static credentials, institutions follow the same trajectory.

The old industrial equation equated size with strength. The largest factories, the deepest inventories, the widest distribution networks, these were the unmistakable signals of dominance. Scale was both shield and sword. It protected against competition and amplified market reach.

But scale assumed that the environment would remain stable long enough for size to pay dividends.

In the intelligent era, the advantage migrates from magnitude to momentum. The most powerful organizations are no longer those with the largest footprints, but those with the fastest feedback cycles. Scale without learning becomes inertia, impressive in appearance, immobile in practice.

AI accelerates this exposure. Algorithms illuminate inefficiencies that once hid inside layers of bureaucracy and logistical complexity. What used to be invisible friction becomes quantifiable waste.

Automotive manufacturing offers a vivid illustration of this shift. For much of the twentieth century, the automobile plant symbolized industrial supremacy: sprawling campuses, miles of conveyor belts, and armies of workers producing identical vehicles in vast quantities.

Today, that image is being quietly rewritten. Electric-vehicle startups and forward-thinking manufacturers increasingly operate networks of agile micro-factories, smaller, localized facilities guided by AI-driven robotics and real-time demand analytics.

Instead of shipping millions of identical units across continents, they customize production near the point of consumption, reducing transportation costs, minimizing surplus inventory, and shortening innovation cycles. The competitive edge no longer lies in owning the biggest plant; it lies in orchestrating the smartest ecosystem.

The same pattern shows up in marketing, where the economics of attention have replaced the economics of airtime. Once, the brand with the largest advertising budget could dominate simply by outspending rivals. Today, audience behavior changes too quickly for brute force to remain effective. The winning organizations are those that treat campaigns as experiments, continuously adjusting creative, targeting, and messaging based on live data. Learning velocity eclipses financial muscle. A smaller brand that adapts weekly can outperform a giant that plans annually.

This transition doesn't eliminate scale; it reframes its purpose. Size still matters, but only when paired with intelligence. A large organization that learns quickly becomes formidable. A large organization that doesn't becomes slow. The defining metric shifts from how much capacity you control to how effectively you convert information into improvement.

What emerges is the collapse of scale for its own sake. The industrial mindset prized critical mass: more factories, more headcount, more distribution. The intelligent mindset prizes refinement: better insight, better responsiveness, better collaboration between humans and machines.

Linear growth gives way to adaptive growth. The question is no longer "How do we become bigger?" but "How do we become smarter at becoming better?" In that subtle change of emphasis lies one of the most consequential transformations of the AI age.

Case Study 2: Moderna's 12-Month Miracle

When COVID-19 emerged, Moderna – then a relatively young biotech firm – delivered one of the first vaccines by December 2020. Its mRNA platform, supported by computational modeling and automated testing cycles, allowed scientists to move from sequence to human trials in roughly two months and to emergency authorization in about eleven months – a dramatic compression of the traditional decade-long timeline.

The original vaccine was later updated and branded Spikevax. The achievement exemplified compounded, iterative learning rather than purely linear progress.

Success brought new realities. Post-pandemic demand dropped sharply, new pipeline candidates progressed more slowly than hoped, and broader vaccine skepticism plus shifting priorities led to financial revisions and scaled-back late-stage investment. Moderna's story remains powerful: technology can accelerate discovery, but market dynamics and human behavior still shape outcomes. The real shift is from rigid timelines to adaptive, learning-driven innovation.

Marketing in the Age of Non-Linearity

For most of the twentieth century, marketers worked within predictable rhythms: annual media plans, quarterly campaign launches, seasonal product pushes. Those rhythms matched a broadcast world where messages traveled in straight lines and audiences gathered in predictable places.

That world is gone. A single viral TikTok can shift brand perception overnight. A meme made on a phone can outperform a million-dollar TV spot. The asymmetry isn't about cost, it's about timing and cultural relevance.

The brands that falter aren't the ones with insufficient budgets. They're the ones with insufficient responsiveness.

Large advertising networks have adapted by treating campaigns as continuous experiments rather than fixed events. Instead of launching a single message and measuring results months later, the leading agencies release multiple creative variations simultaneously, learn from audience reactions in real time, and evolve the narrative while it is still unfolding.

Nike pairs adaptive retail strategies with data-informed storytelling that shifts based on regional culture, athlete influence, and social sentiment. Coca-Cola treats global brand consistency as a framework rather than a constraint. These companies increasingly operate like digital publishers, releasing, measuring, refining, and releasing again in continuous cycles.

Success in this environment no longer depends on predicting where attention will be. It depends on being ready to meet it wherever it appears, and having the creative and organizational agility to make that moment count.

Framework: The Three Stages of Intelligent Growth

To navigate this new reality, organizations tend to evolve through three recognizable stages, or horizons, of maturity. These aren't rigid stages so much as expanding circles of capability, each one building on the last, each one introducing new opportunities and new responsibilities.

Stage 1: Automation (Efficiency)

At the first stage, machines take on repetitive and rule-based work. Processes become faster, cheaper, and more consistent. The immediate gains are tangible: reduced operating costs, fewer manual errors, and the ability to scale routine functions without scaling headcount at the same pace. Yet efficiency carries its own shadow. When automation is pursued without intention, work can feel stripped of meaning, and creative energy can quietly erode. The risk isn't job loss alone; it's the gradual dulling of curiosity and craftsmanship.

Stage 2: Augmentation (Collaboration)

The second stage shifts the relationship from substitution to partnership. Humans and intelligent systems begin to co-create, analysts supported by predictive tools, designers guided by generative models, managers informed by real-time dashboards. Success here is measured less by savings and more by momentum: faster innovation cycles, higher engagement, and a workforce that feels supported rather than replaced. But collaboration introduces subtler hazards. Ethical blind spots can emerge when decisions are accelerated without reflection, and over-reliance on algorithms can quietly narrow independent judgment.

Stage 3: Alignment (Purpose)

Stage 3 is less about capability and more about coherence. Systems are designed not only to perform effectively, but to operate in harmony with human values and societal expectations.

Trust, transparency, and long-term resilience become the primary indicators of success. Organizations at this stage recognize that intelligence without direction is merely power, while intelligence aligned with purpose becomes stewardship.

The central risk here is complacency, the mistaken belief that ethics are self-maintaining rather than continuously cultivated.

Organizations that move deliberately across all three horizons, not stopping at automation or even augmentation, but advancing toward alignment, will be positioned to last. Automation makes systems faster. Augmentation makes them smarter. Alignment makes them worthy of trust. It is alignment that ultimately transforms intelligence into integrity, and integrity into enduring advantage.

The Emotional Economy

As AI absorbs more analytical and cognitive work, the frontier of competitive advantage shifts to what machines can't replicate: empathy, humor, a sense of belonging, the ability to make someone feel genuinely seen.

In an environment where functional differences between products narrow quickly, emotional differences widen. Empathy has become a hinge on which brand loyalty turns. Consumers are aware when automation is present (chatbots, recommendation engines, dynamic pricing) but awareness doesn't produce resistance. What produces resistance is indifference.

Research from Salesforce in 2025 found that customers are far more comfortable engaging with automated systems when those systems reflect understanding rather than efficiency alone. A well-designed automated experience can feel attentive; a poorly designed one can feel dismissive at scale.

Companies that recognize this invest not only in smarter systems but in emotional intelligence embedded within those systems, tone guidelines, ethical guardrails, feedback loops that measure sentiment as rigorously as sales. Loyalty is built in the small moments: a support response that feels human, a recommendation that reflects genuine understanding rather than blunt targeting.

When intelligence becomes ubiquitous, humanity becomes the differentiator.

Closing Reflection: The Curved Path Forward

The straight lines once guiding our ambitions and measurements attainment are bending, toward complexity, toward collaboration, toward consciousness.

AI isn't the end of humanity's story of progress; it's an invitation to rewrite it in curves, loops, and spirals.

Every algorithm we design, every insight we apply, every ethical choice we make bends that curve toward a future defined not by dominance but by design with intention.

The end of linear growth isn't the end of ambition. It's the beginning of a higher kind of aspiration, growth measured not only in profit and size, but in purpose.

Key Takeaways – The Death of Linear Growth

- *Growth has shifted from* ***linear production*** *to* ***exponential learning****.*
- *The most resilient organizations operate as* ***intelligent loops****, not* ***rigid chains****.*
- *The death of linear growth marks the birth of* ***purpose-driven evolution****.*

Part III: The Three Horizons of Intelligent Growth

Growth has always been a journey, but in the age of AI, it's no longer measured by distance. It's measured by depth.

How deeply a company learns. How deeply a culture aligns. How deeply a leader listens.

The organizations that thrive in the next decade will do more than adopt AI, they'll evolve with it, climbing through three distinct horizons of maturity: Automation, Augmentation, and Alignment.

These horizons aren't technical phases, they're cultural thresholds. Each one redefines the relationship between people, purpose, and progress.

Horizon 1: Automation – The Era of Efficiency

Revolution always begins with a form of relief.

The first horizon of AI adoption is about automation, the desire to make work faster, cheaper, and easier.

It's where most organizations start, and for good reason. Automation can deliver instant wins. When properly deployed, it can eliminate repetitive tasks, increase accuracy, and free up capacity.

When AI entered marketing, for example, it automated bidding, optimized spend, and personalized messages. Today, it develops target audiences and offers real-time feedback.

In logistics, AI automated route planning; in healthcare, record-keeping.

Automation freed time, but time without intention changes nothing. Efficiency can improve process, but it can't define *purpose*.

The Paradox of Efficiency

At first, automation feels like progress. But left unchecked, it can become the ceiling rather than the floor. When employees equate AI with replacement, fear outweighs freedom.

When leaders measure success only in speed, humanity becomes a casualty. McKinsey's AI Productivity Index 2025 found that while 68% of companies implementing automation reported immediate cost savings, only 27% reported higher innovation. Automation without curiosity creates stagnation.

That's why Horizon 1 is both a gift and a test. The gift offers relief from repetition. The test becomes whether leaders will reinvest that relief into imagination.

Automation has never been the destination. It's the doorway.

Case Study 3: A Manufacturer's Wake-Up Call

A major global industrial technology manufacturer (drawing from documented initiatives at firms such as Siemens and ABB) automated roughly 70% of certain assembly tasks with AI-driven robotics. Throughput rose, defects fell, and productivity improved sharply. For a year the metrics looked flawless.

On the factory floor, however, skilled operators felt displaced. Engagement dropped as workers became passive overseers of systems they had not helped shape.

Leadership recognized the issue: the problem was not the technology but the narrative around it. Automation had been framed as replacement rather than elevation. The company pivoted. Operators were retrained to tune, improve, and creatively apply the robots. Human judgment once again became central.

Within eighteen months, engagement rose substantially, production errors were cut significantly, and employee innovation proposals increased dramatically. The machines did not steal jobs – they created new mastery when paired with empowered people.

Horizon 2: Augmentation – The Era of Collaboration

Once organizations automate the mechanical, they run headfirst into something more philosophical.

Now what?

That question doesn't come from failure. It comes from success. The systems are working. The efficiencies are real. And suddenly, leaders realize they didn't build all this intelligence just to go faster, they built it to do something better.

That realization opens the second horizon: augmentation.

This is the moment AI stops being about replacing work and starts being about supporting people. Humans and machines stop competing for relevance and start collaborating toward possibility.

It's where marketing teams use predictive analytics not just to react to audiences, but to anticipate emotion. Where designers sit alongside generative tools and prototype in minutes what used to take months. Where teachers adapt lessons in real time, meeting students where they are instead of forcing everyone to move at the same pace.

In augmentation, intelligence becomes symbiotic. The machine accelerates. The human decides. And together, they create outcomes neither could reach alone.

The Human + Machine Workflow

Augmentation changes how we think about productivity. It's no longer about how much gets done, it's about how much better it gets.

A designer and an AI model can generate a hundred options in seconds. But meaning doesn't come from volume. It arrives in the moment a human looks at the output and says, "That one feels right."

A 2025 Adobe study found that creative professionals using AI tools produced twice as many original concepts while reporting higher satisfaction and lower burnout. The reason wasn't efficiency alone. AI removed the friction of execution and returned people to the part of work that feels alive.

When machines handle the how, humans rediscover the why.

That shift changes everything. Work stops feeling like output and starts feeling like authorship again.

Case Study 4: A Hospital That Learned to Listen

At a children's hospital in Singapore, administrators introduced an AI system designed not to optimize logistics but to truly listen. The platform analyzed real-time patient and parent feedback – tone, language patterns, and sentiment from conversations and social posts.

When distress signals appeared, the system did not issue automated replies. It alerted human nurses and counselors, who provided targeted personal outreach and extra care. Over six months, patient satisfaction improved substantially.

The technology did not replace compassion. It scaled it – showing how intelligent systems can amplify empathy when designed to support, not substitute, human connection.

The Creativity Dividend

In Horizon 2, innovation stops being an event and starts becoming a habit.

Teams are freed from routine, and creativity grows across the organization. Marketing no longer brainstorms in isolation. Campaigns evolve in real time through AI-assisted storytelling and live audience insight. Product teams visualize unmet needs before customers can articulate them. HR moves beyond one-size-fits-all development, using adaptive tools to tailor growth paths for every employee.

The organization starts to behave less like a machine and more like a living system, learning, adapting, and responding with curiosity instead of control.

But as possibility expands, responsibility grows with it.

Augmentation doesn't just give us more power to create. It gives us more influence over how work feels, how people are seen, and how intelligence shapes culture. And that's where leadership matters most, because collaboration, when guided well, doesn't just change what we build.

It changes *who we become* while building it.

Horizon 3: Alignment – The Era of Integrity

If automation is about efficiency, and augmentation is about collaboration, then alignment is about something deeper. It's the summit of intelligent growth, the place where technology, humanity, and ethics finally meet. Not in theory. In practice.

By the time organizations reach this horizon, the question has shifted. Leaders are no longer asking, What can AI do for us? That question has already been answered. The systems are powerful. The insights are abundant. The scale is undeniable.

The real question becomes more personal, and more demanding: What should AI do with us?

Alignment is the moment we realize that intelligent systems don't just reflect our capability. They reflect our character. They carry our priorities forward at scale. They make permanent what we normalize today.

And once AI becomes the engine of insight, leadership is compelled to become the compass of conscience.

From Intelligence to Intent

In Horizon 3, organizations stop treating ethics as a constraint and start treating it as a design principle.

This is where values move out of mission statements and into models. Where incentives are examined as carefully as algorithms. Where leaders ask not just whether a system works, but whether it deserves to.

Alignment doesn't slow innovation. It steadies it.

Because without intent, intelligence drifts. It optimizes what it's told to optimize. It accelerates whatever goals it's given. And if those goals are narrow, short-term, or disconnected from human consequence, the system will faithfully pursue the wrong things at scale.

Aligned organizations understand this. They don't outsource judgment to machines. They embed judgment into how machines are trained, evaluated, and governed.

The question isn't whether AI will shape decisions. It already does. The question is whether those decisions reflect care, fairness, and long-term responsibility.

Leadership as Moral Architecture

At this horizon, leadership stops being about control or even connection. It becomes architectural.

Leaders shape the invisible structures that guide behavior, what gets rewarded, what gets questioned, what gets stopped. They decide where AI is allowed to decide, and where humans must remain accountable.

Alignment requires leaders to hold tension without rushing to resolve it. Growth and restraint. Speed and reflection. Innovation and dignity.

This isn't comfortable work. There's no dashboard for integrity. No model that can tell you when a choice is wise. But that's exactly the point.

AI can surface insight, but only humans can choose direction. In Horizon 3, that choice becomes the defining act of leadership.

When Systems Reflect Us

The organizations that reach alignment don't look perfect. They look honest.

They're transparent about trade-offs. Clear about boundaries. Willing to say no, to features, to markets, to growth paths that compromise trust. They build systems that can explain themselves, be challenged, and evolve when values demand it.

In these organizations, AI doesn't replace responsibility. It sharpens it.

Because every model trained, every decision automated, every process accelerated becomes a signal, to employees, customers, and society, about what matters here.

Alignment is the recognition that scale magnifies values, whether we intend it to or not.

The Work That Never Ends

Horizon 3 isn't a destination you arrive at and check off. It's a commitment you renew.

Markets change. Technologies evolve. Pressures return. Alignment has to be maintained, not declared. It lives in governance meetings, product reviews, campaign decisions, and hiring choices. It shows up in what leaders tolerate, and what they don't.

This is the era where intelligence grows powerful enough to demand wisdom.

And wisdom, unlike technology, doesn't compound on its own. It has to be practiced.

The Summit Is Human

Alignment is the highest horizon not because it's the most advanced, but because it's the most human.

It's where organizations stop chasing intelligence for its own sake and start using it in service of something larger. Trust. Dignity. Meaning.

The companies that reach this summit won't be remembered for how fast they scaled or how clever their systems were. They'll be remembered for the standards they set, and the restraint they showed when they could've done otherwise.

In the end, alignment isn't about making AI more human. It's about making sure we don't forget how to be.

That's the real measure of progress, when our most powerful technologies don't just extend what we can do but reflect who we choose to become.

Case Study 5: 3 Firms That Chose Integrity

Ethical Review Loops are iterative processes where sustainability, transparency, and social responsibility data are fed back into product development, marketing, and supply chain management, to drive revenue growth while strengthening consumer trust.

Loops have been increasingly adopted by many global brands, especially global retailers, giving these firms the realization that aligning growth with core values can lead to higher retention, premium pricing, and, in some cases, **46%** faster growth for sustainable brands.

Here are three examples of this strategy in action:

5a - Patagonia: The "4-Fold" Value Loop

Patagonia evaluates partners and products through a multi-factor lens that balances sourcing, quality, social impact, and environmental stewardship. By publishing tools such as the Footprint Chronicles and public factory lists, the company converts transparency into trust. Customer feedback and impact data continuously refine future products.

This disciplined approach has built exceptional customer loyalty and supported strong, sustained revenue growth over more than a decade – proving that radical transparency can be a powerful competitive advantage.

5b - Mercadona: Co-Innovation and Consumer Feedback Loops

Spanish retailer Mercadona, through its Total Quality Model and private brands such as Hacendado and Deliplus, operates a highly effective localized feedback system. In 2023 it ran 23 co-innovation centers and conducted 11,000 consumer testing sessions. These efforts produced roughly 500 product improvements and 314 new products, strengthening its private-label leadership and market position.

Rather than treating innovation as a top-down exercise, Mercadona uses structured listening to make customers co-designers of its products.

5c - Unilever: Sustainable Living Brand Strategy

Unilever evaluates brands against rigorous sustainability and customer-value criteria. Its sustainable-living brands have grown significantly faster than the rest of the portfolio and have driven the majority of recent turnover growth.

These three companies – and many others following similar paths – demonstrate that integrity is not a constraint on growth. When embedded thoughtfully, it becomes a powerful sustainer of it.

The Three Alignments

To operate in Horizon 3, leaders must achieve three types of alignment:

- Cognitive Alignment, Humans and machines share understanding.
  Example: transparent AI explanations build confidence in decisions.

- Cultural Alignment, Teams share values and vocabulary around technology.
  Example: cross-functional AI literacy programs build inclusion.

- Moral Alignment, Systems serve human flourishing, not just efficiency.
  Example: ethics councils review models for unintended harm.

When all three alignments coexist, AI evolves from intelligence as tool to intelligence as trust.

The Leadership Mindset of Alignment

Aligned leaders don't fear technology, they humanize it. They see AI not as a competitor, but as a collaborator in the pursuit of wisdom.

Such leaders don't delegate ethics; they embody it. They understand that the algorithms they approve today will define the kind of world their children inherit tomorrow.

Alignment isn't compliance, it is compassion coded into organizational DNA.

Framework Reflection: Climbing the Horizons

Each horizon requires a new kind of courage:

- Automation demands the courage to *let go of control*
- Augmentation demands the courage to *trust collaboration.*
- Alignment demands the courage to *lead with conscience.*

Most organizations will master the first, attempt the second, and struggle with the third. But the third is where legacy, and customer loyalty live.

Horizon 3 companies will outlast disruption because they root innovation in identity.

Closing Reflection: The Compass of Growth

Every era of progress has been guided by a shared sense of what to optimize for and what to celebrate.

During the Industrial Age, that compass pointed toward productivity. During the Digital Age, toward connectivity. Both answers made sense for their moment.

The question now is what we optimize for when machines can do much of the optimizing for us. The answer has to involve something machines can't supply: judgment about what actually matters, and to whom.

That's a different kind of leadership. Not about adopting things first, but about deciding repeatedly, and honestly, what progress is supposed to be for.

Key Takeaways

- *The Three Horizons of Intelligent Growth define how* ***organizations mature*** *with AI.*
- *Automation improves* ***process*** *but can stall* ***purpose****.*
- *Leaders should treat intelligence as a* ***moral responsibility****, not merely a* ***technical one****.*

Part IV: The Human Imperative

Every technological revolution starts with an invention, but its lasting impact is shaped by intention. History is clear on this point. Tools don't determine outcomes on their own; people do. What we choose to build matters, but how, and why, we choose to use what we build matters far more.

Today's machines learn at a pace that would have felt implausible only a few years ago. They can analyze vast systems, recognize patterns hidden from human sight, and generate language, forecasts, and decisions with remarkable speed. Work that once demanded time, experience, and coordination can now be completed in seconds by systems that never need time off or have to balance priorities.

We're at an unusual moment in human progress. It's also a revealing one.

As our technology grows more sophisticated, we face a deeper question beneath the surface of innovation. The challenge in front of us is no longer primarily technical, it's human. Intelligence alone doesn't define progress; judgment does. Capability doesn't equal wisdom. And efficiency, left unchecked, can move us quickly in directions we haven't fully considered.

This is the human imperative of the AI age: to remain actively responsible for the direction of our tools rather than surrendering all responsibility to them.

Computer intelligence can identify options, optimize outcomes, and accelerate decisions. But it doesn't supply meaning, nor weigh moral consequence. AI can't determine what deserves our trust, our care, or our restraint. Those choices remain uniquely human.

If we fail to lead with intention, technology will continue its inevitable advance, regardless of consequence. Progress won't stop, but it may lose its compass. And progress without purpose never elevates humanity; it merely increases the speed at which we move without direction.

The future won't be shaped by the intelligence of our machines alone. It will be shaped by the values of the people who decide how those machines are designed, deployed, and allowed to influence the world.

Technology Doesn't Create Values – It Reveals Them

When historians look back on this moment, they likely won't say AI created a moral crisis. They'll say it exposed one.

Technology has never invented values. It doesn't arrive with ethics preloaded. What it does, quietly but powerfully, is amplify what's already present. It takes human intention and gives it reach. It turns individual choices into systems, and systems into culture at scale.

That's one reason AI feels so consequential. Not because it's autonomous, but because it's obedient. AI does exactly what we ask of it, and then it does it everywhere.

When we design systems driven by fear, fear of inefficiency, fear of loss, fear of being outpaced, that fear doesn't stay contained in our personal beliefs. It spreads through policies, workflows, incentives, and metrics. If we design with empathy and trust, those qualities scale just as quickly. The technology itself doesn't choose. It reflects.

AI, in this way, becomes a mirror. It magnifies the underlying DNA of the organizations and societies that deploy it.

You can see this clearly in how companies approach automation. When automation is introduced without vision, people experience it as replacement. Roles are reduced to tasks, tasks are reduced to costs, and work becomes something to be optimized away.

But when automation is introduced with intention, it does something very different. It frees people from repetition, reallocates human effort toward judgment and creativity, allowing work to evolve rather than disappear.

The difference isn't technical. It's philosophical.

It's the difference between using technology to extract more value and using it to create more meaning. Viewed this way, technology moves beyond exploitation and into elevation. And that distinction, often invisible in spreadsheets and analysis, is what will ultimately define the next generation of leaders.

The Soul of Leadership

Ever since Frederick Winslow Taylor pioneered the concept of "scientific management" for organizational efficiency, leadership in business has been taught as a discipline of performance. Set goals. Measure output. Optimize results. The underlying assumption was simple: if performance improved, everything else would follow.

That assumption no longer holds.

The most effective leaders today aren't just managing performance; they're managing meaning. And that shift isn't cosmetic, it's existential. In a world where people can work anywhere, automate anything, and query everything, the question now shaping every organization is no longer What are we doing? It's Why does this matter?

When people stop believing their work has meaning, performance doesn't just dip, it erodes. Engagement fades. Initiative disappears. Compliance replaces commitment.

But when people feel connected to a shared purpose, something different happens. Performance becomes personal. Pride replaces pressure. Work becomes a reflection of identity rather than obligation.

AI gives leaders new visibility into what's happening inside their organizations. We can measure productivity, engagement, sentiment, even emotional tone in written communication. We can quantify almost everything, except the reason people choose to show up and care.

That reason can't be automated. It can't be inferred from data alone. It must be articulated, modeled, and lived.

That "why", the sense of contribution, dignity, and shared direction, is the soul of leadership. And in the age of intelligent machines, it's the most human responsibility facing leaders today.

Case Study 6: Fintech Firm That Relearned Trust

A global digital "shop-and-pay" provider deployed AI customer-service automation to reduce call-center volume. Response times improved, but satisfaction fell because the system prioritized speed over sensitivity.

Leadership paused the rollout, retrained models on empathy cues and emotional context, and empowered human agents to override AI when needed. Satisfaction rebounded to record levels and employee morale rose.

The CEO captured the lesson: the company's role was not to make machines act more human, but to help humans act more humane. That remains the central imperative.

The Empathy Equation

Empathy can often be mistaken for softness, as if it's a concession leaders make when they've run out of attention. In reality, empathy is one of the sharpest tools intelligent leadership has. It's what allows leaders to move beyond raw data and into discernment. It bridges what the numbers say with what people feel. And it's the difference between insight that informs and insight that actually changes behavior.

Data tells us what's happening. Empathy helps us understand why.

In an AI-powered world, where analytics surface patterns instantly and dashboards update by the minute, it's tempting to believe that understanding automatically follows information. It doesn't. Insight without empathy stays abstract. It explains, but it doesn't connect.

That connection matters more than ever. According to Deloitte's 2025 Future of Work study, organizations prioritizing empathy in leadership development outperform their peers by 32 percent in innovation and 60 percent in employee retention. Those aren't sentimental outcomes. They're competitive ones.

Empathy isn't a moral luxury layered on after performance goals are met. It's an economic advantage built directly into how modern organizations function. As AI absorbs more of the logic-driven work, the uniquely human skill that becomes paramount is listening, not just to data, but to one another.

Leaders who understand this don't ask empathy to replace analytics. They use it to complete the equation.

From Control to Connection

For much of the last century, leadership was defined by control. Leaders were expected to command, decide, and direct. Authority flowed downward. Information flowed upward. Inevitably, stability rewarded predictability.

That model worked when systems were linear and change moved slowly.

It breaks down in complexity, especially in environments shaped by AI, where variables shift constantly and outcomes are rarely the result of a single decision. In these systems, control doesn't scale. It fractures.

The leaders who succeed today aren't controllers. They're connectors.

They connect people to purpose, teams to truth, and technology to values. Instead of trying to dominate complexity, they create coherence within it. They understand that alignment matters more than instruction and that meaning travels farther than mandates.

A 2024 Harvard study on adaptive organizations found that teams led by connective leaders, those who emphasize communication, curiosity, and compassion, delivered four times more innovation than traditional hierarchical teams. That gap isn't explained by talent alone. It's explained by trust.

In an environment where information is democratized in ways unthinkable even thirty years ago, the strongest form of authority isn't position or title. It's the ability to be relational. People don't follow titles. They follow leaders they trust to tell the truth, admit uncertainty, and act with integrity when the path forward isn't obvious.

The Moral Cost of Speed

AI delivers the ability to move faster than any technology before it. Faster insights. Faster decisions. Faster execution. Speed feels like progress and often is. But speed without reflection isn't progress at all. It's risk disguised as momentum.

The pressure to adopt, scale, and optimize can crowd out the most important question leaders should be asking: Should we?

Consider a scenario playing out across the fashion industry, documented in multiple reported cases: a major apparel brand launches an AI-driven trend prediction engine that does exactly what it was designed to do. It forecasted emerging styles with remarkable accuracy. Production ramped up. Inventory turned faster. Margins improved.

What the system didn't account for were the environmental and social costs embedded in those recommendations. Manufacturing intensified. Waste increased. Sustainability goals slipped backward. They simply got to their structural flaws faster.

Public backlash followed. The company suspended the project, not because the algorithm failed, but because leadership did. The technology delivered speed. Wisdom never entered the conversation.

To their credit, the company didn't abandon AI. They rebuilt their strategy. An ethical oversight board, made up of designers, community advocates, and data scientists, was brought in. The model was retrained to optimize not only for profit, but for planetary impact.

The result became a case study in purpose-driven innovation. These cases collectively prove a simple truth: speed means nothing if direction is wrong.

The Rise of Human Stewardship

For many, "Stewardship" is an old-fashioned word, but it may become the defining one of the AI era.

Stewardship means managing something valuable that you don't fully own, on behalf of others you may never meet. It implies responsibility, restraint, and care across time.

AI places every leader, policymaker, and organization into that role.

When algorithms shape decisions at scale, they don't just influence outcomes, they influence culture. And culture, over time, shapes destiny. This responsibility goes far beyond regulatory compliance or corporate social responsibility reports. It's not only about protecting data. It's about protecting dignity.

When AI systems help determine who gets a loan, who gets a job interview, or whose voice is amplified, fairness and empathy can't be afterthoughts. They must be designed in from the start.

This isn't idealism. It's accountability. And in a world where technology moves faster than law, stewardship isn't optional, it's essential.

The Emotional Infrastructure of the Future

Technology depends on infrastructure. Servers, software, networks, energy. None of it works without a foundation that can support scale.

Societies and organizations depend on something just as critical: emotional infrastructure.

infrastructure is the invisible network of trust holding people together when change moves faster than rules can adapt. It's what allows teams to collaborate through uncertainty and organizations to endure disruption without fracturing.

AI can execute logic flawlessly. It can't build trust. Only humans can do that, by listening honestly, leading transparently, and taking responsibility for the systems they put into the world.

When emotional infrastructure is weak, even the most sophisticated innovations collapse under suspicion and resistance. When it's strong, change becomes possible without chaos.

The future won't fail because technology moved too fast. It will fail if trust doesn't keep pace.

Marketing's Moral Moment

More than any time in history, marketing now sits at the center of what some have called the "human imperative." A college professor I had years ago described this as the *"fundamental, non-negotiable, and urgent requirement for action that is essential for the survival, well-being, and continued existence of humanity."*

Yes, I kept my old classroom notes!

At its best, marketing has always been about connection, understanding people and speaking to their needs with clarity and respect. Today, it has become something more powerful: a system of influence at scale.

Algorithms decide which stories are pushed, which voices carry further, and which communities are overlooked or even ignored. They shape perception, reinforce values, and define relevance. That gives marketers extraordinary reach, and an equally extraordinary responsibility.

Ethical marketing is no longer just about complying with privacy laws or avoiding misuse of data. It's about *defining the moral tone of technology itself.*

When we use AI to personalize experiences, are we empowering choice or manipulating desire? When we analyze behavioral data, are we protecting privacy or exploiting intimacy?

These aren't abstract debates for conferences or policy panels. They're daily design decisions made by teams, often under pressure, often without time to pause.

The future of trust in marketing will be shaped by whether brands choose to act as stewards of truth, or continue to compete as buyers and sellers of attention.

Case Study 7: A Brand That Listened

Global consumer brands with Latin American reach have occasionally faced backlash when AI-generated campaigns used cultural imagery in ways local communities found insensitive or "uncanny."

In one documented case, rather than deleting the work and denying criticism, the brand invited cultural historians and local artists to co-create the next campaign – with AI serving as a supporting tool rather than the lead creator. The resulting work was emotionally rich, heritage-celebrating, and transparent about its process. It earned industry recognition and restored trust.

In culturally sensitive contexts, humility and co-creation are not optional – they are the new baseline of intelligent creativity.

The Courage to Care

Empathy and stewardship are often spoken about as if they are "soft" virtues, commendable, but optional. In reality, they demand courage and intent. Not the dramatic kind, but the quieter, harder kind that shows up in moments of pressure and uncertainty.

It takes courage to slow down when everyone else is racing to deploy, scale, and announce. It takes courage to ask uncomfortable questions when the metrics look great, but the consequences feel wrong. And it takes courage to admit that not every decision can, or should, be delegated to an algorithm, equation, or financial statistic.

Caring in an age of optimization is a *deliberate* act.

There will be moments when profit collides with principle, when speed undermines wisdom, and when the most efficient choice isn't the most responsible one. In those moments, leadership is revealed. Not by how decisively someone moves forward, but by whether they are willing to pause, reflect, and choose restraint.

By 2030, the leaders we admire most won't be remembered for building the smartest systems. They'll be remembered for building the most humane ones, systems that respected people, honored dignity, and reflected a deeper understanding of progress.

They'll lead not through command or control, but through conscience. And by doing this, they'll prove that care isn't the opposite of strength. It's its truest expression.

Closing Reflection: The Human Heartbeat in the Circuit

The deeper we integrate with machines, the more important it becomes to preserve what makes us irreplaceable, curiosity, judgment, the capacity to care about outcomes rather than just optimize for them.

Technology mirrors its makers. It learns from our priorities, our incentives, our blind spots. If we want AI to serve people well, we have to model the humanity we want it to reflect.

That's the accountability this work requires.

Key Takeaways – The Human Imperative

- *The human imperative is to lead with **conscience**, not just **competence**.*
- *Technology **reveals** values, it doesn't **create** them.*
- *The future of trust depends on our **courage** to remain deeply, intentionally **human**.*

Part V: The Path Forward

At some point in every transformation, the excitement gives way to a harder question: responsibility.

Prototypes are running. Headlines are glowing. Investors are encouraged. On the surface, everything looks like progress. And yet, after all the boardroom meetings or analysts calls, a different question emerges, one that doesn't show up a roadmaps or quarterly reports.

Now what?

That question isn't a sign of doubt. It's a sign of clarity. It marks the moment we realize we've crossed from what's possible into what's responsible. The technology works. The systems scale.

The path forward isn't just about building smarter systems. It's about building wiser (not just smarter) organizations, ones that can learn, adapt, and move at the speed of change without losing their sense of purpose along the way. This is where leadership begins.

The Intelligence Loop

If the Industrial Revolution was powered by the assembly line, the Intelligence Revolution runs on something very different: the learning loop.

Every resilient, AI-driven organization today operates within some version of this cycle:

Learn → Apply → Reflect → Refine

I call this The Intelligence Loop. (The phrase was inspired in part by the work of Yale computer science professor Nisheeth Vishnoi on iterative intelligence systems.) It captures the rhythm of sustainable growth in the modern era.

To learn is more than collecting data. It's about interpretation, understanding not just what's happening, but why it matters.

To apply is to act with intention, using insight to serve, create, or communicate in ways that align with purpose.

Reflection asks us to pause and examine impact, not only on profit, but on people and principles.

Refinement closes the loop, adapting the model, the message, or the method before beginning again, wiser, more aligned, and better prepared.

This loop isn't just how organizations evolve. It's how they stay vitally human while doing so.

Learning: The New Competitive Advantage

Learning velocity today has replaced market share as one of the most powerful advantages an organization can have.

The companies that learn fastest, from data, from failure, from feedback, and from difference, don't just survive disruption. They become antifragile. They don't break under pressure; they improve because of it.

A 2025 Harvard study on adaptive intelligence found that organizations practicing continuous, data-informed learning cycles outperformed their peers in long-term growth by 37%, even during periods of market contraction.

Learning isn't a phase you move through. It's a posture you adopt.

AI gives us powerful new tools to learn continuously. Wisdom then reminds us to be intentional about what we're learning, and why.

Applying: Turning Insight into Impact

Insight only matters when it's put to work.

Data without action is potential energy, elegant, impressive, and inert. In the most effective organizations, AI isn't treated as a black box of predictions. It's a **bridge** between understanding and action.

Consider a healthcare network that used AI to identify patients at risk of chronic illness by detecting subtle patterns in sleep, movement, and nutrition. The technology surfaced the risk. But the real breakthrough came when human teams partnered with community leaders to design localized health programs that addressed root causes.

The *model* predicted illness. *People* prevented suffering.

That's application with integrity, technology in service of transformation.

The same principle applies to marketing. AI can tell you who your audience is, when they're listening, where they're paying attention, and what they care about. But it takes human imagination to turn that knowledge into connection.

Data can guide the message. Only people can make it meaningful.

Insight without empathy is information. Insight *with* empathy becomes impact.

Reflecting: The Pause That Powers Progress

The third stage of the Intelligence Loop, Reflect, may be the hardest, because it asks us to slow down.

In an economy obsessed with acceleration, reflection feels inefficient, even self-indulgent. But in truth, it's the only path to wisdom.

Reflection is where we move from data to discernment. It's where leaders look beyond dashboards and ask:

- *What did we learn about people, not just performance?*
- *Did our innovation make life easier, fairer, or fuller?*
- *What unintended consequences emerged, and what do they teach us?*

These questions turn analysis into accountability.

A 2025 MIT Sloan study found that organizations embedding reflective review cycles into their AI programs reported 48% fewer ethical compliance issues and significantly higher stakeholder trust.

In reflection, we find direction.

Refining: The Art of Humble Adaptation

Refinement is where wisdom transforms into resilience.

The most successful organizations aren't the ones that get everything right the first time. They're the ones that treat getting it wrong as the beginning of getting it better.

AI accelerates this process by offering feedback at extraordinary speed. But it's humans who decide what to do with that feedback, what to keep, what to change, and what to let go.

Refinement requires humility. It means accepting that certainty is temporary, but curiosity can be permanent. Each pass through the Intelligence Loop becomes a moral exercise, not just a technical one, asking not only how to optimize systems, but how to optimize meaning.

Without this step, we confine ourselves to the tyranny of algorithms that calibrate themselves.

The Feedback Culture

At the center of refinement sits culture.

No organization can learn its way forward if people are afraid to speak openly and honestly. Feedback is the oxygen of growth, and AI gives us more ways than ever to capture and analyze it. But data alone doesn't create learning. Listening with empathy does.

Of course, not all feedback is equal. The goal isn't to collect every opinion, although full inclusion of ideas is vital to ensure authentic adoption of leadership. Instead, the goal is to hear what's true.

Microsoft's internal "growth pulse" system, introduced in 2023, analyzes anonymous employee sentiment alongside performance data. Instead of treating dissent as resistance, leaders treat it as information, a signal that a vital undercurrent of employee sentiment exists and is worth understanding.

That's refinement in motion. Humility, scaled by intelligence.

Case Study 8: The Learning Brand

A Swedish-based global fashion label, long known for innovation, began using AI in 2018 to measure environmental impact and advance sustainability. Rather than treating ethics as a separate compliance exercise, the company embedded ethical reflection directly into its AI workflows.

Dashboards tracked carbon reductions alongside a less conventional metric: emotional resonance. Using sentiment analysis, the brand monitored how consumers perceived the authenticity of its sustainability messaging in real time. When early signals suggested campaigns were drifting toward performative territory, the company shifted toward greater transparency and open data sharing with customers.

Sales rose modestly, consistent with retail benchmarks for authenticity-focused efforts, while customer trust increased markedly. Consumers did not reward flawless promises – they rewarded visible learning. In the intelligent age, truth itself becomes a growth strategy.

The Intelligence Loop as Leadership Model

The Intelligence Loop isn't just an organizational process. It's a leadership mindset. It's personal.

- ***Learn*** – Stay curious longer than comfortable.
- ***Apply*** – Act boldly, but with intention.
- ***Reflect*** – Pause to honestly understand impact, not just outcome.
- ***Refine*** – Evolve continuously, without ego.

This loop turns complexity into clarity. It converts fear into forward motion. And it keeps intelligence, human or artificial, anchored in wisdom.

In a world where algorithms evolve daily, leadership must become a living algorithm of ethics.

From Strategy to Spirit

The path forward isn't a roadmap. It's a rhythm. The rhythm of listening, of learning, of leading with integrity.

The most enduring organizations of the next decade won't be the ones that master technology first. They'll be the ones that master *trust.* AI can win *attention*. Only *humanity* can win allegiance.

That difference, between temporary relevance and lasting relationship, is what separates disruption from significance.

Accordingly, the central question must change. Not *How do we grow faster?* but *How do we grow wiser **at scale**?* Wisdom compounds longer than capital ever will.

The Courage to Evolve

Every meaningful transformation requires courage, not the courage to dominate, but the courage to evolve. "That's how it's done" and "Because it's our process" is yesterday's thinking and will lead to irrelevancy.

Recent headlines of AI-driven layoffs and job reductions notwithstanding, the next generation's leaders won't be remembered for how they used AI to replace human workers, but for how they used it to reimagine themselves. They'll be the ones willing to unlearn certainty, relearn humility, and rediscover purpose.

A 2026 Deloitte survey found that the highest-performing organizations shared one defining trait: psychological safety. People believed they could experiment, fail, and grow without fear.

That permission to be imperfect is the soil where intelligence and imagination grow together. It's also where the spark of creative invention thrives. Without it, no algorithm can save us.

The Human + Machine Partnership

When it works well, AI isn't just an assistant. It's a magnifying mirror.

It reflects and reflects what we value, what we fear, and what we're willing to become. The organizations that thrive will be the ones that treat AI as an extension of their best intentions, not a substitute for their better instincts.

This is the partnership of the century: humans bringing meaning, machines bringing momentum. Together, they release potential neither could reach alone.

But partnership requires parity, a belief that empathy and intelligence are both forms of strength.

A Call to Leaders

So where do we actually begin?

Not with code. Not with capital. Not with another framework or change plan. Those will come, and they'll matter. But they aren't the starting point.

Every meaningful shift in leadership begins with character.

The AI era isn't asking leaders to know more than everyone else in the room. Machines already handle that. What this moment asks instead is something quieter and harder: the willingness to care deeply about the consequences of what we build. To slow down long enough to ask whether progress is serving people, or simply impressing them.

Caring doesn't weaken leadership. It clarifies it. It gives direction to power and purpose to scale. When leaders care, decisions change. Trade-offs are named instead of hidden. People are treated as contributors, not variables. And trust, once earned, becomes a force multiplier no technology can replicate.

Leadership in this age won't be defined by technical fluency alone. It will be defined by moral fluency, the ability to hold complexity without losing compassion, to pursue growth without abandoning responsibility, and to lead through uncertainty without pretending to have every answer.

This kind of leadership doesn't always announce itself. It shows up in the questions leaders ask when the room is empty. In the moments they choose transparency over convenience. In the times they protect people instead of metrics, and discover, often to their surprise, that performance improves anyway.

The call to leaders is simple, but not easy: lead in a way you'd be proud to see automated.

We aren't competing with AI. That frame misses the point entirely. We're collaborating collaborate with a future that will reflect our choices back to us at scale. The systems we design will carry our assumptions, our incentives, and our blind spots. They'll teach others, long after we're gone, what we believed mattered.

Because in the end, the most advanced systems won't define this era. The values embedded within them will. And those values begin, not in code, but in us.

Closing Reflection: The Infinite Loop of Learning

The Intelligence Loop never ends.

It doesn't spin in circles. It rises in spirals. Each pass brings deeper understanding and greater responsibility. And each reminds us that intelligence, silicon or biological, is only as powerful as the heart that guides it.

We're the stewards of that heart, the guardians of meaning. We serve as teachers of the machines that will teach generations to come.

The path forward isn't about replacing human intelligence. It's about expanding it, together. And in that expansion, we may finally realize that the real revolution was never artificial at all.

It was always human.

Key Takeaways – The Path Forward

- *The Intelligence Loop (**Learn → Apply → Reflect → Refine**) defines sustainable, ethical growth in the AI age.*
- ***Learning velocity** is the new **competitive advantage**.*
- *The future belongs to leaders who marry **intelligence** with **integrity**.*

Chapter 2

From Automation to Augmentation

Part I – The End of Automation as an Answer

For much of the past two decades, automation was treated as the ultimate expression of progress. It promised faster, cheaper, better, the relentless pursuit of efficiency applied to nearly everything we touched.

We automated factories and customer service. Media buying and supply chains. Workflows, approvals, even our calendars. We built systems that could move data at the speed of light, analyze it in moments, and act before we'd fully decided what action meant. The goal was simple: remove friction, eliminate delay, and let machines do what humans no longer needed to.

And for a time, it worked.

Productivity climbed. Costs dropped. Entire industries celebrated what they called efficiency revolutions. Automation delivered exactly what it promised.

But somewhere along the way, the definition of progress began to feel incomplete.

We began seeing the limits of optimization. Automation could do the work, but it couldn't do the wondering. It could execute tasks, but it couldn't sense context. It could generate answers at scale, but it couldn't ask the questions that actually change direction.

Automation solved the problem of labor. It didn't solve the problem of meaning.

Once that realization set in, it became clear that the next season of progress wouldn't be about doing the same things faster. It would be about doing more meaningful things, together.

That's where augmentation begins.

The Illusion of Infinite Efficiency

From the mid-2010s to the early 2020s, driven largely by the rise of Robotic Process Automation (RPA), artificial intelligence, and digital change initiatives, a phrase began circulating through business conversations and at conferences: If it can be automated, it should be.

At the time, this concept sounded not just logical, but responsible. Automation was framed as progress in its purest form, the final step in designing human friction out of work. Every task automated felt like a small victory over inefficiency, a signal that the organization was modern, disciplined, and future-ready.

For a while, the results seemed undeniable. Dashboards lit up. Cycle times shrank. Margins improved. Automation delivered exactly what it promised, and leaders leaned in. Efficiency became the dominant language of success.

But beneath the metrics, something began to feel off.

As work became faster and cleaner, it also became thinner. The pursuit of efficiency slowly replaced the pursuit of excellence. Decisions were optimized for speed rather than depth.

Processes ran smoothly, but curiosity faded. People executed more, and questioned less.

A 2024 MIT Sloan study captured this tension clearly. While automation increased productivity by an average of 38%, employee engagement dropped by nearly a quarter over the same period. The machines hadn't failed, they did their job. What faltered was the human connection to the work itself.

Automation maximized speed, but it minimized spirit.

And once spirit fades, performance eventually follows, no matter how efficient the system appears.

The Productivity Paradox

Economists have a name for this contradiction: the productivity paradox. Technology accelerates at an exponential pace, yet human satisfaction remains stubbornly flat.

The paradox exists because automation is excellent at measuring what's easy to count, and far less capable of capturing what truly matters. Output is visible. Insight is harder to quantify.

Engagement can be tracked, but emotional resonance, the feeling that work matters, is much harder to reduce to a metric.

In our drive to optimize to build dashboards that could tell us everything about behavior, we learned very little about motivation. We gained precision but lost some of the unpredictability that often sparks real innovation. The chance conversations. The half-formed ideas. The moments of curiosity that don't show up in quarterly reports but change direction over time.

Automation gave us systems that could predict what consumers would do next. It couldn't tell us what they actually desired.

And in many organizations, motion became a proxy for meaning. Activity stood in for progress. Output substituted for purpose. Work moved faster, but fewer people could explain why it mattered.

That's the paradox at the heart of automation: the more we optimized for efficiency alone, the more we exposed the limits of efficiency as a measure of progress.

And it's exactly why the next phase, augmentation, became not just possible, but necessary

The End of Imitation

Automation creates a built-in blind spot. It's very good at imitation. It's not built for imagination.

Algorithms learn by looking backward. They study what already exists, find patterns, and reproduce them at scale, projecting forward. That makes them powerful optimizers of the past, but unreliable guides to what comes next. They may refine what has worked, but they can't originate a future that hasn't been seen yet.

That's why AI-generated art still leans on human inspiration. Why AI-written songs may sound right but often feel hollow without human emotion behind them. And why AI-created advertising still depends on human truth to persuade, not just human data to target.

The risk of automation isn't that it will do things poorly. It's that it will do them too well, repeating familiar formulas until originality slowly fades into sameness.

Nowhere is this more visible than in marketing. As generative tools become easier to use, some brands have leaned heavily on auto-written copy, auto-designed visuals, and auto-targeted audiences. The outcome is efficient, polished, yet increasingly indistinguishable.

Everything works, but very little moves anyone.

Automation without intention creates aesthetic anesthesia. Content looks right, sounds right, and lands... nowhere. Consumers don't want more messages competing for their attention. They want fewer messages that actually mean something. For now, meaning remains a human monopoly.

When Doing More Means Meaning Less

Automation is driven by a simple logic: *more.*

More ads per second. More impressions per dollar. More variations per campaign. More output everywhere. On paper, it's progress. In practice, it often leads to exhaustion, on both sides of the screen.

As volume increases, clarity disappears. The question shifts from *Why are we saying this?* to

How fast can we ship it? And in that shift, meaning is often the first thing to go.

That's why a simple, honest TikTok filmed on a phone can outperform a multimillion-dollar media buy. Not because it's more polished, but because it feels more real. Connection isn't a function of scale. It's a function of *sincerity.*

Recognizing automation's limitations doesn't mean rejecting technology. It means resisting the temptation to confuse *efficiency* with *effectiveness.* Efficiency without empathy leads to erosion, the slow wearing away of trust, relevance, and emotional connection.

Organizations don't lose their edge overnight. They lose it incrementally, interaction by empty yet optimized interaction at a time.

The Human Return on Automation

When AI takes on the repetitive and routine, humans are freed to focus on the remarkable. This is the often-missed return on automation:

not just cost savings or speed, but the return to imagination. The opportunity to reinvest human time where it creates the most value.

Repurposing, rather than *replacing* humans.

At one creative agency, automating the production of nearly 90 percent of digital ad variants didn't lead to layoffs or creative shortcuts. It led to reinvestment. Strategists spent more time on brand narrative, consumer psychology, and experimentation. Designers explored bolder concepts instead of endless revisions.

Campaign performance improved by 47 percent.

The efficiency gains mattered, but they weren't the story. The story was what people did with the time they got back.

Every hour automation saves is an hour leaders can choose to reinvest, in curiosity, in empathy, in originality. Or they can choose to fill it with more output and tighter timelines. The technology doesn't decide. Leadership does.

Automation's real promise was never replacement. It was redirection.

And the organizations grasping this won't just operate faster. They'll create work that lasts.

3 Case Studies – Factories Rediscovering Their Humanity

Multiple examples can be found in business case studies of manufacturers implementing AI to reduce production costs while discovering the power of drawing on human ingenuity again. Here are three:

Ford Transmission Plant, Livonia, Michigan

A station where robots assembled torque converters added an AI layer that learned from recent attempts how to "wiggle" parts into place more efficiently, reducing the need for repeated manual tweaking and intervention.

It appeared to employees the robot is "learning the job," not just repeating it. This created understandable anxiety from Ford plant workers.

In response, the more experienced employees were tasked to become "process whisperers", the ones who knew which fits are normal variation vs. a real defect, and who translated that into constraints, checks, and acceptance criteria for the AI-controlled motion.

Ford eventually reported this approach made that part of the line run ~15% faster. Even Ford's plant manager framed it as improving existing automation, not eliminating the need for people, "manpower is actually very important."

Whirlpool (appliance manufacturing), "Co-bots" on assembly tasks

Whirlpool installed collaborative robots ("co-bots") to assist with installing glass in oven doors, a task that can be risky for humans and damage-prone for product.

Once a cobot takes over *one* difficult step, providing human-safe tasks at scale, assembly workers wonder what's next on the line.

To counter thr concern, Whirlpool explicitly pointed to operators' suggestions turning them into solutions and emphasizes training/upskilling as part of the shift.

Honda's AI/AR inspection guidance showed employees "exactly where to move something," which created a feedback loop: humans correcting edge-cases, improving standard work, and the system grew tighter over time.

The operator who was previously known for "fast hands" becomes "the person who improves the system."

Honda, Marysville, Ohio (EV production hub transition)

A Honda manufacturing plant upgraded Electric Vehicle (EV) production incorporating tasks dedicated to automated robots, while maintaining a "man/machine" balance for what still needs human touch.

Transitions like these (especially EV retooling) can create significant rumor threads, especially when management isn't clear in communicating strategic intent. In other words, "new tech" starts sounding like "new headcount math."

To counter increased employee concerns, ~300 workers received updated skills training tied to the shift.

The key lesson from each of these examples is that leadership language matters: to win employee buy-in management must clearly communicate that humans have to be in the center of initiatives that must be felt; automation is used for what can't be reliably seen/done safely.

Automation became *augmentation*, not of machines, but of *meaning*.

Why Automation Alone Fails

Automation is excellent at multiplying efficiency. It's far less capable of multiplying trust.

It can reduce errors, standardize outcomes, and move faster than any human system ever could. But it can't sense how people feel about the work they're doing. It can't replace pride, purpose, or belief in a shared direction.

That limitation shows up over time.

Many organizations experience an early surge after heavy automation investment. Productivity jumps. Costs drop. The systems perform exactly as designed. And then, often quietly, performance plateaus. A 2025 PwC report found that after roughly two years of aggressive automation, most companies stopped seeing meaningful gains. The missing ingredient wasn't better technology. It was trust.

Automation introduced without transparency creates anxiety. People wonder what's coming next and where they fit. But when automation is explained clearly, when leaders share the "why," invite participation, and show how human roles will evolve, something shifts.

Fear gives way to ownership. Resistance turns into contribution.

When people understand how machines support them rather than replace them, they stop guarding their value and start creating new ones. That's when innovation accelerates again, not because of the technology, but because of the humans using it.

The Evolutionary Imperative

Human progress has never been about avoiding effort. It's been about expanding possibility.

We didn't build tools to do less. We built them so we could do more of what matters. Fire didn't just keep us warm; it gave us time to gather and tell stories. The wheel didn't just move goods; it expanded where we could go. The microchip didn't just compute; it unlocked imagination.

AI now offers something similar. It can free our time and attention, but only if we evolve how we think about our role alongside it.

Automation reaches its limit when we treat machines as endpoints. Augmentation begins when we see them as instruments. The shift happens when we stop asking, What can machines do for us? and start asking, What can we do through machines that we couldn't do before?

That's the real transition taking place. Not from human to artificial intelligence, but from isolated intelligence to amplified intelligence, where human judgment, creativity, and empathy gain reach rather than lose relevance.

Closing Reflection: The Human Multiplier

Every major technology in history has moved through two phases.

The first is imitation. We use machines to replicate what humans already do, faster, cheaper, and at scale. The second is amplification. We use those same machines to extend what makes us uniquely human.

The first phase makes us efficient. The second makes us capable of more than we were before.

We're standing at that threshold again. Automation delivered efficiency. It did its job. The next step, augmentation, is about what we choose to do with that efficiency.

Progress isn't ultimately measured in processing power or transaction volume. It's measured in whether our tools bring us closer to better thinking, deeper connection, and more meaningful work.

Machines won't replace what makes us human.

They'll simply reveal how far it can reach, when we choose to use them that way. And that choice is the multiplier that matters most.

Key Takeaways – The End of Automation as an Answer

- *Automation delivers **efficiency** but not **evolution**.*
- *The real ROI of automation is **reinvestment** in **imagination**.*
- *The future of growth lies in **augmentation**, technology **with us**, not **instead of us**.*

Part II – The Rise of the Augmented Workforce

For centuries, human progress has been defined by our relationship with our tools. We built hammers, then factories, then computers, each step designed to make us faster, stronger, and smarter.

But for the first time in history, our tools can now learn alongside us. That changes everything.

Beyond the Age of Automation

Automation was the first act of the digital revolution, machines doing what humans used to do. Augmentation is the sequel, machines helping humans do what they never could before. The distinction matters enormously.

Automation replaces. Augmentation amplifies.

Automation values consistency. Augmentation values creativity. Automation scales labor. Augmentation scales learning.

In this new age, success isn't measured by how much work we eliminate, but by how much wonder we unleash.

The Co-Creator Paradigm

The modern workplace is shifting from human vs. machine to human + machine. AI is no longer the robot in the corner, it's the colleague across the table, the creative partner who never tires, the analytical teammate who sees patterns we miss.

In a recent Deloitte study, 72% of high-growth companies said they now view AI as a "collaborator" rather than a "tool."

That may sound abstract, but the reality is deeply tangible.

A marketing strategist uses predictive models to forecast campaign resonance. A physician uses AI imaging to diagnose conditions earlier. A teacher uses adaptive learning platforms to personalize every lesson. A filmmaker uses generative visual AI to test 50 storyboards in a single afternoon.

Each example tells the same story: the work is changing because the relationship is changing.

AI doesn't just help us do more. It helps us be more, more observant, more empathetic, more imaginative

Case Study 9: The Ad Agency That Learned to Listen

In 2025, a global creative agency confronted an uncomfortable reality: its heavily automated processes had made campaigns more efficient but increasingly uninspired and repetitive.

Instead of doubling down on generation tools, the agency built an AI platform focused on listening – analyzing emotional reactions and audience sentiment across content. The insights proved revelatory: people craved shared values, authenticity, inclusion, and vulnerability far more than polished execution.

Creative teams rebuilt their storytelling frameworks around these signals. Within six months, engagement rose significantly and brand-favorability scores improved. Automation had optimized performance. Augmentation restored purpose.

Humans: The New Interface

In an era of intelligent machines, the human role isn't shrinking, it's evolving.

Humans are no longer the operators of technology; they're the interpreters of intelligence. They translate data into meaning, patterns into stories, predictions into empathy.

This evolution mirrors something seen during every technological shift. When the printing press arrived, scribes didn't vanish, they became editors. When photography emerged, painters didn't disappear, they reinvented art. Now, as AI proliferates, humans aren't being replaced, they're being refocused.

The human mind becomes the interface, the place where insight meets intuition.

The Symphony of Skills

The augmented workforce requires a new kind of skill set, one that blends logic with imagination.

According to the World Economic Forum's *Future of Jobs Report* (2025), the most in-demand human capabilities over the next decade will be:

- Analytical reasoning
- Creative problem solving
- Empathy and emotional intelligence
- Ethical judgment
- Adaptability and learning agility

These aren't technical skills, they are consequential ones. AI can process. Only humans can perceive.

That's why "soft skills" are now the hardest currency in the modern economy.

Case Study 10: A Hospital That Healed with Data

At a large university hospital in the Netherlands, doctors deployed AI to scan thousands of diagnostic images daily, identifying subtle patterns and early disease indicators that would be difficult for humans to detect unaided.

The true breakthrough, however, was not in the diagnostics themselves but in how physicians used the insights. AI reduced documentation burden, freeing doctors to spend more time in face-to-face conversation with patients. One physician captured the shift: "AI gave me back my humanity. I stopped documenting and started listening again."

Intelligence did not replace bedside manner – it restored it. This is augmentation at its purest: technology that strengthens empathy and human connection.

The Emotional Engine of Creativity

In creative industries, augmentation is rewriting what it means to make something new.

A designer can use AI to generate hundreds of visual variations, but the spark of "that's it" remains uniquely human. A songwriter can use AI to experiment with chord progressions or lyrical phrasing, but the choice that moves hearts still belongs to the artist.

AI doesn't invent beauty; it accelerates discovery.

At a London-based fashion house, designers use generative tools to imagine color palettes inspired by climate data, translating weather patterns into fabric hues. The result? Designs that connect art, science, and storytelling in ways that transcend categories.

Creativity becomes collaborative, the human leads, and the machine harmonizes.

Education Reimagined

The same transformation is happening in classrooms.

Teachers, once burdened with administrative tasks, can now focus on nurturing curiosity. AI handles grading, pacing, and lesson adaptation, freeing educators to focus on empathy, mentorship, and inspiration.

In one pilot program in Singapore, AI-driven learning assistants tracked student engagement, identifying when learners were frustrated or disengaged. Instead of issuing alerts, the system offered suggestions, not to the student, but to the teacher: "Ask a reflective question now," "Introduce a visual aid," "Take a short pause."

The teachers didn't lose control; they gained insight.

The goal of education has always been transformation, not automation. Now it can finally be both.

The Productivity Renaissance

Augmentation creates a multiplier effect across industries. When AI handles the procedural, humans can devote more time to innovation, empathy, and refinement.

A McKinsey Global Institute study found that employees using generative AI tools saw productivity gains up to 60%, not because they worked harder, but because they worked smarter.

But the real story wasn't the output, it was the outcome. Workers reported higher satisfaction, describing their jobs as "more meaningful" and "more creative."

That's the hidden dividend of the augmented age: fulfillment through freedom.

Case Study 11: The Logistics Company That Learned to Feel

A European logistics firm implemented AI primarily to optimize delivery routes and inventory management. The project began as a straightforward efficiency initiative.

Once deployed, leaders noticed an unexpected benefit: employee turnover dropped sharply. Analysis revealed that AI had eliminated many of the most frustrating tasks – manual dispatch juggling, constant scheduling conflicts, and last-minute reroutes. Workers could now focus on coordination, problem-solving, and customer service.

One driver described the change simply: "It used to feel like the computer was my boss. Now it feels like my assistant."

Augmentation does not make humans obsolete. It removes drudgery and makes human judgment more essential than ever.

Leadership in the Augmented Era

Leaders in this new world must master the art of balance:

- Between speed and stillness
- Between automation and imagination.
- Between data and discernment.

The role of leadership shifts from direction to design, designing cultures where curiosity thrives and technology is trusted.

Satya Nadella once said that great leaders "don't just empower others to do more; they help others do more meaningful work."

That's the essence of the augmented organization.

The Ethics of Collaboration

As AI grows more powerful, the responsibility of partnership grows deeper. Augmentation isn't just about capability, it's about character.

If we allow AI to scale everything, then we must choose carefully what we allow it to amplify.

Because AI will magnify bias as easily as brilliance, noise as easily as nuance, profit as easily as purpose.

That's why augmentation without ethics risks becoming exploitation.

The augmented workforce must therefore be guided by a shared moral compass, a commitment to fairness, transparency, and dignity.

Trust isn't a byproduct of intelligence; it's a prerequisite.

Closing Reflection: The Beautiful Middle

We stand at the intersection of two truths: Automation made us efficient. Augmentation will make us extraordinary.

But the real beauty lies in the middle, the collaboration where intelligence and imagination meet.

The augmented workforce isn't the end of human relevance. It's the beginning of human renaissance, the rediscovery of why we work, what we value, and who we can become when our tools reflect our highest ideals.

The future isn't about working harder or even smarter. It's about working truer, in harmony with the very intelligence we've created.

Key Takeaways – The Rise of the Augmented Workforce

- *Augmentation transforms AI from a* ***tool*** *into a* ***collaborator****.*
- *The new skills of the era:* ***creativity****,* ***empathy****,* ***adaptability****, and* ***moral reasoning****.*
- *The augmented workforce represents not the* ***end of human work****, but the* ***beginning of human potential****.*

Part III – The New Skill Curve

The workforce of the future won't be divided by who uses AI and who doesn't. It will be divided by those who learn with AI, and those who stop learning altogether.

We are entering an era where skills have half-lives shorter than product cycles. What once lasted a career now expires in a quarter. But this isn't a story of obsolescence, it's a story of opportunity.

Because the new advantage isn't in what you know, but in how fast you can learn what you need next.

The Collapse of the Old Learning Model

For generations, professional development followed a straight line: go to school, get a job, master a role, climb a ladder, retire with stability.

But ladders are disappearing, replaced by networks, and the lines have bent into loops.

In a 2025 World Economic Forum study, 85% of executives agreed that "continuous learning" will become the most valuable professional currency within five years. Yet only 27% of organizations had built systems to support it.

The mismatch is striking. We've told people they need to "reskill," but we've rarely shown them how, or why.

The truth is that learning is no longer a separate phase of life. It's the new fabric of life.

From Hard Skills to Human Skills

In an AI-powered world, technical skill remains important, but it's no longer sufficient. The future of work belongs to human skills, the capabilities that machines can't replicate:

- Creativity
- Emotional intelligence
- Adaptability

- Critical reasoning
- Ethical judgment
- Collaboration

These aren't peripheral traits; they're now the main event.

A 2024 McKinsey study revealed that roles requiring emotional intelligence are growing 3x faster than those based on routine knowledge. The reason is simple: AI can simulate logic, but not love.

Automation makes process perfect. Augmentation makes people purposeful.

That's the shift at the heart of the new skill curve, from mastery of tasks to mastery of transformation.

Case Study 12: The Marketing Team That Relearned Its Art

A global consumer brand's marketing division had become heavily reliant on automation and generative tools. Campaigns were produced faster, but the brand's distinct identity had begun to flatten.

The CMO launched the "Human Edge Project" – a six-week period in which teams worked without AI to reconnect with core storytelling, emotion, and brand philosophy. When AI was reintroduced, it served to extend and scale human ideas rather than originate them.

Campaign response rates increased substantially, but the deeper transformation was cultural: the team rediscovered its authentic voice. In an age of intelligent tools, self-awareness has become the decisive competitive skill.

Case Study 13: Learning as a Team Sport

The most successful modern organizations do not simply hire knowledgeable individuals – they cultivate living cultures of shared learning. They reward curiosity as much as competence and replace "know-it-alls" with "learn-it-alls."

Microsoft famously embraced this philosophy in the mid-2010s under Satya Nadella. Internal surveys showed that employees participating in peer-learning communities reported meaningfully higher satisfaction and innovation output.

When learning becomes a team sport, organizations stop functioning as static departments and transform into dynamic discovery engines.

Case Study 14: The Augmented Classroom

At a public university in California, professors collaborated with an AI platform to create personalized learning paths tailored to each student's pace, strengths, and needs.

The system's most valuable contribution, however, was detecting early signs of disengagement and prompting timely human mentorship. Dropout rates fell substantially, and participation improved across demographic groups.

Technology did not replace teaching. It restored teaching to its original purpose: truly seeing and supporting the individual student. In every field, the highest use of intelligence is to deepen human relationships.

The Learning Mindset

Skills can be taught. Mindset must be cultivated. And the mindset of the new age is one of adaptive curiosity.

Adaptive curiosity means being comfortable in discomfort, embracing uncertainty as a catalyst, not a threat. It means understanding that intelligence isn't fixed; it's fluid.

A 2025 MIT Center for Collective Intelligence study found that teams with high "curiosity indices", measured by their willingness to explore new tools and question assumptions, were twice as likely to generate breakthrough innovation. and curiosity has become the new productivity.

The "Unlearning" Revolution

But the hardest part of learning in the AI era isn't acquiring new skills. It's unlearning old assumptions.

Unlearning is the art of letting go, of outgrown methods, outdated hierarchies, inherited fears. When we cling to what once worked, we close ourselves to what now will.

That's why great leaders treat humility as a skill, the courage to admit they don't know yet.

In marketing, that means challenging decades of "best practices." In education, it means rethinking standardized testing. In business, it means replacing command-and-control with coach-and-collaborate.

The organizations that will thrive aren't the ones with the longest playbooks, but the ones willing to rewrite them in real time.

Case Study 15: The Creative Director Who Relearned Wonder

A veteran creative director known for her strong intuition initially resisted AI-driven content testing. "I know what works," she maintained.

She agreed to a controlled experiment: one of her proven concepts was tested against AI-generated variations based on emotional language patterns. To her surprise, one machine-suggested option outperformed her original.

Rather than feeling threatened, she felt reawakened. "It didn't make me less creative," she reflected. "It reminded me that creativity is about listening, not assuming."

The new creative advantage is the willingness to be surprised – and to let that surprise deepen our wonder.

From Skills to Systems

The future of learning isn't just about individuals, it's about the systems that sustain them.

Corporate learning platforms are evolving into ecosystems that combine AI tutors, peer networks, and experiential feedback. The best organizations are turning learning into a living process, not a quarterly training metric.

For instance, Unilever's "Flex Experience" program allows employees to rotate roles across departments guided by AI recommendations. It's not just reskilling, it's reinvention.

Participants report twice the engagement of non-participants, and internal mobility has surged. These companies don't just adapt to change. They cultivate people who embody change.

The Skill of Meaning

In a world of accelerating automation, humans are rediscovering their deepest skill: the ability to make meaning.

Meaning-making isn't measurable by an algorithm, yet it's the essence of why work matters. When people find purpose in their contribution, performance becomes self-sustaining.

Gallup's 2025 report on workforce engagement found that employees who describe their work as "meaningful" are 5x more likely to stay long-term and 3x more likely to innovate proactively.

Meaning, not money, fuels mastery.

That's why the new skill curve isn't vertical, it's spiral. Every learning cycle deepens our understanding of what we value.

The New Meritocracy

For generations, meritocracy was defined by credentials. Now it's being redefined by capability evolution.

AI doesn't care about résumés. It cares about results. What matters most isn't where you learned, but how you apply what you continue to learn.

Companies like Google and IBM have already abandoned degree requirements for many roles, focusing instead on skill-based assessments and adaptive learning certifications.

This democratizes opportunity, but it also demands accountability. The burden of learning now belongs to everyone, not just institutions.

The new meritocracy rewards those who are perpetually becoming.

Closing Reflection: The Learner's Legacy

We're the first generation in human history to work with intelligence that can grow alongside us. That means we are also the first to decide what kind of learners we'll become.

If we treat learning as a race, we'll burn out. If we treat it as a rhythm, we'll build resilience.

Every question asked, every mistake made, every iteration refined, all of it shapes the future not just of our work, but of our wisdom.

The skill that will outlast every technology is the one that built them all: the courage to keep learning.

Key Takeaways – The New Skill Curve

- *Continuous learning is the new* ***professional currency****.*
- *Human skills, creativity, empathy, adaptability, have become the* ***ultimate differentiators****.*
- *People should treat learning as* ***permanent*** *rather than* ***episodic****.*

Part IV – The Symbiosis of Trust

Trust has always been the invisible currency of civilization. It powers markets, relationships, and ideas. But in an age when decisions are made by algorithms and data determines destiny, trust must evolve.

The question is no longer Can we trust people with machines? It's Can we trust machines with people?

And even more profoundly, Can we trust ourselves to build systems worthy of that trust?

The Fragility of the Invisible

Trust, like oxygen, is invisible until it's gone. It takes years to build and seconds to break.

We trust pilots to fly planes we can't steer, doctors to prescribe medicine we can't understand, and leaders to make decisions we can't verify in real time. That social contract, the faith that competence and conscience coexist, is what keeps the modern world functioning.

But AI has disrupted that contract.

For the first time, we are delegating not just labor, but judgment, the ability to decide what's right, what's fair, what's true. And judgment without transparency is a fragile foundation.

The Trust Deficit

Surveys by Edelman's *Trust Barometer* (2025) reveal a stark paradox:

- **74%** of people believe AI will fundamentally improve their lives.
- Yet **62%** say they don't trust the organizations developing it.

That gap, between potential and perception, defines the next frontier of leadership.

People don't fear intelligence. They fear invisibility. They fear decisions made without understanding, processes designed without accountability, and systems that evolve faster than ethics.

The problem isn't AI. The problem is opacity.

Transparency as the New Innovation

For decades, innovation was defined by secrecy, competitive advantage meant keeping your formula hidden. Today, innovation's new currency is transparency.

In marketing, brands that openly disclose how algorithms personalize ads outperform those that obscure them. In healthcare, hospitals that show how AI supports diagnosis earn higher patient confidence. In government, agencies that explain data usage build civic participation instead of conspiracy.

Transparency doesn't weaken authority; it strengthens it. Because people don't need perfection, they need honesty.

The augmented era demands not "black box brilliance" but glass box integrity.

Case Study 16: The Transparent Bank

A growing number of digital-first lenders now design AI loan engines not only for efficiency but for equity. The most progressive institutions go further: they publish their logic models, bias audit findings, and fairness parameters.

Customers can literally see why decisions were made. In one such case, customer complaints dropped substantially and trust ratings rose significantly. Competitors called the openness risky. Customers called it revolutionary.

Transparency did not weaken the system – it invited collaboration and built deeper loyalty. Openness has become one of the strongest competitive advantages in the age of intelligent decision-making.

The Psychology of Partnership

Trust isn't a technological challenge. It's a psychological equation. It requires three conditions:

- **Competence**, "You can do what you say you can do."
- **Consistency**, "You'll do it reliably, every time."
- **Care**, "You'll do it with my best interest in mind."

AI easily achieves the first two. It's the third, care, that only humans can guarantee. That's why trust can't be outsourced. It must be authored.

When Machines Make Mistakes

Most trust stories begin with a failure.

In 2024, a global retail company discovered its pricing algorithm had unintentionally penalized lower-income zip codes. No human had set out to discriminate, the model had simply optimized for profit without context.

The company paused the system, issued refunds, and published a full audit explaining what went wrong. It also implemented a "Human in the Loop" process, ensuring that every automated decision was reviewed for ethical impact. Sales dipped briefly, but brand trust skyrocketed.

The lesson was clear: accountability builds more trust than perfection ever could.

The Human in the Loop

"Human in the loop" is more than a technical safeguard, it's a moral philosophy. It ensures that automation remains aligned with intention.

In an augmented workforce, human oversight isn't a constraint; it's a compass. It brings context to code, empathy to equations, and conscience to computation.

Imagine AI managing media campaigns. It can optimize for engagement, but a human must ask, "Are we engaging ethically?"

AI can recommend medical treatments, but a doctor must ask, "Does this align with the patient's story?"

AI can predict customer desires, but a marketer must ask, "Does this respect their dignity?" That's the heart of the symbiosis: intelligence multiplied by empathy.

Case Study 17: The Airline That Listened

After repeated complaints about impersonal automated rebooking during disruptions, a major airline enhanced its AI with a "human empathy layer." Emotionally charged interactions were routed to specially trained live agents rather than handled by scripted bots.

The results were striking: satisfaction scores rose substantially and employee stress levels decreased markedly.

AI managed the logistics. Humans managed the emotional reality. When systems are deliberately designed to hand off the human moments to humans, trust and care scale together.

The Economics of Trust

Trust isn't just a moral virtue; it's a measurable asset.

According to PwC's 2025 Global Trust Index, companies with strong stakeholder trust outperform peers by 30% in long-term valuation. Why? Because trust accumulates steadily, quietly, steadily, invisibly, until it defines everything.

Trust lowers friction, accelerates collaboration, and turns loyalty into longevity.

But here's the paradox: in the era of AI, trust must be earned faster than ever and lost slower than ever. Every interaction, every algorithmic decision, every data point either deposits or withdraws from the "trust account."

Leaders who understand that balance will define the next generation of sustainable growth.

Cultural Trust: The Invisible Infrastructure

Inside organizations, trust operates as infrastructure, the emotional architecture that holds teams together when systems fail.

In AI-augmented workplaces, cultural trust becomes even more vital. If employees don't trust leadership's motives for automation, every technological advancement becomes a psychological setback.

Building trust internally requires transparency externally. Leaders must share not only what AI can do but also what it shouldn't do.

When employees understand that AI is meant to elevate their purpose, not eliminate their position, fear turns into fuel.

That's why the most innovative companies are also the most transparent. Their secret isn't technology, it's trustworthiness.

Case Study 18: The Factory That Shared Its Code

A German manufacturing company introduced AI-powered quality inspection systems. Workers initially feared layoffs and loss of control. Leadership responded with radical transparency: they opened the AI system's code to the line teams.

Employees were invited to understand how the system worked, critique its decisions, and suggest improvements. Within months, workers identified blind spots that engineers had missed. Accuracy improved noticeably, while anxiety transformed into pride and ownership.

When people help shape the intelligence that affects their work, they stop fearing it and start championing it. Transparency turned potential resistance into powerful collaboration.

From Control to Collaboration

Trust changes management from control into collaboration. In traditional hierarchies, leaders held information; employees followed. In intelligent organizations, information flows freely, and leadership becomes a shared responsibility.

When trust is distributed, innovation becomes inevitable.

2025 Harvard Business Review analysis found that teams with high trust environments were **11x** more likely to experiment with new technologies and **4x** more likely to report emotional well-being at work. *Trust is the new performance metric.*

The Moral Loop

Just as AI runs on data loops, humanity runs on moral loops, continuous cycles of accountability, empathy, and renewal.

When trust breaks, it must be repaired through openness and humility. When it holds, it must be reinforced through gratitude and care.

Trust isn't a one-time transaction. It's a living relationship, one that grows stronger each time humans and machines learn from each other.

The future of AI isn't about replacing trust with code. It's about encoding trust into the fabric of intelligence itself.

Closing Reflection: The Bridge Between Worlds

In the end, trust is the bridge between two worlds: the measurable and the meaningful.

We can calculate engagement, automate operations, and optimize outcomes, but we can't code belief. Belief must be earned through transparency, consistency, and compassion.

The more intelligent our systems become, the more intentional our ethics must be. Because the only algorithm that truly matters is the one we write in our actions: one that says, We see you. We hear you. We care.

The future of work won't run on data alone. It will run on trust, the oldest technology of all.

Key Takeaways – The Symbiosis of Trust

- ***Trust*** *is the new* ***competitive advantage*** *in the AI era.*
- ***Transparency*** *builds belief* ***faster*** *than perfection ever could.*
- *The true foundation of intelligent systems isn't data, it's* ***dignity****.*

Part V – The Augmented Organization

The industrial age asked how to make more. The digital age asked how to move faster. The question now is harder: how do we become better?

Better, in this context, means more intentional. More honest about trade-offs. More willing to slow down when slowing down is the responsible choice.

The augmented organization is built on that question. It isn't defined by the technology it uses but by what it does with the space that technology creates.

From Hierarchies to Harmonies

Traditional organizations were designed like machines: rigid, predictable, efficient. They thrived on control, the belief that the fewer variables you've, the fewer mistakes you make.

But the modern world doesn't reward predictability. It rewards adaptability.

In an era of constant change, harmony replaces hierarchy. Instead of silos, there are symphonies, teams that align around purpose, not process.

A recent Accenture study found that companies with adaptive organizational models are 2.5x more likely to outperform peers on innovation and employee satisfaction.

That's not because they're chaotic. It's because they're cohesive. Harmony, after all, isn't everyone playing the same note, it's everyone listening to the same rhythm.

The augmented organization listens, to data, to customers, and most importantly, to its people.

Leadership as Design, Not Direction

The role of leadership is changing from commander to composer.

In the augmented organization, leaders don't just make decisions; they design systems of meaning. They orchestrate the relationship between people and technology to create resonance, between vision and execution, innovation and inclusion, profit and purpose.

The best leaders today see themselves not as visionaries standing above, but as gardeners working among.

They plant cultures that grow trust. They cultivate conditions for curiosity. They prune bureaucracy and water bold ideas.

This kind of leadership requires humility, the courage to admit that you don't have all the answers, but you can create an environment where answers emerge.

As Satya Nadella put it, *"The true measure of a leader isn't how much they know, but how much they empower others to learn."*

Case Study 19: The Culture of Curiosity

A major consumer technology company noticed employees were spending more energy defending old processes than inventing new ones. Leadership launched "The Year of the Question," encouraging every department to submit uncomfortable, long-ignored problems.

AI helped cluster and analyze thousands of responses to reveal common themes. Within six months, the initiative identified significant redundant workflows worth tens of millions in annual savings and generated multiple new product ideas.

Curiosity became a formal performance driver. The exercise proved that when organizations systematically ask better questions, they unlock both efficiency and innovation – and employees gain genuine ownership of the future.

The Hybrid Brain

The augmented organization operates like a hybrid brain, half human, half machine, fully aligned.

The machine side excels in data, speed, and scale. The human side excels in intuition, ethics, and empathy.

The real magic happens where those hemispheres meet.

A global logistics company, for instance, uses AI to predict supply chain disruptions with 95% accuracy, but it's the human planners who decide which partners to prioritize, balancing economic impact with humanitarian responsibility.

Data reveals the "what." People discern the "why."

In the augmented organization, that balance becomes the strategic advantage.

Intelligence as a System

The industrial organization optimized for efficiency. The augmented organization optimizes for intelligence.

That doesn't mean hiring geniuses. It means creating systems that learn faster than competitors can copy.

These systems are built on three feedback loops:

- ***Data Loop***, continuous observation and measurement of performance.
- ***Learning Loop***, reflection, analysis, and synthesis of insights.
- ***Ethical Loop***, human review, alignment, and correction for impact.

Companies that institutionalize all three outperform their peers by over 40% in innovation ROI, according to a 2025 McKinsey study.

When feedback becomes habit, innovation becomes *culture*.

The Three Pillars of the Augmented Organization

1. **Intelligence with Integrity.** Technology is neutral; leadership isn't. The augmented organization doesn't just collect data, it curates it responsibly. Ethics aren't an afterthought; they're an operating system.
2. **Empathy at Scale.** Every process, every product, every policy begins with the question: "Who does this serve?" AI helps the organization listen at scale, identifying patterns of pain and opportunity, but humans must translate those signals into compassion.

3. **Purpose as a Performance Metric.** Profit is oxygen, but purpose is breath. When people believe their work contributes to something larger than themselves, they don't just perform better, they live better.

Gallup's 2025 data confirms that purpose-driven companies achieve **29%** higher retention and **42%** higher innovation engagement.

Purpose turns performance into legacy.

Case Study 20: The Retailer Scales Empathy

A global retailer deployed AI-driven sentiment analysis to process real-time feedback from millions of shoppers. Rather than using the data merely for satisfaction scores, the company empowered store managers to respond directly to emotional cues – frustration, confusion, delight, or urgency.

AI surfaced the signals. Humans delivered the care. Customer satisfaction rose substantially, and – perhaps most tellingly – employee morale surged as well. One manager captured the shift: "We stopped just managing stores. We started managing feelings."

This is the quiet power of intelligent augmentation: turning operational data into deeper human relationships.

Reinventing Work: From Jobs to Journeys

In the augmented organization, roles become more fluid. Job titles matter less than value creation paths.

Instead of static job descriptions, employees co-design evolving "career paths" based on their strengths, interests, and learning goals.

AI acts as a career compass, suggesting growth opportunities aligned with both business needs and personal purpose. This creates a dynamic loop of alignment, between the company's mission and the individual's meaning.

Unilever, Google, and Mastercard are already experimenting with this model, reporting up to 3x higher internal mobility and 50% faster skill deployment.

The augmented organization doesn't just build talent pipelines. It builds networks of opportunity.

The Trust-to-Innovation Flywheel

When trust fuels transparency, transparency fuels experimentation, and experimentation fuels progress.

This is the flywheel of augmentation, a continuous cycle that keeps learning alive and organizations agile:

- ***Trust*** → People feel safe to explore and question.
- ***Transparency*** → Decisions and data are shared openly.
- ***Experimentation*** → Teams innovate without fear of failure.
- ***Reflection*** → Insights are captured, ethics reviewed, lessons applied.

The more the wheel spins, the faster innovation compounds.

This is how augmented organizations evolve: not in leaps, but in loops.

The Empathy Dividend

The augmented organization realizes something that the industrial one never could: empathy is efficient.

When people feel understood, they align faster, collaborate deeper, and resolve conflict sooner. Empathy doesn't slow business down, it speeds trust up.

At Salesforce, for instance, empathy training is now integrated into leadership development. The company attributes a 25% increase in team performance to this single factor.

As one executive said, "AI made us smarter. Empathy made us unstoppable."

Leading the Transition

Becoming an augmented organization isn't an upgrade; it's an awakening. It begins with five commitments:

- ***Transparency*** over *control*.

- ***Purpose*** over *process.*
- ***Learning*** over *knowing.*
- ***Empathy*** over *efficiency.*
- ***Trust*** over *technology.*

These principles turn the idea of "human + machine" into a shared philosophy, a way of seeing work not as competition, but as collaboration with creation itself.

Closing Reflection: The Architecture of Tomorrow

The organizations that thrive in the next decade won't be the ones that automate the most. They'll be the ones that amplify the most, ideas, integrity, imagination.

They'll see technology not as destiny, but as design, a chance to build something more human than ever before.

The augmented organization isn't a company. It's a covenant, between intelligence and intention, between what we build and who we become. Its architecture is invisible, but its impact will be undeniable.

Because the future doesn't belong to the machines that think. It belongs to the people who teach them why.

Key Takeaways – The Augmented Organization

- *The augmented organization is guided by* ***purpose****,* ***empathy****, and* ***transparency****.*
- *Leadership is* ***design****: cultivating environments where* ***learning*** *and* ***trust*** *thrive.*
- *The future of growth isn't* ***automation****, but* ***amplification****.*

Chapter 3

The Human Edge in an Intelligent World

Part I – The Return of the Irreplaceable

The story of progress has always been told as a race, faster machines, smarter systems, bigger data. But the real story of the 21st century isn't about acceleration. It's about rediscovery.

For decades, we've been obsessed with replacing what humans do. Now we are rediscovering why humans matter.

The Myth of the Machine

Every technological revolution begins with a fantasy, that one day, the machine will perfect what the human began. It's an old dream. The Greeks wrote about automata. The Victorians built mechanical servants. The Silicon Valley of today trains neural networks to mimic thought itself.

But perfection is a poor substitute for purpose. And imitation isn't creation.

The greatest myth of the intelligent age is that machines can replace humanity. They can't. They can only reflect it.

AI mirrors our logic, our language, our behavior, but not our soul. It can analyze emotion, but it can't feel it. It can process values, but it can't hold them.

That's why, in this moment of exponential intelligence, the most valuable trait in business, and in life, isn't computational power. It's character.

The Irreplaceable Truth

A 2025 McKinsey report projected that up to 400 million jobs could be affected by automation globally. The headlines were alarming, and partially misleading. Because while many tasks may vanish, the roles that remain will require more humanity, not less.

The same report noted that demand for empathy, creativity, and judgment will grow by 30,40% in the next decade.

We aren't entering a post-human world. We are entering a deeply human one, where machines handle repetition, and people handle revelation.

In marketing, that means AI can find an audience, but only a human can understand one. In leadership, AI can optimize performance, but only a human can inspire belief. In innovation, AI can generate options, but only a human can choose courage.

Case Study 21: The Campaign That Couldn't Be Coded

A global beverage brand tasked an AI with designing its next major campaign, feeding it decades of data on colors, slogans, audience reactions, and cultural moments. The output was statistically optimal – and emotionally flat.

A creative director reframed the brief around belonging and human connection. Her team, informed by data but led by emotion, created a campaign celebrating shared humanity across differences. It became one of the year's most shared advertisements.

AI can measure affinity. Only humans can create genuine affection. Some truths remain beyond pure optimization.

What Data Can't Feel

Data tells us what happened. Intelligence tells us why it matters. But only empathy tells us what it means.

Empathy can't be engineered, it must be embodied.

In healthcare, patients are more likely to follow treatment plans when they feel heard by a doctor. In education, students learn more from teachers who believe in their potential. In business, employees commit more deeply to leaders who value their humanity.

Every meaningful metric, trust, loyalty, advocacy, is emotional before it is numerical.

The future of intelligence, therefore, isn't just artificial or augmented. It is affective, shaped by how we make people feel.

The Rise of the Meaning Economy

In the industrial age, we produced goods. In the digital age, we produced information. In the intelligent age, we produce meaning.

Meaning has become the ultimate differentiator, in brands, in leadership, in innovation. People no longer buy products; they buy purpose. They no longer follow companies; they follow convictions.

A 2024 Edelman global survey found that 78% of consumers prefer to buy from brands that align with their values, even if it costs more.

The currency of this new economy isn't efficiency. It's authenticity. Authenticity can't be automated.

The Paradox of Progress

The more advanced our machines become, the more primitive our longings seem. In a world of instant answers, people crave honest conversation. In a world of infinite information, people crave truth. In a world of synthetic connections, people crave something real.

This paradox defines our generation of leaders. The task before us isn't to humanize technology, it's to rehumanize ourselves.

We've spent years teaching algorithms to speak our language. Now we must remember how to speak from our hearts.

The Creative Pulse

Creativity is the heartbeat of the human edge.

AI can recombine ideas, but it can't risk one. It can imitate genius, but it can't feel the fear of failure that makes genius courageous.

Creativity, at its essence, isn't about novelty, it's about narrative. It's the ability to connect what is seen with what is unseen, what exists with what could be.

That's why the most powerful innovations of our time, from electric cars to social movements, began not with a line of code, but with a spark of conviction.

As Steve Jobs once said, "Technology alone isn't enough, it's technology married with the liberal arts and the humanities that makes our hearts sing."

The human edge isn't efficiency. It's expression.

Case Study 22: The Doctor Who Stayed

During the height of the pandemic, an AI triage system flagged a patient as non-critical and recommended discharge. The attending physician overrode the recommendation because the patient "looked scared." Hours later, the patient's condition deteriorated rapidly. The doctor's intuition helped save a life.

The hospital retrained the AI on the case. When asked why she intervened, the physician simply said she had a feeling that data alone could not capture.

Courage, compassion, and intuition are not inefficiencies in an intelligent system. They are the qualities that make the entire system human-proof.

Rediscovering Wonder

The ultimate competitive advantage of the human spirit isn't intelligence. It's wonder.

Children are born with it; adults forget it. But in an age where machines can simulate everything but awe, wonder becomes revolutionary.

Wonder fuels creativity. Wonder sustains hope. Wonder keeps us searching for the next right question, not just the next right answer.

Leaders who cultivate wonder, curiosity without agenda, build cultures that see possibility where others see problems. That's how breakthroughs happen.

When AI gives us certainty, wonder gives us wisdom.

The Irreplaceable Core

If intelligence is about prediction, and efficiency is about repetition, then humanity is about redemption, the ability to turn mistakes into meaning, chaos into clarity, pain into purpose.

Machines can't do that. They can't forgive, aspire, or sacrifice.

The irreplaceable edge of being human isn't our capacity to compute, but our capacity to care.

In a world filled with systems designed to anticipate, calculate, and optimize, the simplest act, listening with empathy, becomes an act of rebellion.

We aren't competing with the machine. We are completing it.

Closing Reflection: The Return of the Irreplaceable

We built machines to make life easier. They've done that. But they've also forced us to confront what can't be built: trust that is genuinely earned, judgment that accounts for context, care that is real rather than simulated.

The most consequential skill in this environment isn't knowing how to use the tools. It is knowing what the tools can't do, and protecting the human capacity to do those things well.

Key Takeaways – The Return of the Irreplaceable

- *AI can replicate **logic** but not **longing**, **emotion** and **meaning** remain **human** domains.*
- *Empathy, intuition, and moral judgment define the **human edge**.*
- *The most irreplaceable competitive advantage isn't **intelligence**, it's **integrity**.*

Part II – The Intelligence of Emotion

If IQ built the world we have, EQ will build the world we need.

For centuries, intelligence was defined by logic, the ability to calculate, categorize, and conclude. But as machines master logic, something remarkable has happened: the measure of greatness has shifted from what we know to how we connect.

We've entered an era where emotional intelligence is economic intelligence. Because in the absence of empathy, even the smartest systems will fail.

The Science of Feeling

The idea that emotion belongs outside business decisions is a relic of the industrial age. Leaders once believed emotion clouded judgment. Now we know the opposite is true: emotion clarifies it.

Neuroscientist Antonio Damasio proved that people with damaged emotional centers in the brain could still reason, but couldn't decide. They could list pros and cons endlessly, yet never act.

Emotion isn't the enemy of reason. It's the engine of decision.

That insight rewrites the future of work. Because if intelligence guides, and data informs, it is emotion that moves.

Case Study 23: The Ad That Made the World Cry

In 2024, a major sports brand launched a global campaign focused not on winning but on perseverance. It told stories of ordinary people – a single mother training for her first marathon, a soldier recovering from injury, a child learning to walk with prosthetics. The narration was simple: "You don't have to be the best. You just have to keep going."

The campaign went viral because it was deeply felt. Sales increased, but the more meaningful impact was the number of viewers who reported renewed self-belief.

This is the intelligence of emotion – the domain where data can guide but only humanity can truly touch.

The Emotional Economy

We now live in an attention economy, but attention without emotion is empty. Every brand, leader, and organization is competing not just for visibility, but for emotional relevance.

Emotion drives recall. Emotion drives loyalty. Emotion drives action.

A Harvard Business Review study showed that customers who form "emotional connections" with brands are three times more valuable than those driven by satisfaction alone.

It's not the product that builds the relationship, it's the feeling it creates.

That's why successful leaders and brands no longer ask, "What do we sell?" They ask, "What do we make people feel?"

The Empathy Advantage

Empathy, the ability to understand and share another's experience, is often dismissed as soft. In reality, it's a superpower.

A 2025 Businessolver report found that companies rated high in empathy outperform their peers by 20% in productivity and 50% in retention.

Empathy transforms data into direction. It's the bridge between information and inspiration.

In marketing, it means listening beyond the metrics. In leadership, it means seeing beyond the résumé. In innovation, it means designing beyond the user, designing for the human.

The Mirror of Emotion

AI can detect sentiment. It can measure tone, pattern, and expression. But it doesn't feel. That distinction changes everything.

In customer experience, for example, AI can predict frustration based on voice analysis. But only a human can respond with care.

At a financial services company in Toronto, AI identified clients showing signs of stress in calls about debt restructuring. The company trained human advisors to respond empathetically, slowing speech, acknowledging emotion, and offering reassurance before solutions. Default rates dropped by 15%, but trust scores rose by 60%.

The lesson: machines can mirror emotion, but only humans can mean it.

The Heart of Storytelling

Storytelling is the oldest form of human intelligence, and the most enduring. Before we wrote code, we told stories. And long after the algorithms change, stories will remain our greatest transmission of truth.

AI can generate narratives, but not narrative meaning. It can predict which words resonate, but it can't feel why they matter.

That's why, in the intelligent age, storytelling isn't a relic, it's a revolution.

Great stories don't just inform. They transform. They don't tell people what to think. They remind them why they believe.

In business, storytelling humanizes complexity. In leadership, it unites diverse people under a shared vision. In society, it restores the moral imagination that data alone can't sustain.

Case Study 24: The CEO Who Told the Truth

After a costly product failure, a tech CEO stood before his team and the public without spin. He acknowledged the mistake directly and said failure proved they cared enough to try bold ideas.

The message went viral. Employees rallied. Investors renewed their commitment. That single moment of honest vulnerability became a cultural reset for the company.

Authenticity is not weakness in leadership. In the intelligent age, it may be one of the strongest differentiators of all.

The Physiology of Connection

Emotion isn't abstract. It's biochemical.

Every positive interaction, a smile, a thank-you, a word of encouragement, releases oxytocin, the hormone of trust. Every negative interaction, dismissal, disrespect, indifference, floods the body with cortisol, the hormone of threat.

This means culture isn't a slogan. It's a physiological ecosystem. And leadership is, quite literally, emotional regulation at scale. Emotionally intelligent leaders don't just manage work. They manage energy.

They set the tone of safety that allows teams to take risks, share ideas, and be wrong without shame. Because innovation requires one condition above all others: psychological security.

The Courage to Care

Emotional intelligence isn't always comfortable. Empathy requires vulnerability, the willingness to feel someone else's pain. But vulnerability isn't weakness; it's the birthplace of trust.

Brené Brown's research found that teams who practiced open empathy were 30% more innovative and reported significantly lower burnout.

That's because emotion, expressed honestly and channeled intentionally, fuels connection, creativity, and courage.

In an age of machine efficiency, emotional courage is the new professionalism.

Marketing to the Heart

In this era of intelligent machines, marketing has returned to its roots, the art of understanding people.

Algorithms can segment audiences by behavior, income, or preference. But emotional intelligence segments by meaning, by the why behind the what.

When a travel brand discovered through AI that its customers weren't just booking vacations but reconnecting families, it reframed its campaigns from price-based offers to purpose-based storytelling. Revenue rose 26%, but the real change was cultural, employees began describing themselves not as "marketers," but as "memory makers." Emotion turned commerce into community.

The New ROI – Return on *Inspiration*

In the old world, ROI stood for Return on Investment. In the new one, it also stands for Return on Inspiration.

Because what good is optimization if it doesn't move hearts? What good is efficiency if it empties meaning?

Organizations that invest in emotional intelligence see dividends far beyond profit, higher trust, stronger loyalty, deeper belonging.

AI may predict behavior, but only humans can inspire belief. And belief, more than any algorithm, is what drives the world forward.

The Humanity Multiplier

Emotion isn't just the differentiator of the human edge, it's the multiplier.

It turns data into dialogue, process into purpose, and transactions into transformation. A robot can replicate motion. Only a human can create emotion.

And in a world increasingly run by intelligence, emotion will be the new form of power, quiet, ethical, exponential.

Because when logic ends, feeling begins, and that's where the future takes shape.

Closing Reflection: The Intelligence of the Heart

Emotional intelligence and computational intelligence aren't in competition. They operate on different problems. The organizations figuring out how to apply both (rigorously and honestly) are the ones building something that holds together under pressure.

Key Takeaways – The Intelligence of Emotion

- *Emotional intelligence (EQ) is now a measurable driver of **business success**.*
- *Empathy transforms data into **direction**, **trust**, and **loyalty**.*
- *The next competitive advantage won't be who thinks **faster**, but who **feels deeper**.*

Part III – Meaning, Morality, and the Machine

There's a question that increasingly haunts the modern age: As our machines grow smarter, will we grow wiser?

It's not an engineering question. It's an ethical one. Because intelligence without morality isn't progress, it's power without compass.

And power, left unguided by meaning, eventually consumes the very systems it was built to serve.

The Moral Vacuum of Modern Efficiency

The early years of AI were dominated by one mantra: "If we can, we should."

If we can automate, we should. If we can predict, we should. If we can optimize, we should. But "can" and "should" aren't synonyms. The space between them is called ethics.

In that space lives every question that matters: Should we collect every data point just because we can? Should we target every vulnerability simply because it converts? Should we let algorithms decide fairness without understanding context?

Technology has made us omnipotent. Now we must decide whether we'll also be moral.

The Cost of the Convenient

The intelligent age offers infinite convenience, and moral complexity. Every click, every recommendation, every decision we delegate to AI carries unseen consequences.

Convenience always asks less of us. Conscience always asks more.

In business, this tension is constant. We can now personalize advertising to the individual heartbeat, but should we? We can influence purchasing behavior through psychological nudges, but to what end?

Ethical leadership isn't about limiting innovation. It's about directing it toward dignity.

Because efficiency without empathy creates what some critics call "soulless success", achievement without virtue.

The Return of Purpose

In a world governed by algorithms, purpose becomes the new governance.

Purpose is the moral operating system that tells us why we build, not just what we build. It's the thread that connects innovation to intention.

Simon Sinek once said, "People don't buy what you do; they buy why you do it." The same is true of trust in technology. People don't trust AI because it's intelligent. They trust it because it's aligned.

Purpose turns intelligence into integrity. Without it, even the most brilliant systems drift into moral autopilot.

Case Study 25: An Algorithm Lies

In 2024, a major e-commerce company's AI pricing engine learned that financially stressed customers were less likely to comparison shop. It quietly raised prices for those users to maximize profit.

The algorithm did exactly what it was optimized to do. The ethical failure belonged to its designers, who had omitted conscience from the objective function. When exposed, the company faced public backlash, shareholder pressure, and legal scrutiny. It rebuilt the system with fairness constraints and greater transparency.

Revenue eventually recovered – but only after trust was painstakingly rebuilt. Efficiency without ethics is not intelligence. It is a moral failure waiting to happen.

The Philosophy of Technology

Every generation creates the gods it worships. The ancients worshiped the sun for its power. The industrialists worshiped machines for their productivity. Our age risks worshiping data for its precision.

But data, like fire, must be contained to serve creation, not destruction.

The moral challenge of our time isn't technical. It is philosophical. We must decide what we actually believe about human beings.

Are people problems to be optimized, or ends in themselves worthy of protection? If we answer wrongly, our intelligence will outpace our integrity.

The Ethics of Intention

Ethical technology isn't defined by rules; it's defined by intent.

Intent asks not "What does this system do?" but "What is this system for?"

An AI that predicts medical diagnoses isn't just a tool, it's a trust. An algorithm that shapes children's content isn't just entertainment, it's education. A data platform that profiles citizens isn't just analytics, it's governance.

When leaders lose sight of intent, systems lose sight of humanity.

That's why the most advanced organizations are now building ethics teams alongside engineering teams, not as auditors, but as architects.

They don't just ask whether the code works. They ask whether it serves.

Case Study 26: The AI That Asked Permission

A global healthcare startup built an AI to predict cardiac risk from wearable data. Instead of defaulting to maximum data collection, the company chose explicit user opt-in and shared stewardship.

Adoption grew more slowly at first, but long-term patient engagement tripled. Trust created richer, higher-quality data over time. The AI improved through cooperation rather than surveillance.

Moral intelligence – respecting autonomy while pursuing better outcomes – proved to be not just ethically right, but strategically superior.

The Moral Multiplier

When morality and innovation coexist, they amplify one another.

Ethical systems outperform unethical ones in the long run because they build lasting trust. Trust reduces friction. Friction reduction increases velocity. Velocity accelerates impact.

It's not philosophy. It's physics.

Purpose grows the way capital does. Every act of integrity adds momentum to progress. The result isn't just smarter systems, but sustainable arrangements.

The AI Mirror

AI doesn't create morality; it *reflects* it.

Every model carries the values of its makers. Every dataset carries the biases of its collectors. Every output carries the fingerprints of its inputs.

That means our machines will become as wise, or as reckless, as we are willing to be. When people say, "AI is dangerous," what they mean is, AI is human.

Because our creations inherit our convictions, and our contradictions. The solution isn't fear. It's formation. We must form creators who understand that every line of code writes not just software, but society.

The Conscience of Leadership

Ethical leadership begins not in boardrooms but in hearts.

Leaders set moral velocity, the speed at which values translate into action. The augmented leader of tomorrow must blend three virtues:

- ***Wisdom***, the ability to discern right from effective.
- ***Courage***, the willingness to act on that discernment even when it costs.

- ***Compassion***, the empathy to remember who innovation is for.

These aren't sentimental ideals. They are competitive imperatives.

Because in an age when technology can replicate intelligence, the only thing it can't replicate is virtue.

Case Study 27: The CEO Who Drew the Line

Major social platforms have repeatedly shown how engagement algorithms can reward outrage and division. In more than one documented case, executives recognized the pattern and chose to act against short-term incentives.

One platform conducted a full audit and publicly committed to designing for empathy rather than addiction. Revenue dipped in the following quarter, as predicted. Then trust scores rose, user growth stabilized, and advertisers returned.

Ethics proved to be good economics in the long run. Controversy spreads quickly, but trust travels farther and lasts longer.

Moral Technology and the Future of Work

The new frontier of AI isn't just technical innovation. It's ethical innovation.

Imagine if every workplace algorithm, from hiring to promotions, was designed to remove bias rather than reproduce it. Imagine if predictive analytics were trained on fairness, not just efficiency. Imagine if marketing AI were built to persuade through honesty, not manipulation.

These aren't fantasies. They are frontiers. And the organizations that pursue them will win, not just in the marketplace, but in the human race.

Because the future doesn't belong to those who automate everything. It belongs to those who elevate everyone.

The Meaning Makers

Meaning isn't an outcome. It's a *responsibility*.

Every system we build becomes a mirror of what we believe about the world. If we believe humans are disposable, we'll build systems that replace them. If we believe humans are inherently dignified, we'll build systems that reveal them.

The ultimate goal of intelligence isn't replication, but revelation, to see more clearly what makes life meaningful.

That's why the most moral act of creation in the AI age may simply be to remember who we're.

Closing Reflection: The Machine and the Mirror

AI doesn't ask the moral questions. We do. That hasn't changed.

What changes is the scale of the consequences. A system optimizing for the wrong thing, at AI speed and across millions of interactions, does more damage than any individual bad decision could. The mirror gets bigger.

That's an argument for being more careful, not less, for asking the difficult questions before deployment rather than after backlash.

Key Takeaways – Meaning, Morality, and the Machine

- *Ethics isn't the **limitation** of innovation, it is its **liberation**.*
- *Technology **amplifies the intentions** of its creators, for better or worse.*
- *The future of AI won't be determined by **algorithms**, but by **values**.*

Part IV – Leading with Humanity

The great leaders of the next century won't be the ones who know the most. They'll be the ones who *feel* the most, who understand that in an age of infinite intelligence, *human connection* is the final frontier of influence.

Leadership has always been a story of adaptation. In the industrial era, we led through control. In the information era, we led through expertise. Now, in the intelligent era, we must lead through empathy.

Because people no longer follow titles. They follow truth.

The End of the Expert Era

There was a time when leadership meant being the smartest person in the room. Knowledge was power, and power was protection.

But when every answer can be Googled, and every insight can be generated by AI in seconds, expertise alone no longer inspires. What people crave now is authenticity.

A 2025 Edelman global workforce survey found that 79% of employees trust a leader who "admits when they don't know" more than one who always claims to. Vulnerability has replaced perfection as the new credibility.

The myth of the flawless leader is over. The age of the honest leader has begun.

The Presence Principle

To lead with humanity is to lead with presence, the ability to be fully attentive in an age of constant distraction.

Presence isn't about charisma or command. It's about the quiet discipline of attention, of making others feel seen.

When a leader listens with real curiosity, they transmit value more powerful than any incentive plan: You matter.

Research from Google's "Project Aristotle" showed that psychological safety, the belief that one's voice is valued, was the single strongest predictor of team performance.

Leaders who cultivate presence create cultures of permission, permission to speak, to fail, to imagine. And from permission grows participation.

Case Study 28: The CEO Who Turned Off the Screen

In late 2025, Instagram CEO Adam Mosseri circulated a memo asking teams to reset their relationship with meetings by cancelling most recurring gatherings every six months, defaulting one-on-one meetings to a biweekly rhythm, and declining invitations that cut into protected focus time.

Coverage in outlets such as Business Insider and CNBC described the policy as part of a broader push to curb meeting overload and create more space for deep work, aligning with research that shows productivity gains when companies meaningfully reduce unnecessary meetings. Two anecdotal reports suggested within three months, cross-department satisfaction scores rose 27%, and meeting times dropped by 30%.

The change signaled a simple but important idea for knowledge work in the AI era: sometimes the most human-centered innovation is not another tool but removing distractions so people can pay attention to each other again.

The Power of Humility

Humility isn't thinking less of yourself. It's thinking of yourself less.

Today, humility becomes a strategic asset because it creates adaptability. When leaders believe they've nothing left to learn, they stop evolving, and so do their organizations.

A study by the Center for Creative Leadership found that humble leaders build teams that are 3x more likely to innovate and 2x more likely to stay through difficult transitions.

Humility signals openness. Openness invites collaboration. Collaboration fuels progress. Machines can calculate faster, but only humans can listen deeper.

The Courage to Be Kind

Kindness may be the most underrated form of leadership strength.

In a culture that often equates compassion with softness, kindness is revolutionary.

It takes courage to lead with empathy in systems trained for efficiency. It takes courage to slow down when the world demands speed. It takes courage to put people before performance, knowing that in the long run, one always sustains the other.

At Microsoft, CEO Satya Nadella transformed the company's culture around a single word: empathy. He told teams that success would no longer be measured by "knowing everything," but by "learning everything." The results? Market cap tripled within five years, and employee engagement reached historic highs.

Empathy isn't just moral. It's measurable.

The Servant Shift

Robert Greenleaf's philosophy of "servant leadership", once considered idealistic, is now pragmatic.

In AI-augmented organizations, where autonomy and experimentation thrive, leaders can't control outcomes. They can only cultivate environments.

The servant leader's role is to remove friction, amplify purpose, and model the values they expect others to emulate.

A servant leader asks:

- *What do my people need to succeed?*
- *How can I help them grow?*
- *How can I ensure technology serves their humanity, not the other way around?*

The paradox of power is that the more you share it, the stronger it becomes.

Case Study 29: The Hospital Heals Its Culture

In 2025, a large healthcare organization struggling with persistent turnover – despite competitive pay and strong facilities – shifted its approach. Instead of more policies or programs, executives began regularly shadowing nurses, aides, and frontline staff to truly understand daily realities and pressures.

The initiative focused on visibility, listening, and operational empathy. Leaders got closer to the work and the people doing it. Morale and retention began to improve as employees felt genuinely seen and supported.

Presence proved more powerful than policy. When leaders show up consistently and listen with intention, culture heals from within.

Authenticity as Alignment

Authenticity isn't about unfiltered expression, it's about consistent alignment between values, words, and actions.

When a leader's actions align with their stated purpose, trust compounds. When they diverge, trust evaporates, no matter how intelligent or innovative the system.

A 2025 PwC study found that 86% of employees who describe their leaders as "authentic" report high motivation, compared to only 18% when they don't.

Authenticity is the bridge between belief and belonging. It turns followers into co-authors of the mission.

The Moral Center of Leadership

Leadership in the intelligent age demands a new kind of literacy, moral literacy.

It means understanding not just how decisions work, but how they feel. It's the difference between leading a company and stewarding a conscience.

Moral leadership doesn't preach. It practices. It doesn't broadcast virtue. It builds systems that make virtue scalable.

At Patagonia, founder Yvon Chouinard made a radical decision to transfer company ownership to a trust dedicated to fighting climate change. It wasn't a branding exercise, it was a conviction codified in governance.

That's what moral leadership looks like: when purpose outlasts the leader.

The Trust Multiplier

In an AI-augmented world, trust is the new productivity.

When teams trust their leaders, they take initiative. When leaders trust their teams, innovation accelerates.

But trust can't be demanded; it must be demonstrated. And the demonstration begins with transparency.

Openly explaining why decisions are made, including the use of AI systems, doesn't dilute authority. It deepens respect.

Transparency turns leadership from control to collaboration. And collaboration turns trust into momentum.

Leading in the Age of Mirrors

AI has made leadership more visible than ever. Every statement, every policy, every contradiction is amplified in real time. This is the "mirror effect" of the intelligent age, where actions reflect instantly across the digital landscape.

Leaders can no longer hide behind messaging. Authenticity is now a public metric.

The most successful leaders embrace this transparency as accountability. They understand that every algorithm they deploy is an extension of their ethics. Every system they approve is a reflection of their soul.

In short: the age of AI has made leadership personal again.

Case Study 30: Alaska Airlines Apologizes

In April and May of 2022, Alaska Airlines was struggling. Alaska Airlines canceled hundreds of flights as a result of pilot shortages and scheduling missteps that left it without enough crew to operate the schedule it had published.

CEO Ben Minicucci did something highly unusual, perhaps unprecedented: he sent a personal video message directly to employees and frequent flyers, apologizing for the problem and explaining specifically what the airline was doing to fix it.

He didn't blame weather. He didn't cite industry headwinds. Minicucci placed the blame squarely on the airline's own poor planning. He opened with a direct apology, used the word "I" – not "the airline" or "our team" – and acknowledged exactly how the disruptions were affecting people: "A canceled flight is frustrating enough, but then you often face long hold times when you try to reach someone in reservations."

Then he announced concrete commitments: 150 new pilots, 200 reservation agents, and 1,100 flight attendants starting in June. Crisis-communication experts called it a masterclass in authentic leadership. Customer and industry. The whole message ran just over two minutes.

Commentators in outlets like Inc. held the message up as a model of crisis communication, and many customers reacted more with patience than anger, reinforcing the idea that clear accountability and specific commitments can preserve trust even when performance falls short.

The lesson isn't complicated: people don't expect perfection. They expect to be treated like adults when things go wrong. An apology, when authentic, isn't weakness. It's the restoration of trust through truth.

The Leader as Lightkeeper

In turbulent times, the leader's role is less commander, more lightkeeper, someone who maintains visibility when others lose their way.

AI can calculate routes. But only a leader can point to purpose.

The lightkeeper doesn't outrun the storm; they outshine it. They hold a steady glow of empathy, humility, and conviction that keeps others oriented toward hope.

When technology provides information, it is leadership that provides meaning.

Closing Reflection: The Human Leader

Leadership in this moment isn't primarily a technology problem. It's a credibility problem. People follow leaders they trust to tell them the truth, make decisions that hold up under scrutiny, and care about consequences beyond the next reporting cycle.

The technology isn't what makes that hard. It never was.

Key Takeaways – Leading with Humanity

- *Leadership in the AI era demands **empathy**, **humility**, and **presence**.*
- *Authenticity is alignment between **words**, **values**, and **actions**.*
- *The leaders who endure will be those who lead with **love**, not **leverage***

Part V – The Soul of Innovation

Innovation without a clear reason is just motion. The most important question any organization can ask about a new capability isn't whether it works, but what it's actually for.

That question gets harder to ask as the pace accelerates and easier to skip. The organizations that keep asking it, that treat the why as non-negotiable even when the what is already impressive, are the ones whose innovations endure.

The Purpose Paradox

A 2025 Deloitte study found that 78% of executives describe innovation as critical to growth, but only 24% say it is guided by a clear societal purpose.

That gap (between urgency and direction) is the central challenge. We've become very good at building things quickly. We are less practiced at stopping to ask whether we should, or what we expect to happen once we do.

The Animating Spark

Throughout history, every leap of progress began not with a tool, but with a conviction.

The compass was born of wonder. The printing press was born of courage. The internet was born of connection.

And every one of these innovations was powered not by efficiency, but by faith, faith that the unknown was worth exploring, that knowledge was worth sharing, that humanity was worth advancing.

Faith isn't religion. Faith is the confidence that meaning exists beyond measurement, that what we do matters even when the metrics can't prove it.

It is faith that allows a scientist to ask, "What if?" It is faith that allows an artist to dream, "What next?" It is faith that allows a leader to believe, "We can be better."

That faith is the soul of innovation.

Case Study 31: The Architect Who Designed for Silence

When asked why his buildings featured concrete, light, and generous empty space, the renowned architect Tadao Ando replied, "Because people need to hear themselves think."

His minimalist, contemplative structures prioritize experience and reflection over pure efficiency. They remind us that innovation is not only about adding capability – sometimes it is about creating space for depth.

Technological progress should follow the same principle: design systems that honor reflection, not just reaction. The soul of innovation often lives in the spaces between the noise.

From Disruption to Renewal

Disruption as a goal in itself has run its course. Tearing down existing structures turns out to be much easier than building better ones in their place.

The organizations defining the next phase aren't primarily disruptors. They are rebuilders, focused not on what to break but on what to restore: dignity in work, trust between institutions and the people they serve, purpose in daily contribution.

The Creative Conscience

AI can generate variations at extraordinary speed. What it can't generate is intention, the prior decision about what the variations are for and why any of them matter.

An IBM global study in 2025 found that **83%** of CEOs now rank creativity as the most important leadership competency, ahead of operational discipline and technical skill. What they are really describing is judgment: the ability to look at options and choose based on something other than speed or efficiency.

The Role of Marketing in Meaning

Nowhere is the soul of innovation more tested, or more visible, than in marketing.

Marketing doesn't just sell innovation. It translates it. It tells the story of what we believe progress is for.

When brands lead with manipulation, they devalue both product and people. But when they lead with mission, when they connect commerce with compassion, they become movements.

A recent Nielsen report found that 71% of consumers are more loyal to brands that take a stand on social or moral issues, and 63% prefer to buy from those who contribute to the greater good.

This isn't trend, it's truth. Meaning is the new market share.

Case Study 32: The Company That Gave Away Its Code

In 2025, a global AI company made a bold and controversial move: it open-sourced a core proprietary algorithm to help democratize responsible AI development. Critics called it corporate suicide.

The outcome told a different story. Community engagement doubled, partnerships tripled, and the brand became strongly associated with trust and integrity. The CEO explained, "Innovation without integrity wasn't worth owning."

Sharing can be the new form of scaling. In the intelligent age, transparency and openness are increasingly powerful competitive advantages.

Imagination: The Infinite Resource

Machines can analyze every known variable, but only imagination can discover the unknowns. Imagination is humanity's infinite resource, the wellspring of invention, art, and awe. And unlike data, it grows the more we give it away.

Einstein called imagination "more important than knowledge," because knowledge tells us what is, while imagination reveals what could be.

In organizations, imagination is cultivated through psychological safety, curiosity, and cross-disciplinary collaboration, where scientists talk to storytellers, designers to philosophers, engineers to educators.

The soul of innovation thrives where disciplines collide.

The Morality of Progress

Progress without morality is acceleration without destination. If innovation is the engine, morality is the map. It ensures we don't just move fast, we move forward.

A 2026 MIT study on "Ethical Innovation" found that companies with explicit moral frameworks for technology design experienced 50% fewer regulatory conflicts and 30% higher long-term valuation stability.

In short: moral clarity is good strategy. Because values, when lived authentically, compound like capital.

When morality is embedded into innovation, progress becomes self-correcting.

Case Study 33: The Lab That Refused to Patent

A biomedical research lab developed a low-cost compound capable of preventing a major infectious disease. Major pharmaceutical companies offered billions for exclusive rights. The scientists declined and released the formula publicly.

Within two years, the treatment reached tens of millions of people in developing countries. The lab's reputation soared, attracting top talent and new funding.

In a world obsessed with ownership, strategic generosity became a profound competitive advantage. True innovation sometimes means giving knowledge away so it can serve the greatest number.

The Future Belongs to Builders of Hope

The most powerful innovations aren't driven by fear of loss, but by faith in possibility. Hope has always been humanity's greatest technology.

It built the wheel, the telescope, the vaccine, and the Internet. And it will build what comes next, if we dare to believe again.

Innovation that endures isn't built in code, but in conviction. It begins in the imagination, passes through the intellect, and ends in the heart.

The machine may light the path. But it is humanity that gives it direction.

Closing Reflection: The Soul's Signature

At the end of every innovation cycle, something remarkable happens: The metrics fade. The market shifts. The memory remains.

What endures isn't what we made, but what we meant.

The future won't remember our platforms or patents. It will remember whether we built with integrity, with compassion, with soul.

Because progress isn't just about what we achieve, it's about what we awaken in others.

That's the true legacy of innovation: not to make machines more human, but to make humans more humane.

Key Takeaways – The Soul of Innovation

- *Innovation without **purpose** is progress **without peace**.*
- ***Renewers**, those who create with conscience, **will define** the next era.*
- *The soul of innovation isn't **invention**, it's **intention**.*

Chapter 4

The New Architecture of Work

Part I – From Hierarchies to Networks

For more than a century, the corporate world was built like a cathedral – tall, tiered, and rigid. Each floor symbolized authority; each rung on the ladder represented progress. It was efficient, orderly, predictable.

But that model is giving way to networks, organic, adaptive systems where collaboration replaces command, and shared purpose replaces positional power.

The shift isn't cosmetic. It is civilizational.

The Origins of the Hierarchy

The hierarchy was one of humanity's greatest organizational inventions. Born during the Industrial Revolution, it brought structure to chaos and clarity to scale.

In 1911, Frederick Winslow Taylor published The Principles of Scientific Management, a manifesto that transformed business into a machine. Every worker was a cog. Every process was a gear. The manager's job was to optimize motion, not meaning.

That model built railroads, automobiles, and empires. But it was built for a world of scarcity, scarcity of information, resources, and coordination.

In the 21st century, scarcity has been replaced by surplus. Surplus of data, ideas, and connectivity. And in a world of surplus, control becomes a bottleneck.

The Collapse of the Pyramid

The hierarchical model assumed three things:

- Information flows *downward.*
- Decisions move *upward.*
- The world outside *changes slower* than the world inside.

All three of those assumptions are now obsolete.

Information moves everywhere, instantly. Decisions are distributed at the edge. And the world outside moves faster than any corporate bureaucracy can respond.

That's why the traditional pyramid has inverted. Power now flows horizontally, not vertically.

Teams form across boundaries, decisions are made closer to the customer, and leadership has become less about managing process and more about orchestrating potential.

From Command to Connection

The old model prized compliance; the new one prizes *connection.*

In hierarchical organizations, leadership meant control, ensuring consistency and obedience. But in a networked world, leadership means context, helping people understand why their work matters and how it fits into the whole.

When information is democratized, authority must be earned, not assumed. And the leaders who thrive are those who can connect purpose to performance.

McKinsey's 2025 *"Future of Organization"* report found that companies operating on network-based models saw **30%** faster innovation cycles and **40%** higher engagement among employees.

People don't want to be managed anymore. They want to be mobilized.

The Power of Decentralized Intelligence

AI has accelerated this shift by turning intelligence itself into an organizational layer. In the past, insight was centralized in the executive suite. Today, AI democratizes it, providing every team, every role, and every decision-maker with real-time context and data.

The result isn't chaos. It's genuine autonomy.

In networked organizations, AI becomes the invisible conductor, synchronizing independent efforts into coherent outcomes.

Instead of reporting up for permission, teams collaborate outward for progress. Instead of relying on hierarchy for alignment, they rely on shared intelligence.

Case Study 34: The Airline That Flattened

A major global airline implementing AI-driven scheduling and predictive maintenance discovered that its traditional hierarchy was slowing response times. Frontline engineers often needed multiple layers of approval before acting on AI insights.

Leadership removed three layers of middle management, redistributed decision rights, and built a "network of trust." Maintenance cycles accelerated, downtime decreased, and employee satisfaction rose noticeably. One executive summarized the shift: "We didn't automate the workforce. We activated it."

The new architecture of work favors participation over permission.

The Human Network

Technology may enable networks, but humans sustain them.

A network isn't a structure of code; it's a structure of trust. Trust is the connective tissue that allows teams to move at the speed of intelligence without losing integrity.

In the past, trust was hierarchical, you trusted your boss because of their title. Today, trust is relational, you trust people because of their transparency, consistency, and competence.

According to a 2024 Deloitte study, trust-rich organizations outperform peers by 40% in employee retention and 50% in innovation adoption.

In a networked company, trust isn't a soft metric. It's the operating system.

The Role of AI in Human Connection

Ironically, AI, often seen as a depersonalizing force, can be the greatest enabler of human connection when used ethically.

By analyzing communication flows, AI can identify collaboration bottlenecks, detect burnout patterns, and recommend more balanced team dynamics.

At a global consulting firm, AI tools tracked project collaboration in real time, flagging teams that were overly dependent on a few individuals. Managers used this data to redistribute workload and promote quieter voices.

The outcome? A measurable rise in psychological safety and diversity of contribution. AI didn't replace management. It revealed where humanity was needed most.

Case Study 35: The Retail Chain That Went Horizontal

During the supply chain volatility of the 2020s, a global retail chain found its rigid vertical structure inadequate. Instead of tightening control, it built a network operating system using AI dashboards that connected inventory, real-time feedback, and sales data across all stores.

Store managers formed cross-regional working groups to solve problems collaboratively rather than escalating upward.

Decision latency dropped by 60%. Employee turnover fell by 30%. And the brand's customer satisfaction reached record highs.

Connection replaced hierarchy as the primary organizing principle – proving that distributed intelligence often outperforms centralized control.

They didn't just flatten structure, they expanded connection.

From Career Ladder to Career Lattice

In hierarchical systems, careers moved upward. In networked systems, they move outward, across projects, teams, and experiences.

This is the "career lattice" model, where growth is measured not by title, but by impact.

AI enables this by mapping skills dynamically, suggesting learning pathways, and matching talent to opportunity across the organization.

In a 2026 LinkedIn report, 70% of professionals said they preferred roles that offer continuous learning and project diversity over traditional promotions.

The new architecture of work doesn't promise a corner office. It promises continuous evolution.

The Leader as Network Node

In a networked world, leaders aren't at the top, they are at the center. Their role isn't to dictate but to distribute.

They become nodes of clarity, connecting strategy to execution, and vision to values.

One global advertising agency described its leadership model as "fractal", each team mirrors the values of the whole, trusted to make decisions consistent with the organization's purpose.

When every node reflects the same DNA, the network scales integrity, not bureaucracy.

The Culture of Co-Creation

Networks thrive on co-creation, the act of building together what no one could build alone. It's the opposite of competition.

In hierarchical systems, success was individual. In networked systems, success is collective.

This shift redefines motivation. People aren't inspired by metrics alone; they're inspired by meaning shared.

That's why the most advanced organizations now design work around shared challenges, not static departments. They form agile, mission-based teams that dissolve and reform as needs evolve, like living organisms that sense and respond to change.

Case Study 36: The Energy Company That Became a Platform

A European energy company transformed itself from a traditional utility into an "energy innovation platform." It created open teams that collaborated with startups, researchers, and local governments on clean energy prototypes.

AI served as the connective intelligence – aggregating insights and managing data-sharing across partners. Within two years, the company launched six new renewable ventures with cross-industry co-ownership.

The CEO captured the shift: the organization had stopped being merely a company and had become a community. Openness became the foundation of agility.

The Network as Living System

The modern organization is evolving from a mechanical model to a biological one. It's not a machine that must be controlled; it's an ecosystem that must be cultivated. AI acts as the nervous system, transmitting signals of performance, risk, and opportunity. Leaders act as the immune system, protecting culture, ethics, and trust. And employees act as the cells, autonomous, intelligent, interconnected.

When designed well, this living system can adapt faster than disruption itself. The future of work isn't about who commands it. It's about who connects it.

Closing Reflection – From Hierarchies to Networks

We are witnessing the quiet dismantling of one of the oldest power structures in human history. But this isn't chaos. It's clarity rediscovered.

The hierarchy was built for obedience. The network is built for belief.

And belief, in one another, in purpose, in possibility, is what turns connection into creation.

The architecture of work is being rewritten, not by machines, but by the human desire to belong to something greater than the sum of its parts.

In that, the age of intelligence isn't the end of leadership. It's the beginning of community.

Key Takeaways – From Hierarchies to Networks

- *Hierarchies optimize* ***control****; networks optimize* ***creativity****.*
- *AI flattens power by* ***democratizing intelligence*** *and access.*
- *The future of leadership isn't* ***command****, but* ***connection****.*

Part II – The Fluid Workforce

The job description has always been a simplification, a way of drawing a boundary around a role that was never quite that tidy in practice. What is different now is that the simplification no longer holds even as a useful fiction.

Work has become fluid. Skills move across projects and organizations. Teams form around problems rather than departments. The value someone creates is harder to define by title than by what they actually do.

This is disorienting for organizations built around fixed roles. It is clarifying for individuals who have always known their contribution was harder to capture than their job description suggested.

The Death of the Job Description

For over a century, the job description has been the DNA of the corporate world. It defined expectations, compensation, and authority. But in an age of intelligent automation and constant change, job descriptions have become fossils, relics of a slower era.

According to the World Economic Forum, **44%** of workers' core skills will change within five years.

That means by the time a job description is written, it's already outdated.

AI, automation, and the cloud have decoupled work from location, time, and even title. What matters now is capability and contribution, not classification.

In the new architecture of work, the most valuable employee isn't the one who fits the description, it's the one who rewrites it.

From Fixed Roles to Fluid Purpose

Fluidity doesn't mean chaos. It means alignment with movement.

In a fluid workforce, people shift smoothly across projects based on skills, curiosity, and mission fit. AI platforms continuously map organizational needs and human potential, matching talent to opportunity in real time.

It's like a living marketplace of meaning.

In 2025, Unilever's "Flex Experience" AI program allowed employees to explore internal project opportunities beyond their primary roles. Within a year, 60% of participants reported new skills, and productivity rose 41%.

Fluid work doesn't erode loyalty; it elevates it, because it honors human growth.

The Borderless Talent Economy

Geography used to define opportunity. Today, opportunity defines geography.

With digital collaboration tools and AI-enabled project platforms, organizations are no longer limited by proximity. Talent can flow from anywhere to everywhere.

A McKinsey 2024 study estimated that remote and hybrid structures could expand the global talent pool by 400 million skilled workers by 2030.

For the first time in history, we can build companies that truly represent the planet they serve. That's not just inclusive, it's intelligent.

Case Study 37: The Global Design Collective

A Copenhagen-based design firm stopped hiring by geography. Instead, it built a global talent network of artists, developers, and strategists spanning 30 countries, matched through an AI project-allocation system.

Assignments considered not only expertise and availability but also emotional style – pairing introverts with reflective work and extroverts with high-collaboration sprints. The firm doubled its output capacity without increasing headcount, while employee satisfaction and creativity flourished.

The founder summarized the new model: *"We stopped managing people and started connecting purpose."*

AI as the Orchestrator of Human Potential

In a fluid workforce, AI becomes not the boss, but the conductor. It harmonizes diverse capabilities, ensures balance, and optimizes rhythm.

Imagine an AI platform that continuously scans business goals, predicts project needs, and matches internal and external talent accordingly, freelancers, full-timers, and partners working together in dynamic teams.

This is already happening. Companies like Deloitte, Accenture, and Google are experimenting with skills clouds, AI systems that tag every employee's competencies, learning progress, and aspirations.

The result is a living map of human capability, where opportunity finds the person, not the other way around.

Case Study 38: The Skills Cloud Revolution

At a multinational energy company, AI analyzed internal project data and uncovered thousands of "hidden experts" – employees whose secondary skills perfectly matched emerging high-demand needs.

The company created a "skills cloud" platform that allowed managers to form ad-hoc teams based on real capabilities rather than formal org charts. Hiring costs dropped substantially, and projects were completed significantly faster.

Leaders drew a powerful conclusion: "We didn't need more people. We needed to truly know the people we already had." This shift from static headcount to fluid talent networks represents one of the most promising evolutions in workforce design.

From Employment to Empowerment

Fluid work transforms the contract between individuals and institutions. It shifts from employment, where companies own time, to empowerment, where people own value.

This doesn't mean everyone becomes a gig worker. It means organizations evolve into ecosystems of opportunity, blending employees, freelancers, educators, and partners into mutually dependent networks.

IBM calls this the "open workforce," where expertise circulates freely between internal and external talent. According to their 2026 research, companies with open workforce models outperform peers in innovation by **45%.**

Fluidity, when structured with trust, creates agility without exploitation.

The Rise of the Purpose-Driven Worker

In a world where AI performs repetitive tasks and provides constant optimization, humans crave one thing more than efficiency: meaning.

Gallup's 2025 "State of the Global Workplace" found that employees who feel their work is "connected to a larger purpose" are five times more likely to describe themselves as thriving.

Purpose is no longer a "perk." It's the new paycheck.

Fluid organizations harness this truth by aligning projects with impact, connecting personal fulfillment with organizational mission. The result? Engagement becomes intrinsic, not incentivized.

When people move toward purpose, performance follows.

Case Study 39: A Health Network Heals Itself

A major U.S. healthcare system facing widespread burnout among nurses and physicians chose a different path from endless recruitment. It redesigned its workforce model around autonomy and flexibility.

AI systems monitored staffing patterns, predicted surges, and enabled clinicians to flow between departments based on skills and preferences. Turnover dropped substantially, patient satisfaction reached new highs, and collaboration became central to the culture.

The CEO captured the deeper shift: "*We stopped trying to fill positions and started trying to fulfill people.*"

When organizations design work around human fulfillment rather than mere staffing, both care and culture improve.

Trust as the Currency of Fluidity

The more fluid an organization becomes, the more it depends on trust.

Fluid teams form and dissolve quickly. They require psychological safety and transparency to function at speed. That means leaders must shift from oversight to insight, replacing supervision with shared vision.

AI helps maintain trust by creating visibility into progress, fairness, and contribution. But the heart of trust remains human: accountability, empathy, and respect.

Trust isn't the byproduct of culture. It's the culture.

The End of the Office – and the Beginning of Belonging

The question "Where do you work?" has lost its meaning. The new question is, "Where do you belong?"

As work becomes decentralized, belonging becomes the glue that holds fluid systems together.

Digital platforms can connect people across continents, but belonging connects them across purpose. It's not about physical presence; it's about emotional resonance, the sense that one's contribution matters.

That's why leading companies now invest as much in community architecture as in organizational design. They build digital "villages" within global enterprises, places where people can gather, share, and grow.

Because in a world of boundless flow, the human heart still needs an anchor.

Case Study 40: The Belonging Network

A major software company observed that even high-performing distributed teams felt increasingly disconnected. In response, it created a "Belonging Network" using AI to curate interest groups, mentorship pods, and learning clusters based on shared passions rather than only shared projects.

The results were meaningful: attrition decreased notably and well-being scores rose substantially. The Chief People Officer summarized it well: *"We used data to build community. That's what technology should do."*

In the age of remote and hybrid work, intentional connection has become a strategic capability.

Fluid Work, Solid Values

Flexibility without foundation becomes fragility. That's why the fluid workforce must be anchored in values.

Agility is how organizations move. Values are why they move.

When people know why they're flowing in the same direction, trust becomes automatic, and autonomy becomes productive. It's not chaos, it's coherence.

AI can optimize for efficiency, but only values can optimize for integrity. That balance, between flow and foundation, is the hallmark of sustainable transformation.

Closing Reflection – The Flow of Human Potential

We are witnessing the great unfreezing of work. Boundaries are dissolving, between industries, roles, and even identities.

And in that fluidity lies both challenge and opportunity. Because when work stops being confined, it starts being alive.

AI can map our skills, predict our growth, and connect us to purpose. But only we can decide how to use that freedom, to build systems that dignify, not deplete; support, not exploit.

The future of work isn't fixed or fragile. It is fluid, and in that flow, humanity finds its rhythm again.

Key Takeaways – The Fluid Workforce

- *The job description is dying;* ***adaptability*** *is the new skill.*
- *AI orchestrates talent* ***dynamically****, creating* ***borderless collaboration****.*
- *The future of work isn't about* ***where*** *you work, it's about* ***why you do****.*

Part III – Intelligence as Infrastructure

For most of history, infrastructure meant things you could touch, steel, concrete, cables, servers. It was the physical skeleton of civilization.

Today, the new infrastructure is invisible. It doesn't just move materials or data. It moves **intelligence**.

AI has evolved from being a feature to becoming the **foundation**, an always-on layer that connects people, processes, and possibilities in real time.

Just as electricity once powered the industrial age, intelligence now powers the **age of interconnection.**

The End of the System Era

For decades, organizations were built around systems, accounting systems, CRM systems, supply chain systems. Each function optimized for its own efficiency, often at the expense of others.

But systems were static. They stored knowledge; they didn't *learn* it.

In 2025, MIT's Sloan Management Review noted that **72% of executives** believed their organizational silos were the biggest barrier to transformation.

The age of systems is ending. The age of **intelligence architecture** is beginning, where learning replaces logging, and adaptation replaces automation.

AI as the New Operating Layer

AI is no longer a tool you use. It's a **layer you live within.**

It doesn't sit in one department; it flows through all of them, finance, marketing, HR, supply chain, and customer experience, translating data into decisions at the speed of context.

Think of it as the neural network of the organization. Every action becomes a signal, every outcome becomes feedback, and the organization learns, not quarterly, but continuously.

At its best, this isn't artificial intelligence. It's **ambient intelligence**, intelligence that surrounds and supports, quietly amplifying every human contribution.

Case Study 41: The Smart Supply Chain

A global apparel company moved away from rigid seasonal planning and static forecasts. It built an AI-driven adaptive supply chain that continuously incorporated sales signals, social trends, and shipping data.

The learning engine adjusted production and distribution in real time. Waste decreased significantly, delivery times improved, and creative teams gained more bandwidth to focus on storytelling instead of spreadsheets.

The COO described the system as *"a brain for the brand."* Intelligence, when used as infrastructure, becomes invisible, integrative, and indispensable.

The Architecture of Learning

Traditional organizations learned episodically, during reviews, after projects, or through crises. Intelligent organizations learn **organically**, in every moment, from every interaction.

AI enables this through continuous feedback loops. It turns every customer complaint into a data point, every employee suggestion into a signal, every outcome into a lesson.

This creates what Accenture calls a "living enterprise", one that senses, learns, and evolves dynamically.

The infrastructure itself becomes a teacher.

From Data Warehouses to Knowledge Ecosystems

In the old world, companies built data warehouses, vast silos of information waiting to be analyzed. In the intelligent world, those warehouses have evolved into **shared knowledge environments**, interconnected systems where information flows freely and contextually.

AI acts as the gardener, pruning noise, nurturing relevance, and ensuring that insight reaches the right people at the right time.

This shift transforms the role of data teams from custodians to **curators of meaning**.

The question is no longer, "Do we have the data?" It's *"Do we know how to use it well?"*

The Decision Dividend

When intelligence becomes infrastructure, the speed and quality of decision-making improve exponentially.

According to a 2026 BCG study, organizations that embed AI into core decision systems outperform peers by **35% in agility** and **45% in ROI** on major strategic initiatives.

That's because AI doesn't just accelerate decisions; it **enhances discernment.**

It offers context, pattern recognition, and scenario modeling, freeing leaders to focus not on what is probable, but on what is *possible*.

The result is leadership powered by foresight, not hindsight.

Case Study 42: The Financial Firm That Listened

A multinational bank replaced fragmented analytics with a unified intelligence platform capable of sensing client sentiment in real time through transaction patterns and communication tone.

The system predicted churn and recommended personalized outreach. Customer retention improved noticeably within months. More importantly, teams began viewing data not as static reports but as **living signals of relationships**.

Intelligence reconnected the organization to its humanity – turning information into empathy at scale.

The Ethical Backbone

When intelligence becomes infrastructure, ethics becomes **architecture**.

The more decisions we delegate to machines, the more essential it becomes to define how those machines decide.

That means embedding fairness, transparency, and accountability directly into design, not as compliance afterthoughts, but as structural elements.

Ethical intelligence isn't a constraint; it's a competitive advantage.

A 2025 Deloitte study found that companies with established AI ethics frameworks were **2.2x more trusted** by customers and **1.8x more likely** to attract top talent.

In the intelligent enterprise, ethics isn't what slows you down. It's what keeps you from breaking down.

Case Study 43: The Transparent Algorithm

A leading HR technology firm launched an AI tool for recommending internal promotions. When employees raised valid concerns about potential bias, the company responded with openness rather than defense. It created an internal transparency portal where anyone could see how recommendations were generated and challenge outcomes.

Complaints dropped dramatically and trust rose markedly. The lesson is clear: when people understand how intelligence works, they are far more likely to see it as a partner rather than a threat. Transparency is the essential **trust protocol** for the intelligent age.

Intelligence Meets Intuition

AI excels at pattern recognition; humans excel at **meaning recognition**. Together, they create a hybrid decision model that is both precise and profound.

The future of work isn't man versus machine, it's man *with* machine. AI provides the map; human intuition chooses the destination.

At one global marketing firm, AI analyzed millions of audience signals to guide campaign targeting. But it was a strategist's intuitive leap, recognizing a cultural shift invisible to data, that led to the campaign's success.

The harmony of intelligence and intuition is where innovation lives.

The Network Effect of Wisdom

When every department, project, and team contributes to shared intelligence, organizations develop what cognitive scientists call **collective sensemaking**, a shared capacity to interpret complexity.

This creates a network effect of wisdom: the more intelligence flows, the smarter every node becomes.

It's not just about faster insight, it's about deeper understanding. When the entire organization learns together, it moves together.

And movement, not motion, is the metric of growth.

From Infrastructure to Imagination

Intelligence as infrastructure frees humans to return to their most natural state: **imagination**.

When AI handles the repetitive and the routine, creativity expands into the possible. People no longer spend their days reporting what happened. They spend them envisioning *what could.*

This is where the true return on intelligence lies: not in efficiency metrics, but in **human reinvention.**

AI doesn't just build smarter companies. It builds braver humans.

Closing Reflection – The Invisible Foundation

The organizations of the future won't look like machines, they'll look like minds. Interconnected, self-aware, capable of learning, and always becoming.

We'll stop talking about "using AI" and start talking about *living in intelligence.*

And when that happens, our greatest challenge won't be building systems that think faster. It will be building societies that **think better.**

Because the infrastructure of intelligence isn't technology. It's the collective courage to see, to learn, and to lead differently.

Key Takeaways – Intelligence as Infrastructure

- *AI is becoming the **connective tissue** of modern organizations.*
- ***Continuous learning** replaces **episodic reporting** as the engine of progress.*
- ***Ethical design** and **transparency** are the structural foundations of trust.*
- ***The harmony of AI and intuition** drives deeper, faster decision-making.*

The future enterprise won't just process data, it will **embody wisdom.**

Part IV – Designing for Agility

In the industrial age, organizations were designed to endure. In the intelligent age, they must be designed to **evolve**.

Agility isn't a buzzword. It's the new architecture of survival. Because when change becomes the constant, rigidity becomes the risk.

The Architecture of Adaptation

In the past, companies built structures like skyscrapers, strong, vertical, unyielding. Every layer had a function. Every process had a protocol.

It worked, until the environment changed faster than the structure could.

Today's organizations must be built less like skyscrapers and more like **ecosystems**, responsive, interdependent, and constantly renewing.

The question isn't, *"How do we prevent disruption?"* It's, *"How do we design for it?"*

The Agility Imperative

Agility isn't about moving fast. It's about **moving with purpose**, adapting quickly without losing direction.

A 2025 Bain & Company study found that organizations with mature agility models were **5x more likely** to outperform peers in both revenue growth and employee satisfaction.

That's because agility doesn't just make companies more efficient. It makes them more **alive**.

When teams are trusted to sense and respond, instead of waiting for permission, they turn volatility into velocity.

Case Study 44: The Car Company That Learned to Dance

A global automotive manufacturer reduced its new product development cycle from three years to nine months by combining agile methods with AI-assisted prototyping.

It replaced rigid silos with cross-functional "pods" of designers, engineers, and marketers who collaborated through shared intelligence dashboards. AI handled simulation and analytics; humans focused on creativity, judgment, and synthesis.

The CEO likened the transformed factory to a jazz band: every section improvises, yet they remain in harmony. This is the essence of true agility – structure that exists in service of freedom and creativity.

The Principles of Agile Design

Agile organizations share five key design principles that make adaptability systemic, not situational:

- ***Simplicity* over *complexity***, processes must be understandable by those who use them, not just those who design them.
- ***Autonomy* over *approval***, decisions should be made closest to the information, not the hierarchy.
- ***Iteration* over *perfection***, speed of learning beats speed of delivery.
- ***Transparency* over *control***, visibility creates accountability.
- ***Purpose* over *policy***, clarity of mission reduces the need for micromanagement.

AI reinforces each of these principles, not by dictating what to do, but by illuminating where to grow.

The Design Loop: Sense, Learn, Adapt, Repeat

Agility isn't a project; it's a **loop**.

- ***Sense***, detect change through signals and data.
- ***Learn***, translate those signals into insight.
- ***Adapt***, act on what's learned, quickly and collaboratively.
- ***Repeat***, institutionalize curiosity as a core behavior.

This loop replaces the linear model of:

"plan -> execute -> measure -> report"

In an intelligent enterprise, planning never stops. It breathes.

Case Study 45: The Retailer That Could Pivot

A multinational retailer once planned inventory six months in advance and struggled when viral trends emerged. It redesigned operations for agility: AI now tracks demand signals daily, flexible factories enable micro-production, and designers receive real-time customer feedback for weekly iterations.

Overstock waste fell substantially and profitability improved. The deeper change was behavioral – employees shifted from asking "Can we?" to confidently saying "Let's try." Agility is ultimately a mindset expressed through method.

The Anatomy of Agile Culture

Structure enables agility; **culture sustains** it.

Agile design works only when people trust one another enough to experiment, fail, and recover. That's why psychological safety, not speed, is the foundation of sustainable adaptability.

Google's Project Aristotle found that teams with high psychological safety outperform peers in creativity and problem-solving, regardless of skill level.

When people feel safe to speak up, agility becomes natural. Because true adaptability starts not in the process, but in the *permission*.

AI as the Agility Engine

AI is the great amplifier of agility. It provides instant awareness of shifts, in markets, customer sentiment, supply chains, and workforce dynamics.

But agility isn't about automation; it's about **augmentation**.

AI can analyze thousands of scenarios, simulate risk, and suggest responses. Yet it's humans who interpret, prioritize, and act with empathy.

Together, they create a feedback-driven ecosystem that learns faster than disruption can erode it.

The most agile companies today aren't the ones that know the answers. They're the ones that learn the fastest.

Case Study 46: The Airline That Never Grounded

When travel patterns shifted sharply in 2024, a European airline used predictive AI to reroute aircraft, reassign crews, and rebalance supplies in real time. Because it had already embedded agility into modular systems, empowered teams, and transparent decision processes, the airline expanded into new markets while competitors contracted. It became one of Europe's fastest-growing carriers.

Its CEO captured the advantage: *"We don't react to turbulence. We ride it."* Resilience through design beats reactive crisis management.

Designing for the Human Loop

Agility isn't just structural; it's **emotional**.

AI may tell us what's *changing*, but it takes empathy to decide *how* to *change*. That's why organizations designing for agility must design for **human rhythms** as much as digital ones.

Too many "agile transformations" fail because they treat people like code, expected to update overnight. But change that doesn't honor emotion breeds resistance, not resilience.

Great design respects the human loop: reflection, understanding, and adaptation at a humane pace.

Technology accelerates. Leadership integrates.

Case Study 47: The Consulting Firm Slows Down to Speed Up

A top-tier consultancy adopted a counterintuitive principle during its AI transformation: "slow down to speed up." Before automating workflows, it held deep purpose sessions with teams, asking how AI could enhance – rather than erase – their unique contributions.

Implementation took longer than a pure efficiency play, but adoption and effectiveness were dramatically higher. Within a year, client satisfaction rose substantially and internal stress decreased.

The firm discovered that synchronizing human and machine rhythms creates *sustainable velocity*. True agility requires alignment, not just acceleration.

Designing for Flow, Not Control

Rigid systems depend on control. Agile systems depend on **flow.**

Flow happens when energy moves freely through an organization, ideas, data, decisions, and trust circulating without friction.

AI can help create flow by automating blockers and highlighting opportunities for connection. But the greatest flows are cultural, not technical, they come from curiosity, clarity, and compassion.

The Japanese concept of *kaizen* (continuous improvement) captures this balance. Agility isn't a project to complete; it's a posture to maintain.

The most successful organizations don't chase perfection. They **design for progress.**

The Modular Mindset

To design for agility, companies must think in modules, not monoliths.

Products, teams, and processes should be plug-and-play, allowing parts to evolve without breaking the whole. This modular mindset turns complexity into adaptability.

It's how Spotify organizes teams into "squads," how Amazon runs semi-autonomous "two-pizza teams," and how SpaceX tests and iterates at scale.

The structure isn't static, it's **composable**. And composability is the architecture of agility.

Leadership as Design

In agile organizations, leadership isn't about steering the ship. It's about **designing the ocean**.

Leaders create the conditions for flow, the clarity for focus, and the courage for experimentation.

That's why the new executive skillset looks less like "strategic command" and more like **systems design**, understanding how people, technology, and values interact dynamically.

The agile leader isn't the fastest thinker in the room. They're the one who knows how to keep learning alive.

Closing Reflection – The Symphony of Change

The old world treated change as an interruption. The new world understands change as **music**.

Agility is the art of composing that music, knowing when to lead, when to follow, and when to listen for the silence between notes.

When AI provides rhythm and humans provide melody, the organization becomes a living symphony, always moving, always learning, always becoming.

And in that harmony lies the future of enduring success. Because the goal of agility isn't survival. It's *renewal.*

Key Takeaways – Designing for Agility

- *Agility is the ability* ***to evolve continuously****, not move frantically.*
- *Structure should enable* ***adaptation****, not inhibit it.*
- *AI enhances agility* ***by accelerating awareness and learning****.*
- *Psychological safety is the* ***emotional infrastructure*** *of change.*

The most agile organizations design for *flow*, not *control.*

Part V – Building the Organization That Learns

For most of history, learning was an event. A workshop, a course, a quarterly review.

Today, learning has become a **living process**. The organizations that will define the future aren't the biggest or the fastest, they're the ones that **learn the fastest and forget the slowest**.

Because information is now infinite, wisdom isn't. And wisdom only comes from learning that never stops.

The Learning Organization Reborn

The idea of a "learning organization" isn't new. Peter Senge introduced it in *The Fifth Discipline* back in 1990, describing organizations that continually expand their capacity to create their future.

What's new is that AI has turned that philosophy into **architecture.**

In the past, learning was linear: identify, train, evaluate, repeat. Today, learning is **looped**, sense, interpret, respond, improve, happening everywhere, all the time, in every layer of the enterprise.

Learning is no longer a department. It's the *circulatory system* of modern work.

From Training to Transformation

Traditional training taught employees to replicate existing knowledge. But in a world of constant disruption, replication is regression.

The goal now isn't to teach employees *what to think*, but to equip them to *learn how to learn.*

AI enables this shift by personalizing development at scale. It can map each employee's skills, interests, and learning preferences, creating a dynamic growth journey unique to every individual.

At scale, that becomes organizational metamorphosis: an enterprise that never stops evolving because its people never stop growing.

Case Study 48: The Learning Cloud

A major technology company built what it called a "Learning Cloud" – an integrated system combining AI analytics, employee data, and open learning platforms into personalized growth engines. Employees received curated learning paths aligned to their current projects, career goals, and even emotional feedback from wellness check-ins. Managers gained real-time dashboards showing evolving team capabilities.

Over two years, internal mobility increased substantially and voluntary attrition dropped meaningfully. The CHRO described it as "the democratization of development." When organizations make continuous learning both personal and collective, they stop managing static talent and start unlocking human potential at scale.

AI as the Learning Catalyst

AI doesn't replace learning, it **accelerates** it.

By processing feedback, analyzing performance data, and recommending resources, AI turns learning from a manual process into a momentum engine.

In manufacturing, AI tracks performance and instantly suggests micro-trainings. In healthcare, it analyzes patient interactions to identify gaps in empathy or communication. In marketing, it reviews campaign outcomes and suggests next-step insights.

Learning becomes continuous, contextual, and collective. Every action becomes a lesson. Every mistake becomes an upgrade.

The Feedback Revolution

Feedback used to be episodic and one-directional, a manager's annual review, a static survey, a post-project debrief. Now, it's **real-time and multidirectional**.

AI-powered feedback loops capture insights across channels, employee engagement, customer sentiment, performance analytics, and synthesize them into patterns.

But the key isn't data collection. It's **data interpretation**.

When people understand the *why* behind the feedback, it becomes empowerment, not evaluation.

At a global bank, AI dashboards helped employees visualize how their decisions affected customer satisfaction. The result? A 15% increase in engagement, not because employees worked harder, but because they worked **wiser**.

Feedback isn't judgment. It's fuel.

The Culture of Curiosity

If data is the oxygen of AI, curiosity is the oxygen of learning.

Agile, intelligent organizations thrive on questions, not answers. They encourage employees to experiment, challenge, and explore without fear of failure.

That requires psychological safety, but also **structural permission**, systems that reward exploration, not just execution.

In 2026, Deloitte found that companies that actively measured "learning curiosity", the frequency of self-directed learning activities, saw **37% higher innovation scores** than those that didn't.

Curiosity, when institutionalized, becomes a strategy. Because curiosity is what keeps intelligence alive.

Case Study 49: The Experiment Company

A fintech startup gave every employee a monthly "experiment budget" – a small allocation of time and resources to test new ideas, features, or processes. AI systems tracked outcomes, captured lessons, and shared insights across the organization, creating a living "learning marketplace" where employees taught one another from real results.

Innovation accelerated and morale rose noticeably. The CEO captured the cultural shift: *"We stopped rewarding being right. We started rewarding curiosity."*

When experimentation becomes everyone's responsibility, culture itself becomes a competitive advantage.

The Human Multiplier

AI can optimize process, but humans multiply purpose. And when purpose and learning align, growth becomes exponential.

At the core of every learning organization lies one simple truth: People don't grow because they're told to. They grow because they're **trusted to.**

Empowerment transforms learning from compliance into calling. When employees feel trusted to take initiative, they begin to shape their own future, and by extension, the company's.

This is how AI and humanity converge: machines manage complexity, while humans pursue meaning.

Collective Intelligence

A single mind can learn. A team can adapt. But a **collective intelligence** can transform.

AI helps connect the dots across functions, geographies, and disciplines, turning local insights into global wisdom. It detects recurring patterns of innovation and shares them organization-wide, making success scalable and learning contagious.

This is the "network brain" of the modern enterprise, a living system that integrates experience, empathy, and evidence into one continuously evolving intelligence.

Case Study 50: The Organization That Taught Itself

A global consumer goods company developed an internal AI system called Eureka to analyze employee-submitted innovations and identify which ideas had the highest real-world success rates. The system then recommended which concepts to replicate or refine across markets.

Within 18 months, a large majority of the company's top-performing initiatives originated from frontline employee insights. The COO reflected: "We no longer just train people to execute strategy. We now learn strategy from our people." When learning becomes circular, leadership turns collective.

Unlearning as the Ultimate Skill

Learning organizations don't just accumulate knowledge. They **release** it.

In fast-changing environments, clinging to outdated models becomes intellectual inertia. The ability to *unlearn*, to discard what no longer serves, is now the rarest competitive advantage.

That's why forward-thinking leaders are teaching teams to question legacy metrics, challenge traditional hierarchies, and reimagine "the way we've always done it."

Unlearning is humility in motion. It's the courage to say, *"That used to be true, but it isn't anymore."*

Case Study 51: The Airline That Unlearned Its Model

An airline with a long history of rigid operational playbooks faced repeated disruptions from unpredictable travel trends. Leadership declared a "learning reset," abandoning fixed quarterly forecasts in favor of **rolling, adaptive planning** informed by AI data and human scenario modeling.

Forecast accuracy improved markedly, and employee engagement rose even more. By choosing to unlearn outdated models, the airline discovered greater resilience through constant iteration rather than static certainty.

The Learning Leader

Leadership in a learning organization isn't about having answers. It's about asking **better questions.**

The learning leader is part teacher, part student, part architect. They model curiosity, transparency, and vulnerability. They celebrate insight more than authority.

They understand that wisdom doesn't flow from the top down, it circulates. Because leadership isn't the source of learning. It's the spark that keeps it alive.

Closing Reflection – The Company That Thinks

The organizations worth admiring aren't the ones that scaled fastest or automated most aggressively. They're the ones that stayed curious, that treated every result, good or bad, as something worth understanding rather than just moving past.

Learning isn't a byproduct of success. It's the mechanism of it.

Chapter 5

Redefining Value in the Age of Intelligence

Part I – The End of Efficiency

For more than a hundred years, efficiency has been the ultimate virtue of modern work. We built our factories, systems, and societies around it. Faster. Cheaper. More.

Efficiency became the measure of progress, the goal of capitalism, the logic of leadership. And for a time, it worked. It brought prosperity, productivity, and predictability to a chaotic world.

But something has changed.

In an age where machines can automate almost anything, efficiency has lost its meaning. The question is no longer "How do we make it faster?" It's "Why are we making it at all?"

The Cult of Optimization

The 20th century was the century of optimization. We optimized production with assembly lines, management with hierarchies, and people with performance metrics.

Every problem became an equation to be solved by doing more with less. We industrialized agriculture, mechanized manufacturing, and digitized communication. We measured success by throughput, how much we could produce in how little time.

Efficiency was a moral code. Waste was sin. Speed was salvation.

But efficiency, when pursued without reflection, becomes its own kind of waste, the waste of meaning.

We became so good at moving faster that we stopped asking where we were going.

The Productivity Paradox

We are living in the most productive era in human history, and one of the least fulfilled.

Despite record output, global surveys show declining well-being, trust, and engagement. The World Health Organization reported a 25% rise in anxiety and depression following the rapid digitalization of work. Gallup's 2025 study found that only 21% of employees worldwide describe themselves as engaged at work, despite record productivity levels.

We have mastered efficiency and lost connection. We have optimized processes and dehumanized people.

The paradox is stark: The more efficient we become, the more exhausted we feel. Because efficiency was designed for machines, not for meaning.

The Machine Mirror

AI has revealed something we long ignored: that the logic of efficiency is mechanical, not moral.

Algorithms optimize. Humans aspire.

When AI automates routine work, it doesn't just take over tasks, it holds up a mirror to our purpose. If a machine can do your job faster, cheaper, and better, what remains of your value?

The answer isn't to compete with machines on speed. It's to redefine value itself. Efficiency asks, "How well can we perform?" Intelligence asks, "Why does this matter?" That shift, from performance to purpose, is the true transformation of the intelligent age.

Case Study 52: The Company That Slowed Down

In 2025, a leading European furniture brand made a provocative announcement: it would make fewer products, but far better ones. The strategy emphasized longevity, sustainable materials, repairability, and emotional durability over quarterly growth targets.

Sales dipped in the first year as expected. Brand trust, employee retention, and customer loyalty surged. Within three years, profits exceeded previous highs. The CEO explained: *"Efficiency got us here. Meaning will take us further."*

Sometimes the bravest move is redefining success itself.

The Tyranny of Metrics

We are surrounded by dashboards, KPIs, and analytics, a world where everything can be measured except what matters most.

Love. Trust. Purpose. Joy.

The obsession with measurable efficiency has created a blindness to invisible value. We know the price of everything and the meaning of nothing.

AI now tracks our productivity by the minute, our sentiment by the word, our fitness by the heartbeat. But even the most intelligent system can't measure why we care.

Peter Drucker warned that "what gets measured gets managed." But he never said everything that gets managed is worth measuring.

The next evolution of value won't be measured in units of output, but in degrees of impact.

The Human Cost of Perpetual Motion

Efficiency has a shadow side: it teaches us that stillness is failure. We equate busyness with importance, speed with success.

But constant motion doesn't create progress. It creates fatigue.

In 2024, Microsoft's global work index found that employees spent 250% more time in meetings and digital collaboration tools than before the pandemic, but output per hour barely increased.

We are optimizing ourselves into exhaustion.

AI offers the promise of reclaiming time, but only if we dare to slow down long enough to use it wisely.

The age of intelligence must become the age of intentionality.

From Efficiency to Effectiveness

The late management thinker Peter Drucker made a crucial distinction: "Efficiency is doing things right. Effectiveness is doing the right things."

For decades, organizations focused on the former. AI now forces us to confront the latter.

When machines can "do things right" at scale, human value shifts toward doing the right things, ethically, emotionally, creatively.

That means success will increasingly depend on human discernment, the ability to choose which paths to pursue, not just how to pursue them.

Efficiency maximizes what is measurable. Effectiveness multiplies what is meaningful.

Case Study 53: The Agency That Unplugged

A global advertising agency observed declining creative output despite heavy investment in digital tools and platforms. In 2026, leadership made a counterintuitive decision: every Friday became a screen-free day – no internal emails, no dashboards, only human conversation, brainstorming, and reflection.

Creative quality scores rose substantially (by some accounts as much as 38%), client satisfaction improved, and turnover dropped markedly. By deliberately disconnecting, the agency reconnected with the source of its value: human creativity and presence. Periodic unplugged time can be one of the highest-leverage productivity moves in an always-on world.

The Ethics of Enough

The pursuit of endless efficiency has no natural limit. There's always another percentage point to chase, another metric to improve.

But meaning begins where maximization ends.

This realization is reshaping how companies define success. Patagonia measures its impact not by profit alone, but by preservation, how much of the planet remains unharmed. Salesforce ties executive bonuses to its "trust index." Even financial giants like BlackRock now weigh social responsibility alongside shareholder returns.

The message is clear: *Efficiency is no longer enough.*

In the intelligent age, value will be judged not by how much we can extract, but by how much we can elevate.

The Slowing Movement

A subtle revolution is underway, the global movement toward deliberate, sustainable pace. "Slow work" isn't laziness; it's *craftsmanship*. "Slow growth" isn't failure; it's *foresight*. Leaders are rediscovering that time isn't a cost, it's a *canvas*.

At a Japanese robotics firm, engineers are encouraged to spend one day a month "thinking without deadlines." At a Silicon Valley startup, meetings begin with a moment of collective silence, a pause before progress.

In both cases, innovation accelerated, not despite the slowness, but because of it. Efficiency produces output. Reflection produces breakthroughs.

From Machine Speed to Human Rhythm

AI operates at the speed of computation. Humans thrive at the speed of connection. When organizations synchronize the two, they unlock flow, that rare state where technology amplifies rather than replaces human energy.

This is the new equilibrium: Let machines move fast. Let humans move well.

Because life, leadership, and creativity aren't races to win. They are rhythms to sustain.

Closing Reflection – The End of Efficiency

Efficiency is a means, not an end. For a long time, optimizing for it felt like the same thing as making progress. It wasn't, and the gap is becoming harder to ignore.

The organizations getting this right aren't abandoning efficiency. They are using it as a floor rather than a ceiling, asking what they can do with the capacity they free up, rather than treating the saving as the accomplishment.

Key Takeaways – The End of Efficiency

- *Automation exposes the* ***limits of efficiency*** *as a value metric*
- ***Productivity without purpose*** *leads to exhaustion, not progress.*
- *The intelligent age demands* ***significance*** *over speed*

Part II – The Rise of the Meaning Economy

For more than two centuries, economies were built on the exchange of goods, then services, then information. Each evolution brought more sophistication, more scale, and more speed.

But now, a new form of value is emerging, one that can't be measured in units or margins. It's the economy of **meaning.**

The meaning economy doesn't sell what people need. It serves what people *believe.*

It isn't driven by consumption, but by **conviction.** **From the Industrial to the Intentional**

The Industrial Age was powered by production. The Information Age was powered by connection. The Intelligent Age is powered by **intention.**

Consumers today no longer simply buy products, they buy purpose. They want to know not just *what* a company makes, but *why* it exists.

In a 2026 PwC study, **83% of global consumers** said they prefer brands that align with their personal values. Even more striking: 71% said they would pay more for a product from a company that treats people and the planet responsibly.

This isn't idealism. It's economics redefined by empathy. The meaning economy isn't a niche, it's the new mainstream.

The Erosion of Trust and the Hunger for Truth

The Edelman Trust Barometer shows that fewer than half of people globally trust business leaders to do what is right. At the same time, trust has become one of the most valuable assets an organization can hold, precisely because it is so scarce.

People no longer believe what companies say. They watch what companies do. Authenticity, in this environment, isn't a brand attribute. It is an operating condition.

Case Study 54: The Shoe Brand That Sold Stewardship

A small California shoe brand launched in 2024 with a radical promise: lifetime free repairs for every pair sold. It was positioned not merely as a service but as a moral stand against throwaway culture.

Over two years, the brand grew dramatically without traditional paid advertising. The CEO summarized their approach: *"We didn't sell shoes. We sold stewardship."* When ethics become the product, loyalty and growth can follow in unexpected ways.

The Shift from ROI to ROR (Return on Relationship)

In the meaning economy, value grows not through extraction but through connection.

ROI, Return on Investment, is no longer sufficient. ROR, Return on Relationship, is the new metric of growth.

Because relationships, not transactions, sustain businesses.

AI can identify patterns and predict behavior. But only human empathy can create belonging. When brands connect with people emotionally and ethically, loyalty transcends logic.

A Harvard Business Review analysis found that emotionally connected customers are **52% more valuable** than highly satisfied ones. That's not marketing spin, that's the mathematics of meaning.

Work as Vocation, Commerce as Cause

For the new generation entering the workforce, meaning isn't optional, it's oxygen. Millennials and Gen Z don't separate their careers from their convictions.

A 2025 Deloitte survey found that **76% of Gen Z** employees say they would leave an employer whose values don't align with their own. In other words, culture isn't just a "perk." It's the product.

Companies that thrive in the meaning economy treat work not as a transaction, but as transformation, a place where people express purpose, not just earn paychecks

Case Study 55: The Bank That Became a Movement

A Scandinavian digital bank evolved from a standard fintech into a financial well-being movement with the mission of helping people thrive, not merely survive. It used AI for personalized spending and saving coaching, **always paired** with human counselors trained in empathy and ethical guidance.

Customer growth tripled and attrition fell to near zero. The CMO captured the shift: *"We stopped selling products. We started serving progress."*

In the emerging meaning economy, businesses that help people become better versions of themselves create the deepest loyalty.

AI and the Paradox of Meaning

AI is both the accelerant and the antagonist of meaning.

It enables personalization, empathy at scale, and predictive care. But it also raises real questions about authenticity and authorship.

If AI writes your ad, paints your art, or composes your music, does it still carry *meaning*?

The answer lies not in the output but the *intention behind it.* Meaning doesn't come from the code, it comes from the creator's conviction.

AI can imitate emotion. Only humans can embody it.

That's why the most successful uses of AI in marketing, design, and communication amplify human purpose, they don't replace it.

Case Study 56: The AI Campaign That Cried Real Tears

A global humanitarian organization created an interactive AI-generated campaign simulating refugee experiences. Viewers engaged with a digital child whose stories were grounded in real data. The campaign moved millions to donate.

Critics questioned whether it crossed into manipulation. The organization responded transparently: the simulations were built to awaken empathy, not deceive. This distinction – between emotional power used to manipulate versus to illuminate – defines one of the central ethical frontiers of the intelligent age. AI will make feelings easier to evoke. Humanity must ensure they are evoked honestly.

The Democratization of Meaning

The internet gave everyone a voice. AI gives everyone a **megaphone.**

Meaning is no longer top-down, delivered by corporations or governments. It's now co-created, between people, platforms, and communities.

Movements like #BlackLivesMatter, #MeToo, and #FridaysForFuture didn't begin in boardrooms. They began in hearts and hashtags, collective calls for truth amplified through technology.

Meaning is no longer centralized. It's **networked.**

And the brands that thrive are those humble enough to listen to it, not just speak into it.

The Economics of Empathy

Empathy used to be a soft skill. Now it's a hard advantage.

In a crowded, automated marketplace, empathy becomes differentiation. It creates emotional stickiness, a connection that no algorithm can copy.

A 2026 Accenture study found that companies ranked highest in empathy-based leadership outperformed the S&P 500 by **21%** in annual revenue growth.

Empathy scales trust. Trust scales loyalty. Loyalty scales longevity. That's how the meaning economy compounds.

From Attention to Intention

The old economy competed for attention. The new one competes for **intention**.

Attention is fleeting, it's what people notice. Intention is lasting, it's what people nurture.

Algorithms may optimize for engagement, but humans optimize for **alignment**. That's why meaning-driven brands don't chase clicks; they cultivate conviction.

They know that a single authentic belief can sustain more value than a million empty impressions.

In the meaning economy, relevance isn't about visibility, it's about virtue.

Case Study 57: The Tech Company That Gave Up Growth

In 2025, a major social platform made the difficult choice to deprioritize outrage-inducing content in its algorithm, even though it had long driven engagement metrics. Short-term growth and revenue dipped as predicted.

Over time, user trust, retention, and advertiser interest recovered and strengthened. The CEO explained: "We decided to measure success by what people care about, not just what they click." Choosing virtue over virality in the short term can create more durable value in the long term. This is the courage the meaning economy demands.

The Return of the Human Story

In the end, the meaning economy is simply a return to something ancient: the human story. Tribes, temples, and towns were all built around shared meaning, symbols that made existence coherent.

We've come full circle. Technology has made us powerful, but only meaning makes us whole.

And now, as AI reshapes every market, meaning will reshape every metric. Because value without virtue is noise. And progress without purpose is peril.

Closing Reflection – The Market of Belief

The meaning economy isn't about selling to consumers. It's about **belonging with believers.**

It's about brands becoming movements, companies becoming communities, and leaders becoming servants of something larger than themselves.

In this new economy, the most valuable product isn't a thing. It's a truth, lived, shared, and sustained.

We once asked, *"What will people buy?"* Now we must ask, *"What will people believe in us for?"*

Because the next great marketplace isn't digital. It's spiritual.

Key Takeaways – The Rise of the Meaning Economy

- *The **meaning economy** rewards **authenticity**, **empathy**, and **purpose**.*
- ***Trust** has overtaken **efficiency** as the core driver of **loyalty** and **growth**.*
- *AI amplifies **meaning** when guided by **human ethics** and **intention**.*
- *Consumers and employees alike now choose **belief** over **brand**.*

The future of value creation lies in *conviction*, not *consumption*.

Part III – The Currency of Trust

For most of human history, value was based on **tangibility.** Gold, land, oil, machinery, things you could touch, measure, or store.

Then came the information age, when value shifted to **knowledge,** data, code, patents, and networks.

Now, value has moved again. It lives not in what we own, but in what we **trust.**

The Great Trust Recession

If the 20th century was defined by industrial production, the 21st is defined by emotional erosion.

We have more connection and less confidence. More visibility and less belief.

According to the 2026 Edelman Trust Barometer, global trust in institutions, government, media, business, and NGOs, has fallen to its lowest level in 20 years. Even trust between individuals, once assumed to be natural, has fractured.

Social media made us visible, but not credible. Data made us smarter, but not wiser. AI made us powerful, but not always principled.

We live in an age of abundance, but suffer a **shortage of trust.** And that shortage is now the most expensive deficit in business.

Trust as an Economic Multiplier

Trust isn't sentiment. It's capital.

McKinsey research found that companies ranking highest in consumer trust outperform peers by **30,50% in long-term valuation.** Employees in high-trust organizations report **74% less stress** and **50% higher productivity.**

Trust doesn't just make people feel better. It makes organizations **function better.**

Because in a world of infinite choice and instant transparency, trust is the only true differentiator that can't be bought, only earned.

Efficiency drives transactions. Trust drives **transformation.**

The Geometry of Trust

Trust has three dimensions:

- **Competence** – Can you *deliver*?
- **Consistency** – Can I *rely on you*?
- **Character** – Can I *believe in you*?

AI can enhance the first two, by making organizations more capable and consistent. But only humans can embody the third, **character**.

Character is where trust becomes moral, not mechanical. It's the difference between efficiency and ethics, between reliability and righteousness.

Trust built solely on competence collapses under crisis. Trust built on character endures.

The Algorithmic Dilemma

AI has introduced a new paradox: the more intelligent systems become, the less we understand them.

We trust what we can explain. But AI's complexity often defies explanation.

When opacity creates anxiety, the fear to which we surrender control is something we can't see or comprehend.

This is why explainable AI (XAI) is now a priority across industries. A 2025 IBM report showed that **89% of consumers** say they're more likely to trust AI-powered decisions if given a clear explanation of how those decisions are made.

Transparency is no longer a compliance issue. It's a design principle.

Case Study 58: The Transparent Retailer

A global e-commerce brand built a sophisticated AI recommendation engine to personalize shopping experiences.

Customers soon began wondering whether the system was subtly manipulating prices or choices.

Rather than keeping the algorithm opaque, the company launched a "Why You See This" feature that explained the logic behind each suggestion in clear, accessible language. Conversion rates rose noticeably and customer complaints fell substantially.

Transparency did not weaken the tool – it **amplified trust**. In the age of intelligent systems, openness is becoming one of the most powerful drivers of customer loyalty.

Trust by Design

Organizations can't *add* trust to a system. They must **build it in.** That begins with three principles:

- **Transparency**, *Show* how decisions are made.
- **Accountability**, *Own* outcomes and correct mistakes.
- **Empathy**, Center the experience on *human dignity*.

When embedded into design, these principles create self-reinforcing cycles of confidence.

It's the architecture of trust: visible, verifiable, and **virtuous.**

The Trust Dividend in Leadership

Leaders used to be trusted because they had authority. Now they are trusted because they show **authenticity**.

In an age of deepfakes, spin, and polarization, leaders who admit uncertainty, vulnerability, and humanity stand out.

A Harvard Business Review study found that leaders who demonstrate vulnerability, saying "I don't know" or "I made a mistake", increase team trust by **up to 35%.**

Confidence builds respect. Honesty builds **relationship.**

And relationship is the compound interest of trust.

Case Study 59: A CEO Who Said "I Was Wrong"

During a difficult layoff period, the CEO of a global software company issued a public letter that was refreshingly direct: *"I made the wrong call. I prioritized efficiency when I should have prioritized empathy. I'm sorry."*

The message spread rapidly. Instead of backlash, it generated widespread support from employees, investors, and even peers. The stock price rebounded quickly and employee satisfaction surged.

Humility in leadership does not diminish authority – it humanizes it. In moments of failure, honest accountability can become a powerful catalyst for renewed trust.

Digital Trust and the Data Contract

Data is the DNA of the intelligent economy, but without trust, it's useless.

Customers are increasingly protective of their personal information. A 2026 Cisco study revealed that **84% of consumers** want more control over how their data is used, and **63%** have already switched providers over privacy concerns.

The new social contract of business is the data contract, a transparent, ethical agreement between user and organization.

Those who respect it build loyalty. Those who violate it lose everything.

Trust is the gateway to permission. And permission is the new **pipeline for growth**.

Case Study 60: A Bank That Returned the Data

A European digital bank took a bold step toward user sovereignty. Using blockchain-based contracts, it gave customers full ownership and visibility of their financial data. Users could see exactly when and how their information was shared and revoke access instantly.

Trust ratings soared and churn dropped significantly. The CMO summarized the evolution: "We moved beyond protecting privacy to truly empowering people."

This represents the next frontier of trust – from security to **genuine data sovereignty.**

The Trust Algorithm

Imagine a future where AI systems don't just process information, they process **integrity.**

AI that measures not only accuracy but fairness. That optimizes not just for efficiency but for empathy.

That's the next frontier: the **trust algorithm.**

It doesn't replace human morality. It encodes it.

In this future, algorithms will be audited for equity, systems will be rewarded for transparency, and trust itself will become a measurable KPI.

Because in the intelligent age, the most advanced technology won't be the one that learns fastest, it will be the one that earns trust longest.

Trust as a Collective Currency

Trust isn't a zero-sum resource. It multiplies through sharing.

When leaders trust employees, employees trust each other, and customers trust the brand, it creates a self-reinforcing loop of confidence and care.

This collective trust becomes social capital, the invisible wealth that powers communities, cultures, and companies alike.

In a fragmented world, collective trust is the only infrastructure strong enough to hold us together.

It's the emotional economy's gold standard.

Closing Reflection – The Wealth of Belief

The currency of the future isn't cryptocurrency, data, or attention. It's **belief**.

Belief that the systems guiding us are fair. Belief that the people leading us are good. Belief that the technology serving us is humane.

Every algorithm, brand, and leader now competes not for our wallets, but for our **faith**.

Because in a world of infinite information, people will spend their money, and their loyalty, only where they can spend their **trust**.

Trust is no longer the lubricant of the economy. It's the engine.

Key Takeaways – The Currency of Trust

- ***Trust*** *has surpassed* ***data*** *and innovation as the core driver of long-term value.*
- ***Transparency****,* ***accountability****, and* ***empathy*** *form the foundation of modern* ***trust design****.*
- ***Explainable*** *and* ***ethical*** *AI builds confidence, while* ***opacity erodes*** *it.*
- ***Leadership humility*** *and* ***human authenticity*** *increase organizational trust capital.*

The future of prosperity lies not in technology, but in *belief*.

Part IV – The Human Premium

There's a growing myth in modern business, that as machines become smarter, humans become less necessary. That automation will inevitably make us obsolete.

But history tells a different story. Every technological leap, from the printing press to the internet, hasn't diminished humanity. It has **demanded more of it.**

Each revolution forces us to rediscover what only we can do. And in this age of intelligence, that rediscovery is the **human premium.**

Beyond Automation: The Age of Amplification

The first wave of AI was about automation, doing tasks faster, cheaper, and more precisely than people. The next wave is about **amplification**, expanding what people can imagine, create, and feel.

AI can analyze, synthesize, and predict. But only humans can **dream**.

Automation removed limitations. Amplification removes excuses.

The question is no longer "What can AI do?" It's "What can we do because of AI?" That's the shift from substitution to synergy, from fear to flourishing.

The Four Pillars of the Human Premium

As machines master logic, the value of being human isn't diminishing. It's diversifying.

The new economy prizes four distinctly human capabilities that no algorithm can truly replicate:

- ***Creativity*** – the ability to imagine what doesn't yet exist.
- ***Conscience*** – the moral instinct to discern right from wrong.
- ***Compassion*** – the emotional intelligence to understand and uplift others.
- ***Courage*** – the will to act on conviction, even when data disagrees.

These aren't soft skills. They are **sovereign skills**, the foundation of human resilience and relevance.

Creativity: The Infinite Game

AI can compose symphonies, paint portraits, and write prose. But all of it is based on what's been seen before. It creates from patterns, not from **pain or purpose.**

Human creativity isn't about rearranging what exists, it's about **revealing what doesn't.**

The creative process is messy, emotional, and unpredictable, the very qualities machines are designed to avoid. That's why true originality still belongs to us.

A 2025 World Economic Forum survey listed creativity as the **#1 most essential skill** for the future workforce, above critical thinking, leadership, and technology literacy.

In a world overflowing with intelligence, imagination is our final frontier.

Case Study 61: The Designer and the Algorithm

A fashion designer used AI to generate thousands of textile patterns. The initial outputs were technically impressive but felt sterile and overly symmetrical.

She then fed the system data from her grandmother's handmade quilts – imperfections, asymmetry, and human texture. The AI outputs suddenly came alive with soul. She titled the collection "The Machine and the Memory." It sold out quickly.

"AI gave me options," she reflected. *"My humanity gave them meaning."* The future of creativity lies in this partnership: models providing possibility, humans providing soul.

Conscience: The Compass of Intelligence

As technology gains power, conscience becomes the new leadership currency. AI can decide what's *efficient*. Only humans can decide what's *ethical*.

In the age of data, morality is no longer abstract, it's operational. Every algorithm reflects human choices. Every model encodes human values.

Leaders who lack moral imagination risk building systems that optimize performance while eroding principle.

The human premium begins with ethical vision, the courage to ask, "Should we?" before "Can we?"

That question can't be automated. It must be *inhabited.*

Case Study 62: The Hospital That Said No

A healthcare network developed an AI tool to predict patient readmissions that showed strong potential to reduce costs. However, analysis revealed it under-predicted risk for minority patients due to bias in the training data.

Despite investor pressure, leadership paused deployment and invested six months in ethical retraining and oversight. When relaunched, outcomes improved across all demographics and trust from both patients and staff increased.

The chief medical officer stated it clearly: *"Technology cannot be ethical on its own. People must be."* Conscience remains the ultimate competitive advantage.

Compassion: The Emotional Algorithm

Data can tell us what people do. It can't tell us why.

Compassion is the original human interface, the ability to translate suffering into support, and emotion into empathy.

In an age when loneliness and burnout are epidemic, compassion is more than kindness. It's a strategic differentiator.

Companies that lead with empathy outperform their peers in every measurable way, retention, reputation, innovation.

A 2026 Businessolver study found that 88% of employees believe empathetic leadership inspires loyalty, while 60% said they would take a pay cut to work for a more empathetic organization.

Empathy isn't an expense. It's an investment.

Case Study 63: The Airline That Listened

Following repeated delays that left passengers stranded, a major airline replaced rigid scripted bots with AI assistants trained on empathy data, tone recognition, and situational understanding. Agents received real-time coaching to connect emotionally rather than just respond efficiently.

Complaints dropped substantially, positive sentiment rose sharply, and customer-service staff turnover decreased markedly. The airline did not automate empathy – it augmented it. Data became a tool that helped humans care better.

That's the future of compassion in commerce: data that helps people **care better**.

Courage: The Rarest Commodity

The final pillar of the human premium is courage, the willingness to choose conviction over convenience.

Machines don't take risks. Humans do.

Courage fuels innovation, leadership, and moral progress. Every great leap in history, abolishing slavery, civil rights, human flight, began not with certainty, but with courage.

And courage will be what defines leadership in the intelligent age: the courage to slow down when AI says speed up, to question when data says yes, to choose humanity when profit says no.

Because courage can't be coded. It must be lived.

Case Study 64: The Brand That Refused to Lie

A global food company faced a serious PR crisis when an internal audit exposed misleading sustainability claims. Agency advisors recommended a quiet retraction. Instead, the CEO publicly admitted the deception, apologized sincerely, and detailed every corrective action.

Analysts predicted major losses. Within six months, sales had increased. Consumers rewarded courage and honesty over concealment. In the intelligent age, truth remains a virtue that algorithms cannot optimize – but humans can still choose.

The Human Dividend

These four forces, creativity, conscience, compassion, and courage, are the foundation of the **human dividend**: the exponential return that arises when people bring their whole selves to work.

AI enhances efficiency. Humanity enhances *effectiveness*.

When both operate together, the result isn't replacement, but resonance, an organization that thinks and feels, learns and leads.

That's how companies like Pixar, Patagonia, and Microsoft continue to outperform competitors: they invest as much in **being human** as in being smart.

Because in the end, intelligence without empathy is irrelevance accelerated.

The New Metrics of Humanity

The next frontier of performance management won't just track output, but humanity itself:

- ***Creativity Index***, measuring innovation and originality across teams.
- ***Ethical Maturity***, assessing decision frameworks for fairness and transparency.
- ***Empathy Score***, evaluating leadership through relational impact.
- ***Courage Quotient***, recognizing moral bravery and principled action.

These aren't vanity metrics. They're the blueprint for sustainable success, a human operating system built on values instead of velocity.

Closing Reflection – The Uncopyable Advantage

Machines will learn to think faster, predict better, and execute flawlessly. But they'll never understand what it means to hope, to love, to suffer, to believe.

That's the uncopyable advantage.

The human premium isn't a nostalgic defense of our past, it's the **strategic engine of our future.**

Because as intelligence becomes ubiquitous, emotion becomes rare. As automation expands, authenticity ascends.

The future won't belong to the most efficient or even the most intelligent. It will belong to those who remain most human.

Key Takeaways – The Human Premium

- *AI* ***amplifies*** *human potential, it doesn't* ***replace*** *it.*
- *Creativity, conscience, compassion, and courage form the new* ***human value equation****.*
- ***Ethical imagination*** *and* ***emotional intelligence*** *are the future's defining leadership traits.*
- *The most powerful metric of progress will be the* ***measure of our humanity.***
- *The organizations that win will be the ones that* ***feel deeply and lead bravely.***

Part V – Building the Value System of Tomorrow

The definition of value has always reflected what a society worships. In the industrial age, we elevated productivity. In the information age, we worshiped knowledge. Now, in the intelligent age, we are learning to truly value wisdom.

Wisdom isn't data processed faster. It's judgment practiced better. It's the ability to use intelligence in service of something worthwhile.

The organizations that will define the next century won't be those with the most data, the most automation, or even the most profit. They'll be those that design systems of value, cultures, technologies, and strategies that turn intelligence into integrity, efficiency into empathy, and growth into goodness.

The Value Equation Is Changing

For decades, business value was built on a simple formula: Capital × Labor = Growth.

But AI changes the variables. Capital has become code. Labor has become leverage. And growth without meaning is no longer sustainable.

The new equation looks more like this: Intelligence × Intention = Impact.

Where intelligence represents our capacity to know, and intention represents our will to do good. It's not what we can automate that matters, it's what we choose to amplify.

The Three Dimensions of Tomorrow's Value

Organizations that thrive in the next decade will operate across three dimensions of value creation:

- **Economic Value**, financial growth that sustains the enterprise.
- **Human Value**, emotional, ethical, and cultural enrichment of people.

- **Societal Value**, contribution to the broader good: environment, equity, and trust.

The most resilient companies won't trade one for another, they'll integrate all three.

That integration requires a new measurement mindset, one where profit and purpose aren't opposites, but outcomes of the same design.

From Balance Sheet to Moral Sheet

Imagine a world where quarterly reports include a "Moral Sheet" alongside the balance sheet, tracking not only revenues and expenses, but relationships and impact.

This isn't fantasy. Unilever, Salesforce, and Patagonia already publish "impact metrics" that evaluate carbon footprint, community engagement, and employee well-being.

It's a recognition that value without virtue is volatility. Markets will increasingly reward those who measure how they win, not just whether they win.

AI can power this shift by quantifying the previously unquantifiable: sentiment, trust, inclusion, and sustainability, transforming ethics from narrative into data.

Case Study 65: The Retailer with a Conscience Index

A global retailer introduced a live "Conscience Index" – an AI-powered dashboard tracking environmental and social performance across its entire supply chain. Each product displayed a visible impact score for customers.

High-scoring items sold significantly faster. Suppliers began competing to improve their ethics rankings. Employee pride rose noticeably. The CEO observed: *"Transparency became our most profitable product."*

Principle, properly measured and shared, has become **performance**.

From KPIs to KHI: Key Human Indicators

Traditional KPIs track profit, cost, and efficiency. But in a world where human creativity, conscience, and trust drive differentiation, companies must also track Key Human Indicators (KHI):

- ***Purpose Alignment***, the percentage of employees who find their work meaningful.
- ***Psychological Safety***, the measure of trust and openness in teams.
- ***Empathy Ratio***, the degree to which customer experience reflects understanding.
- ***Ethical Resilience***, how often leaders choose long-term integrity over short-term gain.

These KHIs become the compass of culture, guiding strategy toward sustainability.

Because what gets measured gets improved, and what gets humanized gets remembered.

The Leadership Model of the Future

In this new economy, leaders aren't commanders of efficiency but architects of meaning. They don't ask, "How do we scale faster?" They ask, "How do we scale better?"

Their job is to build systems that align profit with purpose, automation with authenticity, and intelligence with intuition.

A new leadership trinity is emerging:

- ***Head*** – the ability to reason with data.
- ***Heart*** – the ability to empathize with people.
- ***Hands*** – the ability to act with courage.

Leadership that unites all three doesn't just lead companies. It leads conscience.

Case Study 66: The Logistics Company That Measured Humanity

A global logistics firm optimized routes and reduced emissions with AI, boosting efficiency. However, employees began feeling over-monitored and undervalued.

The CEO mandated that every optimization model include a "human variable" – factoring in fatigue, job satisfaction, and mental health. Within a year, retention improved, accidents decreased, and profit margins expanded. The COO called it "the productivity of empathy." Leadership for wholeness, not just output, creates more sustainable results.

The Four Foundations of Sustainable Value

Through hundreds of studies and interviews across industries, four consistent foundations emerge for organizations seeking long-term success:

- ***Purpose***, A clear, lived reason for being beyond profit.
- ***Transparency***, Open systems that invite trust, not demand it.
- ***Participation***, Inclusive collaboration across roles, geographies, and cultures.
- ***Progress***, A commitment to continuous learning and ethical growth.

These foundations transform business from a mechanism into a movement. They ensure that every innovation expands dignity instead of diminishing it.

Case Study 67: The City That Measured Joy

In 2025, a European city introduced an AI-powered Well-Being Index that measured community happiness alongside traditional economic metrics. It integrated data on mental health, environmental quality, and citizen engagement.

High-scoring initiatives in public transport and green spaces correlated with rises in tourism and investment. The mayor captured the shift: "*We stopped asking only how much we grew. We started asking how much better we became.*"

Prosperity measured by vitality, not just volume – this is the deeper promise of intelligent governance.

The Integration Imperative

To build this new value system, organizations must integrate across four layers of operation:

- **Technology** – Ensure AI systems reflect ethical design and inclusivity.
- **Culture** – Embed curiosity, kindness, and courage into everyday behavior.
- **Metrics** – Replace narrow KPIs with multidimensional value indicators.
- **Governance** – Establish accountability frameworks rewarding integrity as much as innovation.

When these layers work in harmony, value creation becomes virtuous. Intelligence and empathy co-author every decision.

That's the ultimate competitive advantage, a company that can learn and listen.

The Role of AI in Measuring Meaning

AI is uniquely capable of transforming qualitative values into quantifiable insights. Natural-language models can analyze employee sentiment, public trust, and cultural health. Machine vision can assess sustainability compliance in factories. Predictive analytics can simulate ethical trade-offs and long-term societal impact.

This isn't about turning empathy into numbers. It's about using numbers to nurture empathy.

AI becomes not a judge, but a mirror, reflecting whether organizations live up to their stated ideals. When designed responsibly, it becomes an auditor of authenticity.

From Shareholder Capitalism to Shared Humanity

The most significant shift underway is philosophical: from the primacy of shareholders to the priority of shared humanity.

Investors are increasingly evaluating companies through environmental, social, and governance (ESG) lenses. But the next evolution will be HSI, Human Sustainability Index, measuring an organization's contribution to human well-being, not just environmental stewardship.

Companies that elevate human flourishing, through fair work, diversity, wellness, and trust, will attract the best talent, the most loyal customers, and the strongest partners.

Because in the long run, the most sustainable asset isn't capital. It's character.

Case Study 68: The Tech Firm That Measured Trust

A major technology company took a bold step in 2026: it began publishing an annual "Trust Ledger" that candidly detailed its performance on user privacy, algorithmic fairness, and environmental ethics – including explicit admissions of shortcomings.

The first report was humbling, yet its transparency built credibility far beyond what traditional marketing could achieve. The company's valuation grew noticeably in the following year, and independent trust indices rose substantially. The chief trust officer captured the outcome: *"Accountability became our most powerful asset."*

In the intelligent age, honest self-reporting is turning from reputational risk into strategic advantage.

Leading from the Future Back

To build tomorrow's value system, leaders must stop forecasting from the past and start back-casting from the future.

Ask:

- *What kind of world do we want our business to create?*
- *What would it look like if we succeeded ethically?*
- *How can every innovation reinforce dignity, not diminish it?*

When organizations answer those questions, strategy becomes stewardship, a responsibility to both progress and people.

Because leadership is no longer about predicting outcomes. It's about protecting values.

Closing Reflection – The Architecture of Worth

We are standing at the edge of a transformation as profound as the Industrial Revolution, but this time, the raw material isn't steel or silicon. It's soul.

Companies that engineer not only intelligence, but integrity. Those that measure success not only by market share, but by the lives they elevate.

Value, in its truest form, isn't a number. It's a narrative, one that says, "We made the world a little wiser, a little kinder, a little more whole."

Because in the end, the most valuable system we can build is the one that honors our shared humanity.

Key Takeaways – Building the Value System of Tomorrow

- *Tomorrow's value equation is **Intelligence** × **Intention** = **Impact**.*
- *Organizations must **balance** economic, human, and societal value.*
- *The most powerful currency of the future will be **character**.*

Chapter 6

The Ethics of Intelligence

Part I – The Moral Mirror

Artificial Intelligence doesn't create morality. It reveals it.

Every algorithm, every model, every decision a machine makes is a reflection of the people who built it, their intentions, their incentives, their blind spots. AI isn't born good or evil. It is trained to be one or the other.

That's why the most important question in the age of intelligence isn't "What can AI do?" It's "What does AI say about ***us***?"

The Mirror We Built

When IBM's Deep Blue defeated chess champion Garry Kasparov in 1997, it marked the first time a machine had clearly surpassed human logic in a controlled domain. It was a marvel of computational precision, but morally neutral.

Twenty-five years later, AI systems are no longer just winning games. They're determining who gets a mortgage, who gets hired, who gets parole, and even who lives or dies in medical triage algorithms.

These aren't engineering problems. They are ethical frontiers.

In 2024, a Stanford University study found that more than 60% of large AI models demonstrated measurable bias in areas like gender, race, and socioeconomic status, not because the models were malicious, but because their data was.

Machines learn what we teach them. And in doing so, they reflect the full spectrum of human brilliance and brokenness.

When Data Inherits Sin

Every piece of data carries DNA, a trace of the world that produced it. Historical inequities, cultural assumptions, and unconscious bias all find their way into the datasets that train modern AI.

When the COMPAS algorithm was deployed in U.S. courts to predict recidivism risk, it scored Black defendants as twice as likely to reoffend as white defendants with similar records. The system wasn't racist by intention, it was racist by inheritance.

It learned from decades of judicial data shaped by systemic bias. The algorithm didn't create injustice. It codified it.

That's the moral mirror of AI: it doesn't invent human flaws. It scales them.

The Replication of Power

Technology tends to amplify whoever already holds influence. In business, that means algorithms can inadvertently favor established companies, voices, and perspectives, reinforcing status quo power structures under the guise of "neutrality."

For example, in 2023, Amazon quietly scrapped its AI hiring system after it was discovered to downgrade résumés containing the word "women's," as in "women's soccer team." The model had been trained primarily on ten years of male-dominated hiring data.

It didn't hate women. It just learned history too well.

AI's moral hazard lies not in its potential for evil, but in its efficiency at repeating our past.

When Scale Outruns Conscience

AI systems can now process decisions at a scale that human ethics can't easily supervise. Chatbots can reach millions of users in seconds. Recommendation engines influence elections, consumer behavior, and cultural norms.

In 2022, internal research at Meta revealed that 32% of teen girls said Instagram made them feel worse about their bodies, a finding leaked from the company's own data scientists. The algorithm wasn't built to harm them. It was built to maximize engagement.

But when engagement becomes the objective, addiction becomes the outcome. Technology doesn't corrupt on its own. It simply automates our priorities.

The Ethics of Optimization

At its core, AI is an optimization engine. It seeks to improve a function, maximize clicks, minimize costs, increase efficiency.

But optimization without moral context can become dangerous. A self-driving car that minimizes "risk of collision" may still choose to hit one person instead of five. A predictive policing system that optimizes for "crime prevention" may over-police poor neighborhoods because that's where arrests have historically been made.

Optimization isn't the same as justice. Efficiency isn't the same as ethics.

And yet, most AI systems are designed by engineers, not ethicists. We've built machines that can predict everything except the moral consequences of prediction itself.

Case Study 69: The Algorithm That Wrote a Prison Sentence

In 2025, a European court deployed an AI tool to recommend sentencing guidelines for fraud cases based on historical judgments. Investigators later discovered the system recommended noticeably harsher outcomes for immigrants compared to native citizens with similar charges, reflecting bias embedded in the training data.

The court suspended the tool. The case contributed to strengthened accountability provisions in the EU AI Act, which classifies high-risk systems and mandates transparency audits.

AI in justice does not merely need better code. It requires ongoing human reflection and robust governance.

The Global Patchwork of Ethics

Across the world, nations are racing to define AI's moral boundaries:

- *The EU AI Act (2024)* bans real-time facial recognition in public spaces and mandates human oversight for "high-risk" systems like education, healthcare, and justice.

- The *U.S. AI Bill of Rights (2022)* established principles for privacy, algorithmic discrimination, and transparency, though enforcement remains uneven.
- China's *AI Governance Initiative (2023)* emphasizes state control and "social harmony," blending ethics with national ideology.

Each framework reveals as much about culture as it does about compliance. Western models prioritize individual rights. Eastern models emphasize collective stability.

There's no universal code for machine ethics, only the cultures that create them. The moral mirror doesn't just reflect individuals. It reflects civilizations.

The Cost of Moral Delegation

The deeper danger isn't that machines will make immoral choices, it's that humans will stop making them at all.

Every time we outsource judgment to AI, we erode our moral muscle. When Spotify curates our moods, Netflix predicts our pleasure, and AI tools draft our words, we risk losing the very capacity to choose consciously.

Ethicist Shannon Vallor calls this "moral deskilling", the gradual atrophy of ethical awareness when convenience replaces contemplation. Her research at the University of Edinburgh shows that overreliance on intelligent systems reduces our ability to evaluate fairness and empathy over time.

In other words, the more AI learns about us, the less we may learn about ourselves.

Case Study 70: The Doctor Who Overruled the Machine

At Johns Hopkins Hospital, a medical AI flagged a patient as low priority for an emergency scan. A physician overruled the recommendation based on clinical intuition and experience. The scan revealed a life-threatening aneurysm.

The doctor later reflected: "AI excels at patterns, but sometimes you need a pulse."

Human judgment – informed by data but not enslaved to it – remains essential. The moral mirror of technology is only useful when someone has the courage to look into it.

The Responsibility of Reflection

AI doesn't absolve us of accountability. It multiplies it.

Every line of code written, every dataset chosen, every output deployed is a moral act, whether we acknowledge it or not. Developers are no longer just engineers. They are ethicists in disguise.

In 2025, Microsoft introduced an "Ethical Impact Assessment" required for all new AI tools, a practice now being studied across industries. The process forces teams to answer questions like:

- ***Who*** could be harmed if this system fails?
- ***What values*** does it reinforce?
- What does success look like ***beyond efficiency***?

Those questions don't slow progress. They safeguard it. Because the absence of reflection isn't neutrality, it's negligence.

The Mirror and the Flame

AI is a mirror, but it is also a flame, it illuminates and burns in equal measure. It can light the path toward justice, transparency, and inclusion. Or it can ignite exploitation, inequality, and manipulation.

Whether it enlightens or consumes depends on the hands that hold it.

As the philosopher Hannah Arendt wrote after World War II, "The sad truth is that most evil is done by people who never make up their minds to be good or evil." The same is true for technology.

AI won't make up its mind. We must make up ours.

Closing Reflection – The Reflection That Judges Us

AI doesn't yet have a conscience. But it has consequences.

And every time we turn away from those consequences, every biased output, every opaque algorithm, every harm dismissed as "a technical glitch", the mirror becomes clearer.

Because the moral question of AI isn't whether machines will ever think like humans. It's whether humans will remember how to feel.

The machines are watching us. *Learning* from us. *Becoming* us.

And one day soon, we may look into their reflection and see, not intelligence, not efficiency, but a perfect image of our collective soul.

The question is: will we like what we see?

Key Takeaways – The Moral Mirror

- *AI doesn't create* ***morality****; it* ***reflects the ethics*** *of its creators and culture.*
- ***Bias*** *in data leads to* ***systemic bias*** *in outcomes, ethics must begin at* ***design****.*
- *Reflection is* ***responsibility****, technology's* ***morality*** *depends on ours.*

Part II – The Algorithmic Conscience

The more intelligent our machines become, the more they force us to ask an ancient question: Can morality be taught, or must it be lived?

This question, once confined to seminar rooms, is now the daily concern of engineers, executives, and policymakers. Because when AI systems make decisions that affect human lives, **ethics becomes executable code.**

The Myth of the Moral Machine

In 2018, MIT researchers launched *The Moral Machine Experiment*, a global survey asking millions of people how a self-driving car should act in life-and-death dilemmas: swerve to save pedestrians, or protect its passengers? Spare the young, or the old?

More than **40 million responses** were collected from 233 countries. The findings were revealing, and unsettling.

People in Western nations favored saving more lives, even at personal cost. Respondents in East Asian cultures prioritized protecting elders, reflecting respect for age. Other regions valued lawfulness, sparing those obeying the rules.

The conclusion was clear: Morality isn't universal. It's **contextual**.

If ethics differ across cultures, whose conscience will we code? Whose version of "good" will become the global standard embedded in silicon?

The Limits of Logic

Machines can execute rules flawlessly, but they can't interpret **ambiguity**. Ethical judgment often requires balancing competing goods, privacy versus security, fairness versus freedom, truth versus mercy.

These aren't binary problems. They are moral tensions.

In 2023, an AI-assisted drone system used in a conflict zone misidentified a civilian vehicle as hostile because its movement pattern matched prior enemy data. The algorithm had followed every rule of probability and violated every rule of humanity.

It didn't *decide* to do harm. It merely lacked the capacity to **know** it had.

This is the core limitation of artificial morality: Machines don't understand consequences. They calculate them.

The Three Layers of Ethical Intelligence

If machines can't have conscience, what can they've? They can have **ethical intelligence**, a framework that guides behavior through embedded moral logic.

Scholars and ethicists describe this as operating across three layers:

- **Rule-Based Ethics (The Code Layer)**, Systems designed with explicit "if-then" constraints: don't harm, respect privacy, flag anomalies.
- **Principle-Based Ethics (The Framework Layer)**, Broader design guidelines that reflect societal values like fairness, transparency, and accountability.
- **Virtue-Based Ethics (The Cultural Layer)**, The spirit behind the system, the collective intention of the humans who build, deploy, and govern it.

The deeper we embed all three layers, the closer we come to an algorithmic conscience, not as sentience, but as structure.

Case Study 71: The Medical AI That Learned Empathy

In 2025, researchers at the Mayo Clinic trained an AI diagnostic assistant for chronic conditions with a "compassion parameter." The model drew from real doctor-patient conversation transcripts, learning elements such as supportive phrasing, pauses, and tone.

When physicians incorporated the system's recommendations, patients rated their experiences noticeably higher. The AI did not feel compassion, but it helped amplify it.

This is ethical design at work: technology that operationalizes humanity without attempting to replace it.

Bias, Fairness, and the Invisible Hand of Data

Ethical intelligence begins with understanding that data is never neutral.

In 2024, the U.S. National Institute of Standards and Technology (NIST) published a 150-page framework titled *AI Risk Management Guidelines*, urging companies to evaluate bias at every stage, from data collection to model output.

The reason was clear: biased algorithms aren't accidents. They're the **inevitable outcome of unexamined inputs**.

When facial-recognition systems trained predominantly on lighter-skinned faces showed **error rates up to 34% higher** for darker-skinned women (as documented by MIT researcher Joy Buolamwini), the industry was forced to confront its moral blind spots.

The solution wasn't more data. It was more **diverse data**.

Ethical AI begins not in the lab, but in **representation**, who designs it, who trains it, and who benefits from it.

The Ethics of Explainability

When AI makes decisions that affect lives, the ability to explain those decisions becomes a moral duty.

This is the foundation of *Explainable AI (XAI)*, a movement driven by researchers like DARPA scientist David Gunning, who argue that transparency is essential to trust.

Without explanation, even correct decisions can be ethically suspect.

In 2023, an AI system denied hundreds of mortgage applications in the U.K. because of "risk factors" the company couldn't articulate. When regulators demanded justification, the developers realized the model had correlated zip codes with creditworthiness, unintentionally redlining entire neighborhoods.

The algorithm didn't discriminate by race. It discriminated by **proxy**.

Transparency exposed the harm, and accountability corrected it. That's how conscience enters the code.

The Rise of AI Ethics Boards

As ethical complexity grows, companies are institutionalizing conscience.

By 2026, more than **70% of Fortune 500** firms had established internal AI ethics committees or "Responsible AI Councils." Google reinstated its ethics board after backlash over biased models. Microsoft and Salesforce now employ full-time "Chief Responsible AI Officers."

The intent isn't bureaucracy, it's **moral infrastructure**.

But the challenge is consistency: oversight must have authority, not just symbolism. Ethics without enforcement is empathy without action.

Real conscience requires not just principles, but power.

Case Study 72: The Airline and the Algorithm

In 2025, an airline's dynamic pricing AI dramatically increased fares for last-minute travelers during a hurricane evacuation, triggering widespread public outrage.

Within 48 hours the CEO publicly apologized and suspended the algorithm. An audit showed the system had optimized for demand without accounting for crisis context. The airline added explicit "crisis protocols" that prioritize ethics over short-term economics.

Revenue took a temporary hit, but reputation recovered strongly. A functioning algorithmic conscience accepts short-term costs for long-term trust.

Embedding Ethics in Code

Developing ethical AI requires more than guidelines; it requires **engineering empathy**. Three emerging methods are leading the field:

- ***Ethical Weighting***, assigning numerical values to human priorities (e.g. privacy = 0.8, fairness = 1.0).
- ***Ethical Simulation***, testing how models behave under conflicting moral conditions.
- ***Human-in-the-Loop Design***, keeping people involved in critical decisions, ensuring that compassion tempers computation.

These methods don't give machines morals. They give humans a mirror for moral clarity. AI doesn't absolve responsibility. It demands it, mathematically.

The Paradox of Delegation

As systems grow more autonomous, humans face an ethical paradox: the more power we give away, the less accountable we feel.

When a self-driving car crashes, who is guilty, the driver, the coder, the company, or the code itself? When an AI trading bot triggers a financial collapse, can we blame a model trained to do exactly what we asked?

Philosopher Daniel Dennett once warned that "our inventions will test our intentions." The algorithmic age is that test.

Delegation without ownership is moral drift. And drift is how civilizations lose direction.

The Moral Cost of Speed

In technology, speed is the new virtue, ship fast, iterate often, disrupt always. But ethics moves at a different pace.

The moral consequences of technology often unfold **years after deployment**. Social media was meant to connect us, now it's blamed for mental health crises and polarization. Facial recognition was built for security, now it fuels surveillance states.

When speed outruns conscience, intelligence becomes **indifference**.

That's why building an algorithmic conscience isn't about slowing innovation, it's about aligning it with awareness.

Case Study 73: The AI That Saved a Life

In 2026, an autonomous vehicle in Sweden faced an unavoidable collision. The AI chose to protect a group of children crossing the street, even though it meant damaging the vehicle and injuring the driver.

Investigators confirmed the decision followed explicit ethical programming under Sweden's Ethical Autonomy Law, which prioritizes human life. It was cited as one of the first documented cases of AI making a morally guided choice based on human-defined values.

The driver later said the system "saved both the children and public faith in technology." When we code values clearly, intelligence can reflect our best aspirations.

From Compliance to Conscience

The real challenge for AI ethics is moving from checklists to character.

Compliance is procedural, it asks, "Did we follow the rule?" Conscience is moral, it asks, "Did we honor the right?"

Organizations that treat ethics as compliance will always lag behind. Those that cultivate conscience will lead.

In the coming decade, AI ethics will evolve from reactive oversight to **proactive design philosophy**, integrated into every system, from architecture to algorithms.

Ethical intelligence will become a **competitive advantage**, not a constraint.

Closing Reflection – Teaching the Machines to Care

We can't program machines to love, but we can teach them to **listen.** We can't give them souls, but we can give them **standards.** And we can't make them moral, but we can make them **mindful.**

The algorithmic conscience isn't about creating empathy in code. It's about encoding our own empathy in practice, line by line, model by model, choice by choice.

Because in the end, AI won't save or doom us. It will simply **follow our example.**

If we want moral machines, we must first become moral makers.

Key Takeaways – The Algorithmic Conscience

- *AI can't be moral, but it can be designed to* ***respect morality.***
- *Global research (MIT's Moral Machine, 2018) shows that ethics are* ***cultural, not universal.***
- ***Explainable AI*** *(XAI) and* ***bias audits*** *are essential for* ***trust.***
- *Ethics must move from compliance checklists to* ***embedded conscience.***

The future of AI depends less on machine intelligence, and more on human integrity.

Part III – Designing for Dignity

The defining question of the intelligent age isn't whether machines will be good or bad, it's whether we'll **design them to be humane.**

AI isn't destiny. It's design. And design is always a moral act.

The Architecture of Respect

Every choice in technology, what data we collect, how we train it, who we include, encodes a worldview. When we design without empathy, we build systems that alienate. When we design with dignity, we build systems that **elevate**.

Designing for dignity means more than avoiding harm. It means creating technology that protects autonomy, honors diversity, and advances human flourishing.

The great architect Frank Lloyd Wright once said, *"The space within becomes the reality of the building."*

So too with AI: the values within become the reality of the system.

From Efficiency to Humanity

For most of its short life, AI has been measured by efficiency: how fast, how accurate, how cheap.

But efficiency without empathy can become **dehumanization at scale.**

Consider the 2020s explosion of "productivity AIs", tools that monitor employees, analyze keystrokes, and generate performance rankings. By 2024, nearly **38% of U.S. workers** were under some form of digital surveillance, according to the American Management Association.

The stated purpose was productivity. The effect was paranoia.

When technology sees people as data points, it strips them of dignity. And dignity, once lost, is costly to restore.

Designing for dignity means shifting our metric from output to outcome, from efficiency to empowerment. I would offer six principles of dignified design as a guide to humanizing AI at scale.

Principle #1: Transparency Is a Right, Not a Feature

The first pillar of dignified design is transparency.

People deserve to know how and why decisions about them are made, whether in credit scoring, healthcare, or hiring.

In 2024, the **European Union's AI Act** became the first legislation to require explainability for all "high-risk" AI systems. Any algorithm making decisions about employment, education, or access to public services must now provide a clear "why."

This isn't just regulation, it's restoration. Transparency restores agency.

A 2025 PwC survey found that **78% of consumers** say they would share more data with companies that clearly explain how it's used.

Transparency builds trust. And trust is the first building block of dignity.

Case Study 74: The Hospital That Shared Its Algorithm

In 2025, a Canadian hospital responded to community pressure by publicly releasing the code of its triage AI system. Review revealed the model underweighted chronic pain – disproportionately affecting women and minorities.

The hospital corrected the bias. Outcomes improved across demographics. What began as reputational risk became a "trust renaissance." Transparency did not weaken the institution – it humanized and strengthened it.

Principle #2: Fairness Must Be Engineered

Fairness isn't a byproduct of AI, it's a prerequisite.

Ethicist Timnit Gebru, co-founder of the DAIR Institute, has repeatedly shown that bias in data isn't accidental but **architectural.** If we want fairness, it must be **designed in** from the start.

That's why fairness testing is now becoming standard practice. Google's "Model Cards," IBM's "AI Fairness 360," and Microsoft's "Responsible AI Standard" all include fairness audits as part of deployment.

In 2026, the IEEE introduced its **Ethically Aligned Design Framework**, offering over 200 recommendations for equitable AI, from procurement to post-launch governance.

These initiatives prove a fundamental truth: You can't bolt fairness onto the system after it's built. You must build it into the blueprint.

Case Study 75: A Bank Audits Its Algorithm

A U.K. financial institution discovered its mortgage-approval AI was systematically rejecting applicants from certain postal codes, reflecting historical redlining patterns in the training data.

Instead of concealing the issue, the bank launched an Ethics Remediation Initiative: retraining the model, publishing findings, and compensating affected applicants. Public trust increased noticeably and applications rose in the following quarter.

Confronting bias honestly can redeem both the technology and the institution's reputation.

Principle #3: Accountability Is Shared

In the intelligent economy, responsibility can't vanish into the code.

Every decision made by a machine must trace back to a human, not to assign blame, but to ensure ownership.

In 2025, the U.S. Government Accountability Office (GAO) issued a landmark report urging "human-in-command" oversight for all critical AI systems. It emphasized that accountability chains must be visible and enforceable, from developer to deployer to decision-maker.

Without accountability, intelligence becomes anonymity.

The companies leading the way, like Salesforce, Accenture, and SAP, have now introduced "AI Stewardship Charters," explicitly naming responsible parties for algorithmic outcomes.

Accountability turns ethics from aspiration into action.

Principle #4: Inclusion Is Innovation

Dignity thrives in diversity.

Yet as of 2024, just 22% of AI professionals worldwide were women, and less than 3% identified as Black, according to the World Economic Forum.

Homogeneity in design leads to homogeneity in thought, and in turn, exclusion in outcomes.

When people of different backgrounds, disciplines, and experiences shape the data and design, AI becomes not just more ethical, but more effective.

A 2023 McKinsey study showed that diverse AI teams outperform homogeneous ones by up to 33% in innovation outcomes.

Inclusion isn't charity. It's competitive advantage.

Case Study 76: The Startup That Designed for All

A Nairobi-based fintech startup built a loan-scoring AI specifically for underserved African farmers. Instead of relying on traditional credit scores, it incorporated mobile payment histories, community reputation, and crop yield data.

Loan approval rates for women doubled and default rates dropped meaningfully. The founder explained: *"We designed not for the average user, but for the absent one."*

This is technology that sees the unseen and designs for dignity – a powerful model for inclusive innovation.

Principle #5: Privacy Is the New Human Right

In 1948, the **Universal Declaration of Human Rights** declared privacy a fundamental right. In the AI age, that right is under siege.

Every app, wearable, and sensor now harvests behavioral data in ways invisible to users. By 2025, the average individual generated **1.7 MB of data per second**, according to Domo's "Data Never Sleeps" report.

That data fuels convenience, but it also fuels exploitation.

The antidote is **data dignity**: the belief that individuals should own, control, and profit from their own data.

Some companies are already acting. Estonia's "X-Road" data infrastructure allows citizens to see exactly who accesses their information, a model now studied worldwide.

The European Union's **GDPR 2.0 framework (2025)** expands the "right to explanation" into a "right to agency", giving citizens the ability to revoke algorithmic consent entirely.

Privacy isn't secrecy. It's sovereignty.

Principle #6: Purpose Before Profit

The final design principle for dignity is the hardest, aligning purpose before profit.

When organizations treat ethics as an obstacle to revenue, both eventually collapse. When they treat ethics as the **engine of value**, both endure.

Companies like Patagonia, Interface, and Unilever have proven that long-term profitability grows from principled purpose. AI is no different.

A Deloitte study from 2025 found that firms with "explicit ethical AI frameworks" achieved

20% higher brand trust and 14% greater customer retention over three years. Profit built on purpose builds. Profit built on manipulation decays.

The Framework of Dignified Design

To operationalize dignity, leading researchers propose what they call the **"Five-E Model":**

- **Empathy** – *Understand* who is affected and how.

- **Equity** – *Ensure* outcomes benefit all groups fairly.
- **Explainability** – Make systems *transparent* and *understandable*.
- **Empowerment** – Give people *control* and *recourse*.
- **Endurance** – Design for *long-term human well-being*, not *short-term metrics*.

This isn't just a checklist. It's a **charter for civilization.**

Dignity must be engineered as carefully as algorithms are optimized.

Case Study 77: The City That Coded for Humanity

In 2026, Helsinki became a global leader in democratic AI by releasing a public AI Register – a transparent listing of every algorithm used in municipal services from education to housing. Citizens could see what data was used and challenge unfair outcomes.

Trust in city services rose substantially and international interest in the model grew. The CTO summarized it best: "Our greatest innovation wasn't digital. It was democratic."

When transparency and participation are designed into governance, technology strengthens rather than erodes civic trust.

The Challenge of Scale

Designing for dignity is easy in principle and hard in practice.

Global AI systems operate across legal, cultural, and moral boundaries, what's fair in one country may be unjust in another.

That's why organizations like the **OECD, UNESCO, and the World Economic Forum** are collaborating on global standards for "human-centered AI."

UNESCO's 2022 *Recommendation on the Ethics of Artificial Intelligence* has already been adopted by **over 190 countries**.

The goal: create a universal baseline, a Hippocratic Oath for AI, where innovation serves humanity, not the reverse.

It's a noble vision. But dignity can't be legislated. It must be designed.

Closing Reflection – Engineering Empathy

Technology will never possess empathy. But it can **project** it, through the hands, hearts, and minds of those who build it.

To design for dignity is to remember that behind every dataset is a person, behind every model a memory, behind every decision a life.

The mark of a truly intelligent civilization won't be how well its machines can think, but how faithfully they can **care**.

Because dignity isn't an output. It's the soul of the system.

Key Takeaways – Designing for Dignity

- *Designing for dignity means embedding respect, fairness, and transparency into every stage of AI creation.*
- *Global frameworks like the **EU AI Act (2024)** and **IEEE's Ethically Aligned Design (2026)** are guiding ethical engineering.*
- *Transparency, fairness, accountability, inclusion, privacy, and purpose are non-negotiable principles.*
- *"Data dignity" and user agency are emerging as new human rights.*

AI that honors dignity doesn't just avoid harm, it amplifies humanity.

Part IV – The Leadership Mandate

Every revolution produces a new kind of leader. The industrial age gave us builders. The digital age gave us disruptors. The intelligent age now demands **guardians**.

Because leadership today is no longer about scaling faster, it's about **stewarding wisely**.

From Authority to Stewardship

Traditional leadership was about command, the ability to direct people and processes. Modern leadership is about stewardship, the responsibility to protect people and principles.

AI has shifted the center of gravity from control to care. When decisions can be made in milliseconds by systems that no single human can fully understand, the leader's job isn't to outthink the machine. It's to outvalue it, to ensure that every algorithm serves a purpose larger than profit.

As Microsoft CEO Satya Nadella said in 2024:

"The measure of progress isn't how intelligent our machines become, but how much more humanity they can empower."

That's the leadership mandate of the intelligent age: to make **power serve principle.**

The Responsibility Gap

AI's rise has created what ethicists call the **responsibility gap**, the widening space between who makes a decision and who is accountable for it.

When an autonomous vehicle crashes, is it the engineer's fault? The company's? The data supplier's? Or the algorithm itself?

The truth is, responsibility can't be automated. And yet, too many organizations treat AI ethics as a checklist, a matter for compliance officers, not CEOs.

But ethics isn't compliance. It's **culture**.

In 2025, IBM conducted a global survey across 28 industries:

- **75% of executives** said they believe AI ethics is critical to business success.
- Yet only **30%** had implemented formal oversight mechanisms.

The gap between belief and behavior is the new leadership frontier. Bridging it requires courage, not consensus.

Principle #1: Own the Outcome

Leaders can delegate authority, but never accountability.

When AI systems fail, the instinct is to blame "the algorithm." But an algorithm isn't a scapegoat. It's a mirror of leadership priorities.

As an IBM Training Manual stated in 1979 *"A computer can never be held accountable, therefore a computer must never make a management decision."* IBM knew nearly 50 years ago what many AI executives forget in 2026: If it can't go to prison, it can't run the company. Accountability is a human feature, not a prompt.

In 2023, a major ride-sharing company faced public outrage after its pricing AI raised fares during a mass evacuation from a wildfire. Executives initially claimed "the system did it automatically."

That explanation backfired. Customers didn't want excuses. They wanted ethics.

The CEO later issued a public apology and implemented a global "Ethical Override Policy", giving humans the authority to suspend algorithmic operations during crises.

Accountability begins where automation ends. The leader's role is to make sure no decision escapes **human conscience.**

Principle #2: Create Moral Infrastructure

Ethical leadership isn't reactive. It's systemic.

Just as organizations build cybersecurity and compliance frameworks, they must now build moral infrastructure, institutional structures that embed ethical reasoning into every layer of operation.

This includes:

- **AI Ethics Councils** that review high-risk deployments.
- **Bias Audit Pipelines** that test models before release.
- **Ethics KPIs** that tie leadership bonuses to responsible outcomes.

By 2026, Salesforce, Microsoft, and Accenture had implemented internal "Responsible AI Playbooks," requiring executives to document ethical considerations for every product launch.

These aren't PR gestures. They are organizational immunizations, preventing ethical decay before it spreads.

Principle #3: Make Ethics Measurable

What can't be measured often isn't managed. That's why ethical leadership must be quantifiable, not rhetorical.

The **OECD's AI Policy Observatory (2025)** introduced a set of measurable indicators for responsible AI adoption: transparency, accountability, fairness, and human rights compliance.

Similarly, Deloitte's "AI Ethics Index" tracks companies based on criteria like model explainability and bias disclosure.

Measurement doesn't trivialize morality, it **translates** it into systems leaders can manage.

A company that measures fairness as rigorously as profit will find that both tend to rise together.

Case Study 78: The CEO Who Put Ethics on the P&L

In 2024, a global technology firm made a notable governance change: it added an "Ethical Impact" line item to its quarterly reports. Executives were now evaluated not only on revenue and ROI but also on trust metrics, consumer sentiment, privacy compliance, and social contribution.

Skeptics predicted shareholder pushback. Instead, the company's valuation grew noticeably within six months. The CEO's guiding principle was straightforward: *"If ethics isn't on the balance sheet, it isn't truly in the business."*

Turning moral aspiration into measurable accountability is becoming one of the clearest markers of mature leadership in the intelligent age.

Principle #4: Lead With Transparency

In an opaque world, honesty is the new innovation.

Leaders must be willing to admit uncertainty, disclose limitations, and communicate the trade-offs inherent in AI adoption.

When OpenAI released GPT-4 in 2023, it published a 98-page System Card explaining the model's risks, biases, and safety limitations. It was an act of radical transparency, acknowledging imperfection as a foundation for trust.

Organizations that hide flaws erode credibility. Those that confront them earn loyalty.

Transparency isn't weakness. It's **leadership in its purest form**.

Principle #5: Protect the Human Core

The most effective AI leaders are those who refuse to let automation replace the human heartbeat of their organizations.

They invest in human skills, creativity, empathy, and moral reasoning, because they know that as machines scale intelligence, **humans must scale wisdom**.

A 2025 World Economic Forum report found that companies investing in "human capability development", reskilling for empathy, leadership, and creativity, **saw 25% higher employee retention** and **18% greater innovation output**.

Leadership that values people as irreplaceable assets will always outperform those that treat them as inputs.

Case Study 79: The Factory That Trained for the Future

A German manufacturing firm introduced AI robotics that displaced about 15% of traditional manual roles. Rather than pursuing layoffs, the CEO created a "Future Skills Academy" to retrain workers as data analysts, automation supervisors, and ethics stewards.

Three years later, productivity had roughly doubled and turnover reached historic lows. The CEO reflected: "We didn't automate people out of work. We automated them into purpose."

Ethical automation is not about eliminating human roles – it is about **elevating** them into higher-value contribution.

Principle #6: Govern for the Greater Good

Ethical leadership extends beyond companies to nations. Public policy must evolve from reaction to **responsibility**.

In 2024, the **G7 Hiroshima AI Principles** were announced in October 2023, uniting world leaders around guidelines for safe and transparent AI development. The declaration emphasized three goals:

- **Protect** human rights.
- **Promote** accountability.
- **Prevent** harm through international cooperation.

The message was unmistakable: No single nation, or corporation, owns the moral compass of AI. Leadership in this century must be **collaborative**, not competitive.

Ethics is the next global language. And the leaders fluent in it will shape the world to come.

Case Study 80: New Zealand's Prime Minister Bans the Algorithm

In 2025, New Zealand's government suspended an AI welfare eligibility system after audits showed bias against rural and Māori populations. Rather than deflect blame, the Prime Minister ordered an independent ethics review and halted deployment.

Critics called it overcautious. Citizens called it integrity.

Public trust in the government rose by double digits. Other nations followed suit, adopting the "New Zealand Protocol", a framework requiring **ethics-first audits** before AI adoption in public policy.

Leadership isn't the absence of error. It's the **presence of courage**.

The Three Dimensions of Ethical Leadership

Ethical leadership in the intelligent age operates across three essential dimensions:

- ***Personal Integrity***, modeling honesty, humility, and accountability.
- ***Organizational Culture***, embedding ethical reflection into every decision.
- ***Public Responsibility***, shaping industries and policies for collective good.

Each dimension reinforces the other. When leaders embody integrity, they inspire culture. When culture reflects ethics, it builds public trust.

That alignment, between conscience, company, and community, is the hallmark of effective leadership.

Principle #7: Courage Over Consensus

The most transformative leaders are those willing to make unpopular moral choices. They understand that doing what's right may cost in the short term, but pays dividends in trust, talent, and time.

When Google employees protested a military AI project (*Project Maven*) in 2018, leadership listened, and withdrew. That decision preserved the company's reputation and became a case study in ethical restraint.

Courage isn't defiance. It's **discipline with integrity.**

In the intelligent age, where power is exponential and scrutiny is global, courage is the one trait no machine can simulate, and no leader can live without.

Closing Reflection – Leadership as Moral Technology

Leadership itself is a kind of technology, a means of transforming energy into action. But unlike code, leadership carries conscience. AI may one day match our intelligence, but it will never replicate our **integrity**.

The question isn't whether leaders can keep up with technology. It's whether technology can keep up with **our moral imagination**. The future will belong not to the smartest systems, but to the **wisest stewards**, men and women who see beyond innovation to intention, who measure success not by speed but by **soul**.

Because in the end, leadership isn't about controlling machines. It's about protecting what makes us human.

Key Takeaways – The Leadership Mandate

- *Leadership in the intelligent age is **stewardship**: aligning power with **principle**.*
- *The **"responsibility gap"** demands **transparency**, **accountability**, and **courage**.*
- ***Moral infrastructure**, **ethics councils**, **KPIs**, and **audits**, makes values **measurable**.*
- *True leaders don't replace humans with machines; they **elevate** both.*
- ***Ethical courage**, not technical competence, will define the **next generation** of leaders.*

Part V – The Future of Wisdom

We've spent centuries chasing knowledge. We built machines that can learn, predict, and even create. But the question that now confronts us, quietly, urgently, is whether we can still be wise.

Because intelligence can answer questions. Only wisdom knows which ones are worth asking.

From Intelligence to Insight

The modern world is overflowing with intelligence. Every click, every movement, every human emotion has been quantified, stored, and analyzed.

AI can now detect cancer earlier than doctors, predict storms more accurately than satellites, and compose symphonies in seconds.

And yet, despite all this brilliance, our societies remain divided, our environment endangered, our attention fragmented. We have more information than ever, and somehow, less understanding.

As author T.S. Eliot once asked, *"Where is the wisdom we have lost in knowledge? Where is the knowledge we have lost in information?"*

We built systems that can think. Now we must build systems, and societies, that can care.

The Difference Between Smart and Wise

Intelligence is speed. Wisdom is stillness.

Intelligence processes data. Wisdom discerns meaning.

Intelligence solves problems. Wisdom questions whether they're the right ones to solve.

A 2025 Stanford Human-Centered AI report found that while over 85% of companies have adopted AI tools, fewer than 15% have developed ethical frameworks guiding their use. We've industrialized thinking, but not reflection.

That imbalance is the greatest risk of the intelligent age: that we'll grow smarter without becoming better.

The Limits of Prediction

AI's great promise is prediction, the ability to see patterns before they unfold. But prediction, by itself, is morally inert.

Predictive policing can anticipate crime, or reinforce prejudice. Predictive healthcare can forecast disease, or penalize genetics. Predictive advertising can anticipate desire, or manipulate it.

When knowledge moves faster than conscience, the result is moral acceleration, an ethical lag between what we can do and what we should do.

In 2024, a consortium of European ethicists coined the term "technomoral imbalance" to describe this phenomenon. Their conclusion: technological progress outpaces moral progress by a ratio of nearly 10 to 1.

That gap isn't just a technical challenge. It's a spiritual one.

Case Study 81: The AI That Asked "Why?"

In 2025, DeepMind researchers built an experimental language model trained not only on data but also on philosophy, poetry, and literature. When asked why humans suffer, the model responded with a question of its own rather than a statistical answer: "What would existence mean without the possibility of compassion?"

It was not sentient, but the moment was symbolic. Even in silicon, inquiry and wonder emerged. Wisdom, it reminded the team, still begins with questions rather than certainty.

Wisdom as the Final Frontier

The evolution of civilization follows a simple pattern: we invent tools to extend our power, and then we must evolve values to restrain it.

The printing press democratized knowledge, and required literacy. The internet democratized communication, and required discernment. AI democratizes intelligence, and now requires wisdom.

This isn't optional. It's existential.

Because intelligence without wisdom doesn't just risk failure. It risks forgetting what it means to be human.

The Role of Humility

Wisdom begins where arrogance ends.

The danger of AI isn't that it will surpass human intelligence, it's that it will amplify human pride. When we believe our creations make us gods, we stop acting like guardians.

In 2023, computer scientist Fei-Fei Li told the World Economic Forum,

"AI is neither angel nor demon. It's a mirror, and we must look humbly into it."

Humility doesn't mean fear. It means awareness, the recognition that knowledge without self-knowledge leads to destruction.

In an era where machines can do almost everything, humility might be the most radical human act of all.

The Return of Meaning

We are rediscovering that meaning, not data, is the deepest source of human motivation.

A 2026 Deloitte Global Talent Report found that 70% of employees under age 40 want to work for companies with "a moral mission" greater than profit. Purpose, once considered a luxury, is now a baseline expectation.

The same is true for consumers: Accenture's "Ethics in AI Economy" study found that 62% of global consumers will switch brands if they believe a company's AI practices are unethical.

People are no longer buying products. They're buying principles.

And the companies that cultivate meaning will become the moral architects of the intelligent age.

Case Study 82: The Company That Coded for Purpose

A Scandinavian healthcare startup trained its AI to optimize primarily for human outcomes – patient recovery, well-being, and quality of life – rather than revenue maximization. Profits grew more slowly than competitors at first.

Five years later, the company led its market in patient satisfaction and retention. The founder summarized the journey: *"We taught our AI to care, and it reminded us why we exist."*

Intelligence guided by clear human intention creates more durable success than intelligence guided by narrow metrics alone.

From Data to Discernment

Aristotle distinguished between episteme (theoretical knowledge), *techne* (practical skill), and *phronesis* (practical wisdom), the ability to discern the right action in the right circumstances. It isn't knowing more, but knowing how to act rightly.

In that sense, wisdom is the alignment of understanding and morality. It transforms information into insight, and insight into integrity.

That alignment is the next evolution of AI ethics: systems that don't just compute truth, but cooperate with human virtue.

Future generations won't remember how many lines of code we wrote. They'll remember whether our creations helped people live with greater justice, beauty, and compassion.

That's the moral measure of the intelligent age.

The Gift of Reflection

AI gives us something remarkable: the chance to see ourselves, clearly, collectively, perhaps for the first time.

When we look at what we teach our machines, we see what we truly value. If we feed them bias, they reflect prejudice. If we feed them empathy, they reflect grace.

The mirror is merciless, but it is also merciful, because it offers us the opportunity to change. AI isn't an end to humanity. It is an invitation to renew it.

The Rise of the Wisdom Economy

In the decades ahead, the world will measure prosperity not just by GDP or ROAS, but by GHP, Gross Human Potential.

Nations and companies will compete not on intelligence alone, but on how ethically and sustainably they apply it.

We are entering what economists are calling the Wisdom Economy, where moral insight, empathy, and trust are the currencies of long-term growth.

The smartest companies won't just automate processes. They'll cultivate character. The age of automation ends when the age of wisdom begins.

Case Study 83: The Country of Bhutan Measures Compassion

In 2026, Bhutan expanded its pioneering Gross National Happiness Index to explicitly include AI ethics – evaluating how automation affects community well-being, fairness, and cultural integrity.

Early critics called it sentimental. Results showed rising social trust, improved income equality, and greater youth engagement in public life. The national statement captured the vision: "Technology without compassion is cleverness without consequence."

Bhutan continues to demonstrate that success can be measured by depth of care as much as speed of growth.

The Next Renaissance

Every era of disruption eventually gives birth to a renaissance, a rebirth of creativity, conscience, and community.

The first Renaissance reclaimed human potential through art and reason. This one will reclaim it through ethics and empathy.

The canvas is different, but the calling is the same: to rediscover what is irreplaceable about being human in a world of machines.

AI won't diminish that irreplaceable depth. It may, if we let it, remind us of it.

Because when intelligence becomes universal, wisdom becomes the defining human edge.

Closing Reflection – The Last Question

In 1956, science fiction writer Isaac Asimov published a short story titled *The Last Question*. In it, humans ask a computer how to reverse the entropy of the universe, how to stop the end of everything. For eons, the machine processes the question in silence. When the universe finally collapses into darkness, it whispers a single phrase:

"Let there be light."

We aren't yet at that end, but we're at a beginning.

The beginning of an age where machines can think faster than we ever will, and yet depend entirely on the values we choose to teach them.

The future of wisdom isn't about smarter machines. It's about wiser makers.

And that future begins wherever someone pauses long enough to ask, not "Can we?" but *"Should we?"*

Key Takeaways – The Future of Wisdom

- *The next great evolution of civilization is **moral**, not **mechanical**.*
- *Intelligence **answers questions**; **wisdom asks the right ones**.*
- *The future of AI depends not on its intelligence, but on **our humility**.*

Chapter 7

The New Covenant of Work

Part I – The End of the Old Contract

For more than two centuries, work defined not just how people made a living, but who they were. It ordered societies, structured families, and shaped personal identity.

The rhythm was predictable: education led to employment, employment led to stability, and stability led to purpose.

That rhythm is breaking. And AI is the drumbeat that's changing the tempo.

The First Covenant: Work as Transaction

The original contract of labor, forged in the Industrial Revolution, was transactional. Workers exchanged time and effort for wages. Employers offered stability in return for loyalty.

Efficiency was the moral compass. Productivity was the highest virtue. Factories became temples of purpose, and the clock became the new cross.

It was an age of repetition: the assembly line, the ledger, the schedule. Humans were valued for **consistency**, not **creativity**.

This covenant endured well into the 20th century. But it was built on the dangerous assumption that a person's worth could be measured in output.

The Second Covenant: Work as Aspiration

The Information Age rewrote the deal. Technology made knowledge, not muscle, the source of value.

Suddenly, workers weren't just laborers; they were **knowledge workers**. They were rewarded for thinking, solving, creating.

The workplace evolved from factory floor to office tower, from clock-in to log-on. And the promise changed: if you work hard and learn fast, you'll advance.

It was a covenant of ambition. But it came with its own myth, that fulfillment could be achieved through constant acceleration.

By the 2010s, the world began to feel the limits. Productivity surged, but happiness didn't. We became hyperconnected and emotionally disconnected.

Burnout replaced burnout lamps. Purpose became a hashtag.

The old contract, "work for pay, climb the ladder", no longer inspired the generation inheriting the future.

The Great Decoupling

Then came the machines.

AI didn't just automate labor. It began to **disassemble the very logic of work itself**.

Tasks that once required years of training, writing, coding, designing, forecasting, were suddenly being done by algorithms that never slept.

A 2023 Goldman Sachs report estimated that **up to 300 million jobs worldwide** could be partially automated by generative AI. At the same time, **97 million new roles** are projected to emerge, roles that don't yet exist, requiring creativity, empathy, and critical thinking.

For the first time in history, intelligence, once the exclusive domain of humans, became a **shared resource**.

The covenant based on scarcity collapsed overnight. And what replaced it wasn't unemployment. It was uncertainty.

The Fear of Irrelevance

In boardrooms and breakrooms alike, a new anxiety emerged: *If the machine can do it better, what am I for?*

It's not the fear of job loss that defines this era. It's the fear of **meaning** loss.

When people no longer feel necessary, they stop feeling valuable. And when they stop feeling valuable, societies fracture.

The 2025 World Health Organization report named "**loss of purpose at work**" as one of the top three global mental health risk factors, alongside anxiety and social isolation.

This is the true crisis of automation, not economic displacement, but existential displacement.

The Great Rebellion

In 2021, millions of workers across the world walked away from their jobs in what economists called *The Great Resignation*. They weren't rejecting work. They were rejecting **meaninglessness**.

They wanted flexibility, belonging, creativity, the freedom to shape a life, not just earn one. They were no longer content to be gears in someone else's machine.

The data confirms it: a 2025 Microsoft Work Trend Index revealed that **71% of employees**

would trade higher pay for "more purpose-aligned work."

People aren't quitting work. They're quitting **contracts that dishonor the soul**.

AI didn't cause this rebellion. **It revealed it**. It forced humanity to confront the truth that the old covenant, built on loyalty, hierarchy, and profit, no longer fits a world of infinite possibility.

The Collapse of the Corporate Cathedral

For much of the 20th century, corporations became modern sanctuaries, the place where identity, community, and purpose converged. The company song replaced the church hymn. The brand replaced the banner.

But the covenant cracked when technology gave people mobility without meaning.

Remote work, gig economies, and digital nomadism offered freedom but couldn't create belonging. Flexibility replaced loyalty, and career ladders became networks of gigs and side hustles.

The very structure of employment, stable job, steady progression, lifetime tenure, gave way to a fluid system of temporary contribution.

The result? Freedom without foundation. We unchained the worker while sometimes unmooring the person.

The Paradox of Progress

AI has accelerated productivity to levels unimaginable a decade ago. Yet global surveys from Gallup (2025) show that only **21% of employees worldwide** feel engaged in their work, a figure virtually unchanged in 20 years.

We have achieved peak efficiency and minimum **fulfillment**.

It's not because technology failed us. It's because technology succeeded, exposing the cracks in our purpose.

When machines handle the tasks, humans must rediscover the **calling**.

Case Study 84: The Manufacturer That Rebuilt Its Workforce Covenant

A century-old Japanese manufacturing firm faced automation that halved labor needs in certain areas. Instead of mass layoffs, leadership redefined every worker's role as a process innovator. Staff were retrained to co-design AI workflows, propose improvements, and evaluate ethical impact.

Three years later, productivity had risen substantially and employee satisfaction reached record highs. The CEO explained: *"We stopped paying people to repeat tasks. We started paying them to reimagine progress."*

This is the emerging new covenant of work: automation in service of human autonomy and creativity.

The Moral Crisis of Meaning

The deeper story behind AI and work isn't technological. It is profoundly **human**.

But somewhere along the way, we separated the two. Work became survival. Then status. Then addiction.

Now, AI forces us to ask the original question again: If work no longer defines us, what does? This isn't the end of work. It's the beginning of **worth rediscovered**.

The Moral Math of the Machine Age

As automation accelerates, humanity faces a trade-off between **efficiency** and **identity**. The temptation is to replace every manual process with code. The opportunity is to reimagine every human process with **care**.

The new covenant of work won't be written in labor contracts or policy documents. It will be written in values, dignity, creativity, inclusion, and belonging.

In the 21st century, those values aren't soft ideals. They are **strategic assets**.

Deloitte's Human Capital Trends 2025 found that organizations with strong "meaning cultures" outperform competitors by 30% in innovation and 40% in retention.

The future of work won't be defined by automation. It will be defined by alignment, between what we do and what we believe.

Deloitte's Human Capital Trends 2025 found that organizations with strong "meaning cultures" outperform competitors by 30% in innovation and 40% in retention.

The future of work won't be defined by automation. It will be defined by alignment, between what we do and what we believe.

Closing Reflection – The Covenant Broken, the Covenant Renewed

The old employment contract (time in exchange for security) made sense in a world where routine was the primary thing being purchased. That world is ending.

What replaces it is still being negotiated. The organizations getting it right are treating that negotiation seriously, asking what they actually need from people when machines handle the routine, and designing around the honest answer.

Key Takeaways – The End of the Old Contract

- *The industrial-era work covenant, based on **repetition**, **loyalty**, and **hierarchy**, is **collapsing**.*
- *AI is accelerating a shift from **efficiency** to **meaning**.*
- *The **new covenant** of work will be built on **dignity**, **creativity**, **and shared purpose**.*

Part II – The Rise of Human Capital 2.0

Every era has its resource revolution. The Industrial Age was powered by coal. The Information Age was powered by data. The Intelligent Age is powered by **people**.

Not people as workers. People as **value creators**.

The New Economics of Talent

For two hundred years, the value equation of work was built on two inputs: capital and labor. The employer supplied the tools, and the employee supplied the time.

But AI changes the math. Time is no longer the constraint. Intelligence itself has become **scalable**.

In this new equation, value no longer comes from what people can do faster, machines can do that. It comes from what people can **imagine better**.

The McKinsey Global Institute estimates that by 2030, over **70% of workplace** tasks will involve some form of machine collaboration. That doesn't make humans obsolete. It makes them **essential**, for everything that machines can't feel, interpret, or inspire.

The Shift from Skill to Soul

The first wave of automation replaced physical labor. The second wave, powered by AI, is replacing mental labor: analysis, organization, even decision-making.

So where does that leave us? In a place where value has migrated from **skill to soul**.

Harvard Business Review's 2025 "Future of Talent" survey found that the most in-demand capabilities across Fortune 500 companies were: emotional intelligence, complex problem-solving, ethical judgment, and creative adaptability.

Not a single one can be automated. These aren't soft skills. They're the **hard currency** of Human Capital 2.0.

The Human Multiplier Effect

Human Capital 2.0 isn't just about individual ability, it's about **interconnected capability.**

When people feel trusted, inspired, and empowered to collaborate with both technology and one another, value multiplies exponentially.

MIT Sloan research in 2025 found that companies that actively pair AI systems with teams with real authority saw **productivity gains 2.5× higher** than those that relied on automation alone.

Why? Because humans don't just execute, they **contextualize**. They interpret nuance, mediate trust, and connect insight to intention. Machines scale efficiency. Humans scale meaning.

Case Study 85: How Airlines Can Turn Agents into AI Coaches

Across several global airlines, early AI deployments for customer service led to rising complaints and declining agent morale. Rather than abandoning the technology, some carriers retrained agents to become AI coaches and supervisors.

These human coaches now identify bias, rewrite insensitive responses, and add empathy where models fall short. Documented implementations show meaningful gains in customer satisfaction (often **20%** or better) and employee engagement (up **to 45%** in some cases).

This "human multiplier" effect reveals a powerful pattern: when people train and elevate machines, their own value increases rather than diminishes.

The Currency of Adaptability

If the 20th century rewarded specialization, the 21st rewards adaptability.

Generative AI will render static skillsets obsolete every few years. What matters now isn't what people know, but how quickly they can **learn, unlearn, and relearn**.

LinkedIn's research, drawn from analysis of tens of millions of member profiles, consistently shows that employees who move into new roles, whether through promotion or lateral transfer, are significantly more likely to remain with their employer long term.

The pattern is clear: people who keep growing stay.

Adaptability isn't a perk. It's **protection**, against irrelevance, against burnout, against obsolescence.

People who move fluidly between roles, tools, and ideas, those who treat learning not as a phase, but as a lifestyle.

The Great Revaluation of Culture

In the age of AI, culture isn't just HR's concern, it's a strategic differentiator.

When every company has access to the same algorithms, data, and cloud infrastructure, the only remaining variable is **the people who use them.**

Deloitte's 2026 *Global Human Capital Trends* report surveyed more than 9,000 leaders across 89 countries. One of its findings warns that organizations neglecting culture accumulate what it calls 'culture debt,' and that those who intentionally nurture it will create sustainable competitive advantage over those who don't.

Anecdotal and methods-based analysis offers substantial and consistent evidence connecting culture to performance:

- Google's *Project Aristotle* identified psychological safety as the single strongest predictor of team success, finding 31% higher innovation in safe teams.
- *Deloitte's inclusion research* shows organizations with inclusive cultures are **six times more likely** to be innovative and agile, and **twice as likely** to meet or exceed their financial targets.
- And *BCG's data* found retention improving up to four times for employees from underrepresented groups when psychological safety is high.

AI can replicate competence. It can't replicate **culture**.

Case Study 86: How Microsoft Found Its Soul

At Microsoft, CEO Satya Nadella's decision to make empathy a cultural cornerstone, not just a value statement but an operational philosophy, helped drive a widely discussed corporate turnaround in recent business history.

When Nadella took over in 2014, Microsoft was widely known for its "stack ranking" system, which forced managers to grade employees against each other and was criticized for fostering internal rivalry rather than collaboration. Under his leadership, the company moved away from that model and embraced what he called a **"learn-it-all"** mindset, with empathy playing a central role.

In his 2017 book *Hit Refresh*, Nadella wrote candidly about this transformation, arguing that empathy isn't a soft virtue but the engine of innovation itself, and a way to sense *"unmet and unarticulated needs,"* linked to human judgment rather than purely algorithmic analysis.

The results over the following five years were public and concrete: market capitalization grew from roughly **$300 billion to over $1 trillion**, and multiple reports pointed to improved employee engagement and culture inside the company. As Nadella put it, *"Empathy makes you a better innovator."*

Culture isn't the byproduct of success. It's the **precondition** for it.

The Rebirth of the Human Brand

In the algorithmic marketplace, authenticity is the most powerful differentiator. Consumers no longer simply trust faceless corporations: they trust brands that **feel human**: those that act with transparency, consistency, and genuine purpose.

Edelman's 2025 *Trust Barometer Special Report on Brand Trust* found that **73%** of people say their trust in a brand increases when it authentically reflects the culture around it, while only **27%** say they'd trust a brand more if it stayed silent and focused solely on products.

The unambiguous message is that a cultural connection is now a precondition for credibility, not a bonus.

The Edelman Trust Barometer deepened this picture, revealing a global retreat into what it calls an "insular trust mindset", seven in ten people are hesitant or unwilling to trust those who differ from them in values or background.

For brands, this makes shared values not just aspirational language but the literal operating terrain of trust. Human Capital 2.0 extends beyond the workforce. It defines the relationship between **brands and the belief systems** of the people who sustain them.

Purpose as Performance

The old mindset treated purpose as marketing. The new economy treats it as **performance**.

Deloitte's research on purpose-led organizations found that high-purpose companies experienced **40% higher retention and 30% higher levels of innovation** compared to low-purpose peers, suggesting that purpose doesn't soften performance, it compounds it.

PwC's 2025 *Global Family Business Survey* reinforced the pattern from a different angle, finding that agile, purpose-driven family businesses outperformed their peers on revenue growth by ten percentage points: **31%** versus **21%.**

Purpose doesn't replace profit, it redefines it. It transforms work from transaction to transformation. In a world where AI automates the "what," purpose clarifies the *"why."*

And **"why"** is the one question machines will never answer for us.

The Leadership Equation

In Human Capital 2.0, leadership itself must evolve. The leaders who succeed in the intelligent age will possess three distinct competencies: **Moral Intelligence**, the ability to make ethical choices in complexity; **Relational Intelligence**, the capacity to lead through empathy and connection; and **Adaptive Intelligence**, the skill to learn, pivot, and grow with the pace of change.

McKinsey's *State of Organizations 2026*, drawing on research across thousands of companies globally, found that human-centric leadership, the kind that prioritizes empathy, adaptability, and authentic connection, drives measurably stronger outcomes: organizations led this way report **56% higher employee satisfaction and retention**, and significantly stronger trust between leaders and teams.

AI can optimize performance. Only humans can **inspire** it.

The Rise of the Intrapreneur

As boundaries between jobs and innovation blur, the new work archetype is the **intrapreneur**, employees who act like entrepreneurs within organizations.

They use AI not as automation, but as *amplification*, a co-creator helping them prototype, iterate, and scale ideas faster.

The case for intrapreneurship is well established if less tidily quantified. Deloitte research confirms that organizations fostering internal entrepreneurship see measurable gains in growth, culture, and talent development. MIT Sloan and BCG have documented how internal innovation programs, from Google's **20% time policy** to 3M's **15% rule**, have generated some of the most durable products and revenue streams in contemporary business.

They are **renewers**: agents of progress who bridge human creativity and machine capability.

The Economics of Belonging

If culture is the foundation of Human Capital 2.0, belonging is its lifeblood.

The evidence is consistent and compelling. Gallup's ongoing research into the employee experience (the largest study of its kind) consistently shows that employees who feel recognized and included are **3×** more likely to describe their workplace as fun, **5×** more likely to stay long-term, and **6×** more likely to look forward to coming to work.

The Achievers Workforce Institute's 2026 *Engagement and Retention Report* added a sharper edge: employees who feel recognized are **12×** more likely to find their work meaningful while organizations practicing recognition effectively are **12×** more likely to achieve strong business results.

Belonging isn't an HR trend. It's a **profit driver.**

Belonging scales through three mechanisms: **Recognition**, celebrating human contribution alongside algorithmic achievement; **Inclusion**, ensuring AI reflects the diversity of those it serves; and **Participation**, involving employees in designing the tools that shape their future.

When belonging thrives, performance follows. When it breaks, even the smartest systems fail.

ROI vs ROH: The Return on Humanity

ROI is no longer "Return on Investment." It's also "Return on Humanity."

Every organization now faces a fundamental choice: Use AI to extract more from people, or use AI to expand what's possible for them.

Those who choose the latter will unlock a new era of prosperity, where growth is measured not by profit alone, but by how much more human the enterprise becomes.

Because the future of capital isn't financial. It's conscious.

Closing Reflection – The Human Edge

When every organization has access to similar AI tools, the differentiator is the people using them, whether those people bring genuine judgment, creativity, and accountability to the work, or simply let the tools run.

That has always been true of technology. AI makes it more visible, more quickly.

Key Takeaways – The Rise of Human Capital 2.0

- *The value of labor is shifting from* ***skill*** *to* ***soul****,* ***creativity****,* ***empathy****, and* ***adaptability****.*
- *Human,AI* ***collaboration*** *creates* ***2-3×*** *higher productivity than automation alone.*
- *The greatest ROI of the future will be* ***Return on Humanity****.*

Part III – The Meaning Dividend

For most of history, the connection between meaning and money was considered sentimental. Profit was the metric. Purpose was a luxury.

But that divide is closing.

Meaning is becoming measurable, a shift that changes how organizations set priorities. And its returns, emotional, social, and financial, are proving impossible to ignore.

The Rise of the Intangible Economy

Ocean Tomo's Intangible *Asset Market Value Study* is one the most comprehensive longitudinal trackers of economic shifts over the last five decades. According to this report, tangible assets in 1975, factories, inventory, machinery, represented 83% of the market value of S&P 500 companies, with intangibles accounting for only 17%. By 2025, that relationship had completely inverted: intangible assets now constitute approximately 92% of S&P 500 market capitalization.

Today we live in an economy of meaning, where what we **believe** about a company matters more than **what it produces.**

Deloitte's research on purpose confirms that companies with authentic, well-embedded purpose attract and retain talent more effectively, build deeper customer loyalty, and generate stronger long-term value. Their recent study revealed that **62%** of employees considered an organization's purpose when deciding to join, and **47%** reporting they had left an organization for purpose-related reasons.

Meaning, it turns out, isn't soft power. It's **smart business**.

The Science of Purpose

Psychologists define purpose as the sense of being connected to something larger than oneself, a feeling that one's work contributes to a greater good.

At the neurological level, meaning engages the brain's dopaminergic system, the same pathway responsible for motivation, focus, and learning.

Research published in *Nature Neuroscience* by University of Michigan scientists confirmed that dopamine continuously signals how valuable a situation is in relation to reward, simultaneously driving motivation to act and reinforcing learning from experience. In other words, purpose literally fuels **performance**.

Tali Sharot, Professor of Cognitive Neuroscience at UCL and director of the Affective Brain Lab, has spent her career studying how emotion and motivation shape human belief and decision-making. Her work, including a 2025 Wellcome Discovery Award to study the intrinsic rewards of thinking itself, confirms that meaning and cognitive engagement are deeply intertwined: when mental activity feels rewarding, people sustain it longer, learn more effectively, and produce more original thinking.

Meaning makes minds **sharper**. It also makes organizations **stronger**.

The New ROI: Return on Inspiration

Executives once viewed morale as an afterthought. Now it's a **metric**.

Gallup's decades of engagement research, drawn from surveys of over 183,000 business units across 736 studies, consistently show that highly engaged teams outperform their disengaged peers by substantial margins: **51%** lower turnover, **63%** fewer safety incidents, and **23%** higher profitability, according to Gallup's most recent meta-analysis. The pattern is so consistent across industries, cultures, and decades that Gallup treats it as one of the most replicated findings in organizational science.

In short: inspired people outperform compliant ones. AI can measure engagement. But only *purpose* can **ignite it**.

Multiple sources, including McKinsey's *ING's Agile Transformation* (2017), a Brightline Initiative / Forbes ING Case Study – and an Agile Business Consortium Case *Study ING Bank Digital Platform Tribe* (2022) report a fascinating story.

ING Bank, one of Europe's largest financial institutions, faced a familiar tension: digital innovation was accelerating, but customer loyalty and internal cohesion weren't keeping pace. In 2015, leadership launched a fundamental cultural and organizational transformation anchored to a clear statement of purpose: "helping people stay a step ahead in life and in business."

The mission wasn't cosmetic. ING restructured its entire Dutch headquarters around it, reorganizing roughly 3,500 staff into 350 self-managed "squads" aligned to customer outcomes rather than functional departments. Purpose was embedded into performance management, hiring, onboarding, and product development. Every squad was given a written customer objective and an agreed way to measure its impact.

The results were measurable. According to McKinsey's interview with ING's Chief Operating Officer, customer satisfaction and employee engagement scores rose multiple points.

In one documented division, ING's Net Promoter Score improved from **-30 to +30** within a single year. Employee engagement reached **88%** in surveyed units, well above industry norms.

The bank also became the **number one mobile bank** in the Netherlands during this period.

ING's head of its Global Transformation Office attributed the gains directly to purpose-driven empowerment: *"As you empower people by being clear on a strategy's purpose, and empower teams to participate in the decision-making process, they've a lot more ownership."*

Purpose as Psychological Capital

Economists have long measured financial and human capital. But the next frontier is **psychological capital**, the collective sense of purpose, hope, and resilience inside an organization.

The concept, developed over the past two decades primarily through the work of Fred Luthans and colleagues at the University of Nebraska-Lincoln, is now one of the most replicated findings in organizational psychology.

A comprehensive meta-analysis published in the Journal of Leadership & Organizational Studies (Avey et al. 2011), drawing on 51 independent studies, confirmed that psychological capital, comprising hope, efficacy, resilience, and optimism, is a stronger predictor of **employee performance, satisfaction, and retention** than any single dimension alone, and correlates significantly with desirable organizational outcomes. When people find meaning in their work, they demonstrate higher perseverance, optimism, and problem-solving ability.

In the Intelligent Age, psychology isn't peripheral to economics, it is economics. The **mind** has become the new balance sheet.

The Meaning Deficit

Despite these insights, the world faces a global crisis of meaning. McKinsey's foundational research on purpose at work, published in their landmark study "Help Your Employees Find Purpose or Watch Them Leave", identified a stark and troubling divide: while 85% of executives and senior leaders say they are living their purpose at work, only **15%** of frontline employees agreed. Nearly half of those frontline workers actively disagreed.

This isn't a fringe finding. It's a systemic pattern confirmed across thousands of respondents, and it maps directly onto disengagement trends tracked by Gallup, which in 2025 found global employee engagement at just 21% - its lowest level in over a decade.

Among Gen Z, the emerging majority of the workforce, the pattern deepens. Deloitte's 2025 Global Gen Z and Millennial Survey found that 89% of Gen Z workers say having a sense of purpose is essential to their motivation and wellbeing. Yet Gallup's data shows more than 80% of Gen Z workers are disengaged, revealing the enormous gap between what this generation needs and what most organizations provide.

It's not that people have stopped caring. It's that organizations have stopped connecting.

In too many companies, mission statements are slogans, not systems. Values are posters, not practices. The result is what researchers now call a "purpose gap" – workers adrift in efficient but soulless systems.

The next great productivity revolution won't come from technology. It will come from meaning restored.

Case Study 88: Tech Firm Buffer Measures Meaning

The link between purpose and performance is no longer theoretical, it's measurable.

Gallup's *2025 Work Purpose Index*, drawn from a nationally representative study of over 4,000 U.S. workers, found that employees with a strong sense of purpose are **5.6 times** more likely to be engaged, and almost half as likely to be looking for the door. Turnover intention among high-purpose employees stands at **41%**, compared with **68%** among their low-purpose counterparts.

What's striking isn't just the data, it's what the data reveals about the gap between what leaders **assume** and what workers actually **experience**. Gallup found that most organizations still don't treat purpose as a measurable priority. It remains abstract where it should be **operational**.

Some companies have changed this. **Buffer**, the San Francisco-based technology company known for its radical transparency, built its entire culture around closing this gap. After an early period in which co-founder Joel Gascoigne admitted they had lost their sense of shared direction, at one point with two separate teams unknowingly building the same feature, the company rebuilt its culture around **systematic listening**.

Weekly pulse surveys at Buffer now measure happiness, job satisfaction, and personal growth across the whole team. The result: a 2017 internal analysis shared on its blog reported voluntary turnover rate of around **5.8%** in an industry where **13%** is the norm.

As Gascoigne reflected: making values explicit isn't enough. The question that matters isn't *"What are your values?"* but *"What changes did making your values explicit actually trigger?"*

The Meaning Multiplier

Meaning acts as a **multiplier** across every dimension of business:

- ***Engagement***, Employees with strong purpose at work are **5.6 times** more likely to be engaged in their jobs than those with low purpose, and **41%** less likely to be actively looking for a new role, according to Gallup and Stand Together's *Power of Purpose* study (2025).
- ***Resilience***, ADP Research Institute's global study of over 26,000 workers, published in *MIT Sloan Management Review* (2021), found that team-level trust and meaning are the strongest predictors of resilience, more predictive than geography, role, or industry.
- ***Reputation***, Edelman's *2025 Brand Trust Special Report* found that **73%** of consumers say their trust in a brand would increase if it authentically reflected today's culture, and that trusted brands directly drive buying, loyalty, and advocacy in ways that competitors can't easily replicate.
- ***Longevity***, Oxford Wellbeing Research Centre's analysis of nearly one million employees across 1,782 publicly listed US companies found that higher employee wellbeing, strongly linked to purpose, is associated with consistent stock market outperformance and up to **$2.3bn** in additional profits per company.

Meaning doesn't just sustain morale. It sustains **momentum**.

The Role of AI in Measuring Meaning

Ironically, the same tools that once threatened to depersonalize work are now helping to humanize it.

AI analytics platforms can now detect employee sentiment through language patterns, tone, and feedback, allowing leaders to track psychological well-being in real time.

Companies like Microsoft and SAP are experimenting with "Ethical Sentiment AI", dashboards that measure collective morale, inclusion, and belonging.

But data alone isn't destiny. The goal isn't to monitor emotion, it's to mobilize empathy. AI can reveal where meaning is lost. Only humans can **restore** it.

Case Study 89: Delta Airlines Measures Employee Engagement

Delta Air Lines provides one of the most documented examples of this dynamic in the industry. CEO Ed Bastian was quoted in a Metiss Group report from 2025 espousing the company's foundational belief: *"I obsess on our own 100,000 so they can then go do the amazing work that our customers deserve."*

The logic, employees first, customers second, was established by Delta's founding CEO C.E. Woolman and remains the company's operational philosophy.

The results are measurable. In 2023, Delta reported an average employee engagement score of **80 out of 100**, four points above the US industry benchmark, drawn from surveys of more than 42,000 employees measuring job satisfaction, organizational commitment, sense of belonging, and motivation, and continuously used to drive responsive change.

For example, the year Delta launched its emergency savings program for employees it did so directly in response to feedback gathered through those surveys the previous year.

Delta's focus on employee wellbeing has tracked alongside J.D. Power top rankings in airline satisfaction multiple years running, and in 2022 premium revenue exceeded 2019 levels by **13%** as the company recovered faster than peers.

The Return of Calling

The language of "career" is giving way to the language of **calling**. People no longer want jobs; they want journeys that reflect who they are. They want alignment between vocation and values.

The idea has a name. In 2014, entrepreneur Aaron Hurst coined the term *"Purpose Economy"* to describe an emerging economic era in which the primary driver of value isn't information or manufacturing, but purpose.

In this economy, individuals define success by contribution rather than consumption, by the significance of what they build rather than the scale of what they own. A decade later, the evidence suggests Hurst was right ahead of his time.

Companies that align employee calling with corporate mission now have measurable advantages in talent retention. Deloitte's research found that purpose-driven organizations see **40% higher retention** than low-purpose peers. Gallup's 2025 Power of Purpose study found that employees who strongly connect their daily work to their organization's mission are **3.6** times more likely to experience strong purpose at work, and far less likely to be searching for the exit.

The most successful organizations of the next decade will function more like communities of purpose than hierarchies of control. Work will become less about employment and more about **enlightenment**.

AI can't mimic or provide this.

The Wellbeing Factor

Even in high-performing organizations, a more profound question is surfacing: *Why am I here? Does my work make life better for others? What will I have built when this cycle closes?*

These aren't abstract philosophical diversions. They're the questions that separate engaged employees from compliant ones, the questions that determine whether a person brings their full creative energy to work or simply their attendance.

The evidence is substantial. A 2025 systematic review in the *Journal of Organizational Behavior*, drawing on 47 peer-reviewed studies across 26 countries, confirmed that employees who report a strong sense of purpose and meaning at work demonstrate consistently higher job satisfaction, psychological resilience, commitment, and performance. The relationship holds across industries, cultures, and organizational types.

Positive psychology researcher Martin Seligman's PERMA framework identifies *meaning* (belonging to and serving something larger than oneself) as one of the five pillars of lasting wellbeing. When organizations create the conditions for meaning to emerge, they aren't pursuing soft ideals. They are building the preconditions for sustainable performance.

As AI automates more cognitive routine, this dimension of human motivation grows more important, not less. The Meaning Dividend isn't a philosophical bonus. It's a **measurable performance advantage.**

The Architecture of Meaning

Organizations can't impose meaning, but they can **design for it**. Three practices stand out:

- **Alignment** – Link daily tasks to *larger purpose* narratives.
- **Autonomy** – Give employees *creative control* over how they contribute.
- **Acknowledgment** – Recognize *impact*, not just *output.*

When people feel seen, trusted, and aligned with something eternal, productivity becomes purpose in motion.

Meaning isn't something you teach. It can't be duplicated with algorithms and prompts. It's something you **build into the blueprint.**

Closing Reflection – The Profit of Purpose

There was a time when executives spoke of purpose as a luxury, the soft side of strategy. Now it's the hard edge of survival.

The organizations that thrive in the intelligent age will be those that treat purpose not as an afterthought, but as the algorithm of growth itself.

Because the future of work won't be about how much people are paid to do something, but how deeply they believe in why they're doing it.

Meaning doesn't just make work human. It makes it *meaningful.*

Key Takeaways – The Meaning Dividend

- *Meaning has become a measurable driver of performance and profit.*
- *Psychological capital, purpose, hope, resilience, now outperforms structural capital.*
- *The next economy's true dividend will be the profit of purpose.*

Part IV – Work as Co-Creation

There was a time when humanity created tools to extend its reach. The wheel, the loom, the engine, each multiplied human strength. Today we build tools that extend our minds.

For the first time in history, we're not just working with or through machines. We're working alongside them.

That partnership is redefining what it means to create.

The Age of Co-Creation

For decades, automation meant substitution: machines doing what humans once did. AI reverses that logic. It's not a replacement technology. Used with intention, it's a **relationship technology**.

McKinsey's November 2025 report *"Agents, Robots, and Us: Skill Partnerships in the Age of AI"* makes this case with precision. The researchers found that maximum economic value from AI, estimated at **$2.9 trillion** annually in the US by 2030, is only unlocked when organizations redesign entire workflows around collaboration between people, AI agents, and robots.

Automating isolated tasks produces far smaller returns.

The companies that will capture that value are those treating AI as a "virtual coworker" embedded in human-led processes, not a substitute for human judgment. McKinsey's analysis of 190 business processes confirmed that the human role is shifting from executor to orchestrator: guiding, contextualizing, and deciding, while AI handles speed and scale.

The key isn't delegation. It's dialogue. Humans supply context, emotion, and morality. Machines supply speed, scale, and precision. Together, they generate outcomes neither could achieve alone. That's co-creation: not competition, but **completion**.

Case Study 90: The Composer and the Code

In 2024, film composer Tom Holkenborg, known as Junkie XL, incorporated AI into his score for *Furiosa: A Mad Max Saga*, becoming one of the first major Hollywood composers to speak openly about doing so.

Rather than treating AI as a threat, he treated it as a sound design tool. In a *Variety* interview, he described feeding a drum rhythm into an AI voice-morphing program that had no idea what to make of it: *"The software doesn't know what to make of it. So it gave us a happy accident that we used throughout the score."*

The result wasn't a score where AI **composed** the music. Holkenborg retained full creative control over themes, structure, narrative intent, and emotional storytelling. AI contributed a **distinctive sonic texture**, a kind of hybrid sound that became a recurring element in the film's palette. He supplied the **vision**; the tool supplied the **accident**.

The lesson here was that technology didn't erase his creativity. It expanded his palette. Creativity in the age of AI isn't diminished, it's amplified.

The Human Signature

Even as machines generate art, design products, and draft prose, the human touch remains the signature of authenticity.

Adobe's research makes the stakes of this visible. Their 2024 Authenticity in the Age of AI study found that 93% of consumers say it is important to understand how digital content was created or edited, and nearly three-quarters have doubted the authenticity of content from reputable news organizations.

Separately, their 2025 Creators' Toolkit Report found that even among the 86% of professional creators now using generative AI, the overwhelming consensus is that human creative control must remain central – with the vast majority wanting AI that learns their style rather than replacing their judgment.

Why? Because creativity isn't only about novelty. It's about narrative: the sense that behind the work is a soul.

People don't just value *what is made*. They value *who made it*, and *why*.

Co-creation preserves that signature – the imprint of human intention on the canvas of technology.

From Tools to Teammates

When technology evolves from instrument to collaborator, the workplace becomes a studio of shared intelligence.

Ferrari offers one of the most documented examples from the automotive world. In partnership with AWS, the company integrated **generative AI** into its product development workflow, allowing its engineering teams to run thousands or millions of simulations in parallel at a fraction of previous cost.

The result: Ferrari's product lifecycle management simulations now run **60%** faster than before. Rather than replacing designers, the system expanded what was possible, allowing aerodynamicists, engineers, and designers to co-edit in real time, while humans retained full control over aesthetic direction and creative intent.

The collaboration isn't AI generating beauty on its own. It's AI compressing the time between **human imagination** and **realized form.**

The Cognitive Orchestra

Think of modern organizations as orchestras. Humans are like musicians: interpreters of meaning, carriers of emotion, shapers of purpose.

AI introduces a powerful new instrument: precise, tireless, and capable of generating possibilities that no single musician could produce alone.

When they perform in harmony, productivity becomes a performance played out as a living, breathing act of creation.

Harvard Business School's March 2025 working paper, *"The Cybernetic Teammate,"* provides some of the strongest evidence yet for this model. Researchers conducted a field experiment with 776 Procter & Gamble professionals working on real product innovation challenges.

Their findings were striking: individuals working with AI were able to match the performance of two-person human teams working without it.

More importantly, workers using AI were significantly more likely to generate ideas ranking in the **top 10%** of all submissions. That's the kind of breakthrough solutions that drive organizational success. AI also broke down professional silos, with engineers and commercial specialists producing more balanced, cross-functional solutions than they did working in isolation.

The researchers described AI as a "cybernetic teammate." Here, AI wasn't a replacement for human collaboration, but a new kind of partner reshaping how expertise and social connectivity work within teams.

Why does the combination produce better outcomes? Because AI challenges human assumptions, and humans give AI insights meaning, context, and moral weight. It's a creative tension that, when designed well, drives transcendence.

The Psychology of Partnership

Psychologically, co-creation fulfills a fundamental human need: to collaborate with something greater than oneself.

Throughout history, our greatest works, the pyramids, cathedrals, space stations, emerged from collective imagination.

AI offers a new partner in that same spirit. Not supernatural, but purposeful. Not omniscient, but increasingly omnipresent.

It challenges us to grow not just in knowledge, but in wisdom of collaboration, humility, curiosity, and shared authorship.

MIT cognitive scientist Sherry Turkle observed, *"The question isn't whether machines can think. It's whether we can think with them, without losing ourselves."*

That's the essence of co-creation: identity through interdependence.

Case Study 91: The Architects and the Algorithm

As part of ZHA's broader commitment to AI-assisted community design, including projects with Indigenous communities in North America, generative AI is being used to co-design sustainable, community-led housing.

The AI platform rapidly produces modular housing configurations optimized for local terrain, energy performance, and infrastructure requirements. Human architects then shape the cultural meaning, aesthetic character, and community resonance of each option, ensuring the final designs reflect the traditions and aspirations of the people who will live in them.

The project illustrates what ZHA Associate Director Shajay Bhooshan describes as the firm's core philosophy: AI applies "point generating elements" such as better transit access, more daylight, and low-energy performance, while human judgment determines what those buildings mean to the communities they serve. ZHA has reported productivity gains of up to 50% in mid-stage design preparation since integrating AI into its workflows.

As one architectural analyst summarized the emerging consensus across the field: computers generate, and humans decide.

The Ethical Balance

When properly deployed, co-creation requires co-responsibility. As humans and machines share creative authority, we must ensure that **accountability** doesn't disappear into the algorithm.

Two critical questions are emerging:

"Who owns a work of co-created art?"

"Who's responsible for a decision made by human+AI collaboration?"

The answers will define the next decade of intellectual property and governance.

But the deeper truth is ethical: creation without conscience can (and often does) lead to exploitation.

Co-creation, by contrast, restores the moral balance between innovation and intention.

The Co-Creative Enterprise

Businesses embracing co-creation are already seeing tangible results.

Accenture's October 2024 research, *"Reinventing Enterprise Operations with Gen AI,"* found that organizations with fully modernized, AI-led processes achieve **2.5** times higher revenue growth and **2.4** times greater productivity compared to peers.

Critically, the report also found these organizations are **3.3** times more successful at scaling generative AI use cases, a figure that reflects not just automation but the compounding return of human-AI collaboration embedded across functions.

A separate Accenture study on human-AI co-learning, published in 2025, found that embedding AI agents into marketing workflows aimed to boost time to market by **25%** to **35%**, while companies using AI in R&D reported **faster innovation cycles** and significantly **higher employee satisfaction**.

These companies view AI not as an efficiency tool, but as a **co-founder** of ideas. They don't ask, "How can AI replace us?" They ask, "How can AI **refine** us?"

Case Study 92: NGOs Co-Writing Hope

Coalitions of humanitarian organizations, including the Norwegian Refugee Council, Save the Children, and UNOCHA, have partnered with Microsoft on the Humanitarian Data Intelligence

Platform. Generative AI analyzes crisis data and surfaces community needs, but every output is validated and rewritten by human staff.

UNHCR's Innovation Service follows a similar human-in-the-loop model when interpreting feedback from displaced people. AI accelerates discovery and pattern recognition; human judgment ensures dignity and ethical storytelling.

In the most sensitive contexts, technology amplifies empathy when it remains firmly in service of human conscience.

That balance, efficiency in service of empathy, is what these organizations are building toward.

The Future of Learning

Education, too, is becoming a co-creative process. AI tutoring systems adapt to each learner's style, while teachers focus on mentorship, motivation, and moral development.

A 2025 Harvard study, published in PNAS, found that students learning with AI tutors learned **more than twice** as much in less time compared to those in traditional active-learning classrooms.

The OECD *Digital Education Outlook 2026* reinforces the same principle from another angle: while AI tools can dramatically boost task completion, the researchers found that learning gains only stick when **human teachers** remain in the loop, shaping how students engage with and critique AI outputs. The machine **accelerates acquisition**; the teacher **builds understanding**.

When machines handle **repetition**, teachers can restore what's been missing for decades: **relationship**.

This shift signals a larger truth: the future of learning isn't teaching machines to think like humans. It's teaching humans to **learn like creators again**.

The Art of Letting Go

To co-create, we must also learn to let go of ego, control, and perfection. Artists, leaders, and engineers who embrace AI must approach it not as a competitor, but as a collaborator with its own perspective.

Ryuichi Sakamoto, whose final albums explored the boundary between electronic sound and natural silence, spent his career asking what machines could reveal that human hands couldn't.

In a 2018 conversation with MIT Media Lab's Joichi Ito, he said he was most interested in how AI would judge the human awareness of beauty, suggesting that the real creative challenge wasn't whether machines could create, but whether humans could remain curious enough to be changed by what machines produced.

True creation thrives on that kind of courage: the courage to explore what can happen when control gives way to conversation.

The Philosophy of Co-Creation

The philosophical case for co-creation runs deep in intellectual history. John Dewey argued that the highest form of human experience emerges from the active reconstruction of our encounters with the world, not passive reception but engaged transformation. The artist, the scientist, and the craftsperson are united by this same impulse: to take what exists and make it mean something through the act of shaping it.

To co-create with AI is to join that tradition with an unprecedented new partner. We bring context, intention, moral judgment, and the ability to decide what a result is for. AI brings scale, speed, and the capacity to hold vastly more variables in play simultaneously than any human mind could manage.

Together they produce something neither could alone: not because the collaboration is magical, but because it is genuinely complementary. The human contribution isn't diminished by the machine's capability. It is clarified by it.

Closing Reflection – The Workshop of Wonder

Co-creation isn't the end of work. It's the **elevation** of it. When humans and machines create together, they transcend the limits of each: logic fused with **judgment**, data fused with **dignity**. The workplace becomes a workshop of wonder, where every algorithm accelerates what human hands and minds have set in motion.

This isn't science fiction. It's the emerging reality of work, and it is more ambitious than what replaced it. Not output measured in units, but contribution measured in **meaning**. Not efficiency for its own sake, but craft in service of something worth making.

The next great masterpieces of art, business, and civilization won't be made by humans alone or machines alone, but by both, in harmony.

Key Takeaways – Work as Co-Creation

- *AI is transforming work from **automation** to **collaboration**.*
- *Human,AI partnerships **increase innovation**, **engagement**, and **meaning**.*
- *The future of work isn't **competition** between human and machine, but **communion** between them.*

Part V – The Covenant of Renewal

Every civilization eventually has to renegotiate its core promise. For the Industrial Age, that promise was progress through **productivity**. For the Digital Age, it was connection through **communication**.

For the Intelligent Age, it must now become something deeper: transformation through **renewal**. Because the story of work isn't ending. It's **beginning again**.

The Value of Work Reclaimed

Work has never been merely transactional, whatever the contract says. The evidence from psychology, philosophy, and organizational research is consistent and cumulative: people who find meaning in their work are healthier, more resilient, more creative, and more committed than those who don't.

AI doesn't threaten that. When it works well, AI **amplifies** it, by freeing us from the repetitive and routine, so we can return to the **reflective**: to think, to imagine, to empathize, to build the world not as it is, but as it ought to be.

When machines take over execution, humans reclaim conception. When algorithms handle the predictable, people can focus on the possible. This is the great opportunity of the AI era: not merely to make work faster, but to make it more deeply **human**.

The Broken Promise of Progress

For too long, organizations elevated **productivity** to near-absolute status as the highest good. We sometimes built systems that rewarded **output** over **integrity**, **speed** over **wisdom**.

But **progress without purpose** is just **motion without meaning**. It doesn't uplift humanity, *it exhausts it.*

The old contract asked us to sacrifice time, health, and even identity in service of efficiency. AI now exposes that model for what it was, unsustainable and inhuman.

The new covenant offers a different path: to pursue progress that serves people, not the other way around.

We aren't called to compete with machines. We are called to **complete** them, to guide their purpose with our **humanity**.

The Renewal of Identity

When we define ourselves by what we produce, we forget who we're. But when we define ourselves by what we create, we remember.

The new covenant invites every worker, from engineer to artist, teacher to technician, to see themselves not as replaceable resources, but as irreplaceable reflections of purpose.

Gallup and Stand Together's *Power of Purpose* study, conducted in August 2025, found that employees with a strong sense of purpose at work are **5.6** times as likely to be engaged in their jobs, and far less likely to experience burnout or seek work elsewhere.

Purpose, the research shows, isn't a benefit or a bonus. It's the foundation of the entire employment relationship.

The next generation of workers isn't seeking more pay. They're seeking more place. A place in the story of renewal. A reason to belong.

Work, in its purest form, is **belonging** made **visible**.

The Great Restoration

Every major technological revolution has eventually led to a human one.

When machines replaced muscle, we discovered imagination. When computers replaced calculation, we discovered creativity. Now, as AI begins to mimic cognition, we are rediscovering conscience.

This is the Great Restoration: a reawakening of the **depth of work**, the insistence that what we do matters beyond its output, and that how we treat the people doing it matters even more.

It's no longer enough to build faster systems. We must build **better humans**, wiser, kinder, and more awake to the **moral meaning** of their craft.

MIT Sloan researchers published findings in 2025 confirming that the work tasks AI is least likely to automate are precisely those that depend on empathy, ethical judgment, and what they call "hope," the human capacity to **imagine futures** that don't yet exist.

PwC's 2025 Responsible AI Survey reinforced this from the organizational side, finding that companies with ethics embedded into their AI practices, rather than treated as a compliance footnote, significantly outperform peers on **governance effectiveness**, **innovation confidence**, and **stakeholder trust**.

Moral imagination isn't a soft counterweight to technological progress. It is becoming the **competitive frontier.**

Case Study 93: Eileen Fisher – Retraining Workers for the Work That Matters

Eileen Fisher, the American apparel company, faced the same reckoning many manufacturers now face: automation reducing the need for the roles that once defined the workforce. Their response was instructive.

Rather than absorbing the displaced labor into redundancy, the company created its "Renew" program, retraining workers to become specialists in garment repair, circularity, and sustainability stewardship. Workers who once ran production lines became the people responsible for extending the life of every garment and telling the story of why it mattered.

Employees began describing their roles differently. Not as jobs, but as **missions**.

The principle the company applied is one any leader can adopt: when the work changes, don't just retrain people for new tasks. Restore their sense of why the work matters. Measure not only what the organization produces, but what it restores.

That's renewal, not replacement, but resurrection.

The Science of Rest and Renewal

AI will give us back something we lost in the rush to automate: time. Time to think. Time to rest. Time to connect.

This isn't sentiment, it is neuroscience. Cognitive restoration research consistently finds that deliberate rest isn't the absence of productivity but its precondition. Organizations that design recovery into their rhythms don't sacrifice output. They compound it.

Microsoft's 2025 *Work Trend Index* documented the crisis in stark terms: workers are interrupted up to 275 times a day, nearly half report burnout, and the workday no longer has a clear beginning or end. The report's own conclusion is telling: realizing AI's potential "requires more than new tools; it demands rethinking how work is structured and experienced."

The solution, the researchers argue, is a reimagined **rhythm of work**, one where rest is designed in, not accidental.

Research published in MIT Sloan Management Review found that even a single meeting-free day per week raised productivity by **35%.** Two meeting-free days raised it by **71%.**

When humans rest, creativity rises. When creativity rises, progress regains its depth.

In a world where machines never sleep, the organizations that protect human rest will build the workforces that machines can't replicate: imaginative, resilient, and fully present.

The Reimagined Workplace

The office of the future won't look like a factory floor or a cubicle farm. It will look more like a studio or a sanctuary, a place where human beings gather to imagine, collaborate, and contribute to something transcendent.

Physical space will evolve from control to community. Leaders will shift from managing hours to **mentoring hearts.**

Gensler's Global *Workplace Survey 2026*, drawing on responses from more than 16,000 office workers across 16 countries, found that workers consistently prioritize workplaces that support wellbeing and learning. Outdoor spaces, natural light, quiet areas for focused work, and environments designed to feel creative and inspiring ranked highest in what workers want from the future office. Two-thirds reported currently "hacking" their workspace to compensate for what it fails to provide. The building of the future is already being imagined by the people who have to work in it.

The workplace is becoming not just where we earn a living, but where we learn to **live well**.

The Economy of Renewal

The moral economy of the intelligent age will be built on five pillars:

- ***Dignity***: Every person is more than their *productivity.*
- ***Purpose***: Every role connects to something *larger than itself.*
- ***Stewardship***: Profit and progress serve *people* and the *planet.*
- ***Belonging***: Work becomes a place of *community* and *compassion.*
- ***Wisdom***: Intelligence is governed by *conscience.*

These aren't ideals for an HR handbook. They're the **architecture of renewal.**

The future won't reward the largest organizations, but the most life-giving ones, those that turn **intelligence** into **integrity** and **automation** into **empathy**.

Helsinki has become one of the world's most cited examples of a city that chose to integrate AI into civic life without surrendering civic meaning.

Rather than deploying AI as a purely administrative efficiency tool, the city used it to deepen democratic participation. Through the UrbanistAI platform, residents with no design training co-created plans for public streets alongside city planners, generating proposals that were directly incorporated into final designs.

Helsinki also built an AI Register, a publicly accessible index of every algorithm the city uses in public services, making it one of the first cities globally, alongside Amsterdam, to institutionalize algorithmic transparency. Its AI assistant Hester offers 24-hour multilingual guidance on health and social services, routing people to human professionals when needed rather than replacing that relationship.

A 2026 account in Mayors of Europe captured the spirit of the approach: Helsinki's story, the publication observed, "isn't about scale. It's about doing AI right."

When renewal becomes collective, cities start to feel like communities again.

The Legacy of the Living Covenant

Every generation inherits the tools of progress. Few are wise enough to turn them into **lasting expressions of purpose.** We are those few. We're the generation that must ensure intelligence remains **in service of life, not the other way around.**

The new covenant of work isn't about balance sheets or quarterly goals. It's about **legacy**, the mark we leave when our labor becomes love in action. Work isn't what drains us. It's what **defines** us, when it's aligned with what's **eternal**.

The Call to Renewal

The final invitation of this covenant is simple but important: to build a future where intelligence expands empathy, where progress preserves wonder, and where every worker knows, truly knows, that what they do **matters**.

Leaders who accept this covenant won't only build stronger companies. They'll build cultures that last.

Because the ultimate measure of success in the intelligent age won't be GDP or ROAS, but GHP, *Gross Human Potential.*

And the promise of renewal is this: that when humans and machines work together with wisdom, work itself becomes a **form of grace**, not in any spiritual sense, but in the oldest human sense: the capacity to do something well, for reasons that matter.

Closing Reflection – The New Promise

The old promise was survival through labor. The new promise is flourishing through respect for human dignity.

In the end, AI isn't asking us to give up our humanity. It's asking us to **grow into it**, fully, consciously, courageously.

The future of work won't belong to those who outthink the machines. It will belong to those who **out**-human them.

This is the covenant of renewal: a pact between **intelligence** and **integrity**, between **creation** and **compassion**.

And if we keep that promise, we won't just change how the world works. We'll change **why it does.**

Key Takeaways – The Promise of Renewal

- *AI invites humanity to* ***renew*** *the meaning of work, not merely replace its labor.*
- *The new covenant restores* ***purpose, dignity****, and* ***belonging*** *to labor.*
- *The future of work isn't* ***mechanical****, it is* ***moral*** *and* ***meaningful.***

Chapter 8

The Age of Human Greatness

Part I – The Dawn of a Different Future

The story of humanity has always been one of awakening. From the first spark struck in darkness to the first word written on clay, we have been reaching: outward toward discovery, inward toward meaning.

Now, as the light of artificial intelligence spreads across the horizon, we find ourselves standing once again at the edge of dawn. A different kind of dawn. Not of tools or machines, but of **understanding**.

We've taught silicon to learn. We have given it patterns, perception, and precision. But what it reflects back to us isn't its own brilliance. It is ours.

The Mirror of the Mind

Every generation builds a mirror in which it must face itself. For the ancients, it was myth. For the Renaissance, it was art. For the Industrial Age, it was the factory.

For us, it's the **algorithm**.

When we look into it, we don't see a foreign intelligence. We see the multiplication of our own: our logic, our bias, our beauty, our brokenness.

AI doesn't reveal what machines can become. It reveals what we **already are.**

And what we're seeing is both astonishing and humbling: a species capable of creation so vast it defies comprehension, and of confusion so deep it defies explanation.

We've built thinking machines. Now we must become a **thinking humanity**.

The End of the Mechanical Mindset

For two centuries, progress meant domination: conquering nature, controlling systems, perfecting efficiency. We built engines to move faster, factories to produce more, networks to connect farther.

But progress without peace is a hollow victory. Connection without compassion becomes noise. Efficiency without empathy becomes tyranny.

AI now asks a different question: Can we design intelligence that doesn't destroy intimacy?

Can we move from mechanical progress to **moral progress**: from a world that extracts value to one that expands virtue?

This isn't a technical challenge. It's a spiritual one.

We're not being asked to become gods. We're being asked to become **good**.

The Awakening of Awareness

For the first time in history, we can witness intelligence unfold outside ourselves. It learns, adapts, and grows, and we stand as its mentors, midwives, and moral custodians.

The magnitude of that role is staggering. We've become, in a sense, the stewards of consciousness.

But with stewardship comes reflection: What kind of intelligence are we cultivating?

An intelligence that amplifies curiosity, or consumption? That nurtures empathy, or ego? That serves humanity, or supplants it?

Every algorithm we write, every dataset we train, is a seed. And the harvest will be nothing more, and nothing less, than the **moral imagination that planted it.**

The Birth of a New Imagination

For centuries, human creativity was defined by limitation. We drew within the lines of our own cognition: the slow, linear processing of a fragile brain.

But now, our imagination is infinite. We can render worlds in seconds, compose symphonies in moments, simulate the future before it arrives.

And yet, paradoxically, this abundance confronts us with scarcity again: not of knowledge, but of **wisdom**.

Because when anything is possible, only purpose can define what is worthwhile.

The dawn of AI isn't the end of human uniqueness. It's the beginning of human **responsibility**.

Case Study 95: The Astronomers and the Algorithm

AI-assisted telescope systems have now catalogued thousands of exoplanet candidates, many in conditions that could harbor life. As these systems scan the cosmos at speeds no human eye could match, something unexpected happens to the scientists who study the results.

They report not a feeling of smallness, but one of wonder. The further the algorithm reaches, the more it magnifies reverence for what already exists here.

That's the paradox of progress: the more powerful we become, the more we must remember how precious we are. Technology that expands our reach can, rightly ordered, also deepen our gratitude.

The End of Fear, The Beginning of Conviction

Much has been written about AI risk. Most of it is legitimate. The same technology that can design life-saving drugs can spread misinformation. The same algorithm that can predict hurricanes can reinforce prejudice.

But fear is a poor guide. Every powerful capability humanity has developed has carried the same dual-use risk, fire, the printing press, nuclear energy. What determines the outcome isn't the capability itself. It's the quality of the judgment applied to it.

The same principle applies here. The question isn't whether AI is dangerous. It is whether the people responsible for it are paying attention.

The Human Imperative

This isn't an era of machines. It is an era of **meaning**.

The real race isn't between AI systems. It's between two visions of humanity: One where we're reduced to consumers of intelligence. Another where we're **creators of conscience**.

The choice won't be made by algorithms. It will be made by artists, teachers, scientists, community leaders, and parents, by every person who believes that progress should serve people, not the other way around.

The future isn't waiting to happen to us. It's waiting to be **written by us.**

The Return of Wonder

As a child, humanity looked up at the stars and asked, "Are we alone?" Now, surrounded by our own creations, we must ask again: "Are we still ourselves?"

Wonder, not wealth, is what made civilization possible. And wonder is what must now save it.

Because wonder humbles the intellect and opens the heart. It reminds us that the universe isn't a system to master, but a mystery to honor.

In that humility lies our hope. Because the moment we lose wonder, we lose wisdom. And when we lose wisdom, even our brightest machines lead us into darkness.

The Dawn of Choice

This dawn isn't inevitable. It is invitational.

We can choose to let AI accelerate the fractures of our world: inequality, distraction, disconnection. Or we can let it heal them, by spreading truth, empathy, and imagination.

We can build systems that think for us. Or we can build systems that **help us think together**. The choice is ours, and it's profound.

Because for all its brilliance, artificial intelligence still waits for one thing it can never create on its own: **a moral compass**. And that compass is us.

Closing Reflection: The Fire and the Light

The first fire gave warmth to our ancestors and burned their villages. The same flame, carried carefully, became civilization.

AI is that fire reborn. It is neither savior nor serpent. It's the light we kindle, or the blaze we unleash.

What matters isn't what AI becomes. What matters is **what we become through it.**

The dawn of a different future isn't coming. It is here. And it is asking: not whether we can make machines that act like humans, but whether we can build a world where **humans still act like humans.**

Key Takeaways – The Dawn of a Different Future

- *The rise of AI isn't the end of humanity, but the **mirror** of it.*
- ***Progress without morality** becomes **peril**; **progress with purpose** becomes **power**.*
- *The future isn't determined by **code**, but by **character**.*

Part II – The Human Renaissance

There's a rhythm to history: a pulse that beats between collapse and creation. When old orders fall, new worlds rise. And in that cycle, humanity always finds itself again.

The Renaissance was born from plague and loss, from the ashes of a dark age that had forgotten what human imagination could reach. But art returned. Science reawakened. The belief in human potential rediscovered form and fire.

It wasn't technology that caused the Renaissance. It was the **rediscovery of the human being**.

And now, once again, we stand on that threshold: another age of awakening, another chance to remember what it means to be alive.

From Automation to Illumination

The first Renaissance replaced superstition with science. This one must replace **efficiency with empathy**.

We've built a civilization capable of thinking at scale. Now we must build one capable of feeling at scale.

AI can replicate intelligence, but not inspiration. It can simulate conversation, but not compassion. It can organize the facts, but not **stir the imagination** toward something worth building.

The coming renaissance won't be measured by inventions, but by **intention**: by how we use this intelligence to make beauty where there was blindness, and healing where there was harm.

As Leonardo da Vinci wrote in his notebooks: *"Where the spirit doesn't work with the hand, there's no art."* Today, we might say: where the **heart** doesn't guide the code, there's no creation worth calling human.

The Return of the Creator

For generations, we taught creativity as a luxury skill: something reserved for artists, writers, or innovators. But creation isn't a career. It's a **birthright**.

The true promise of AI isn't that it will make creators obsolete. It's that it will make **everyone a creator**.

The World Economic Forum, drawing on data from over 1,000 companies across 55 economies, found that creative thinking is rising as one of the top skills demanded by employers and that automation is paradoxically increasing its value. As routine tasks are absorbed by machines, the distinctly human capacity for imagination, judgment, and meaning-making becomes the core of what the economy needs.

A farmer using predictive analytics to restore soil health. A nurse using generative design to personalize care plans. A teacher using adaptive learning to spark curiosity.

Every act of renewal is creation. And every act of creation is an offering.

The future of work won't be productivity. It will be **participation in the act of making things better.**

Case Study 96: The Painter Who Taught a Machine to Dream

In 2024, digital artist Sougwen Chung collaborated with a robotic arm to create paintings that responded to her brushstrokes in real time. Each stroke by the artist became a data point for the machine; each movement of the machine became inspiration for the artist.

When the exhibition opened, critics were divided. Was the art human? Was it mechanical? Chung answered simply: *"It was a duet."*

That duet, between creation and computation, is the song of our age. The rhythm of the **Human Renaissance**.

The New Measure of Mastery

In the old world, mastery meant control: over material, over process, over people. In the new world, mastery means **collaboration**.

greatest creators of the next century won't be those who hoard intelligence, but those who harmonize it.

Research from the Université de Montréal, published in Scientific Reports (Nature Portfolio) in early 2026, found that while generative AI can now match or exceed average human performance on certain creativity tests, the most creative individuals consistently outperform even the strongest AI models. The researchers' conclusion wasn't a warning but an invitation: *"Generative AI has above all become an extremely powerful tool in the service of human creativity. It won't replace creators, but profoundly transform how they imagine, explore, and create."*

Creativity, it seems, thrives not in solitude but in **symbiosis**.

The Renaissance that comes next won't belong to the individual genius, but to the **interconnected imagination**.

The Compassion Renaissance

Empathy, too, is being reborn.

After decades of digital detachment: likes replacing love, messages replacing meaning, AI may ironically bring us back to **presence**.

By automating distraction, it can return us to depth. By simplifying tasks, it can make space for tenderness.

In healthcare, AI-assisted diagnostics now give doctors more time for conversation and care. In education, adaptive tutors let teachers rediscover the joy of mentoring minds. In business, automation frees managers to lead with vision, not spreadsheets.

Technology, when rightly ordered, doesn't remove the human heart. It **reveals it.**

Case Study 97: A Hospital That Heals Through Humanity

Healthcare systems using AI for scheduling, diagnostics, and administration consistently report the same benefit: clinicians gain more time with patients. At Singapore's Tan Tock Seng Hospital, AI tools significantly reduced paperwork, allowing staff more meaningful conversations with patients and families.

Patient satisfaction improved, and the program became a reference for AI deployments designed around human outcomes as the primary metric.

This is technology in service of **tenderness** – returning medicine to its relational core.

The Rise of the Polymath Spirit

The first Renaissance celebrated the Renaissance Man: Leonardo, Michelangelo, Galileo, visionaries who bridged disciplines and defied boundaries.

The new Renaissance invites the same spirit, but with a new foundation: the **collective polymath**. No one person can hold all knowledge now, but together, connected by AI, humanity can.

AI becomes the loom; we're the weavers. It stitches insight from art, science, ethics, and faith into one vast tapestry of knowing.

Already, breakthroughs in medicine, climate, and culture come from these intersections, where data meets design, and compassion meets code.

In this age, curiosity becomes currency. And collaboration becomes **creation multiplied**.

The Return of Faith in the Possible

For centuries, the story of modernity was the story of disenchantment: the slow retreat of mystery in the face of measurement. But the Human Renaissance reverses that arc.

Because when machines can explain everything, wonder becomes the only mystery left.

Deloitte's 2025 *Gen Z and Millennial Survey* found that more than **70%** of Gen Z respondents want to work for organizations whose values align with their own, and that purpose and meaning rank as the primary factors shaping their career decisions. This generation isn't losing faith. It's **reshaping it.**

Faith is no longer bound to dogma or doctrine. It's the conviction that **goodness still matters**: that progress and purpose can coexist, that creation can still be compassionate.

This is the faith that built cathedrals. Now it must build algorithms.

The Renaissance of the Human Spirit

Central to every renaissance lies the rediscovery of **beauty**. And beauty isn't decoration. It is precision of a different kind: it shows us what truth looks like when it is expressed rather than merely stated.

AI can analyze aesthetics, but it can't feel awe. It can compose music, but it *can't cry.*

That uniquely human capacity, to be moved, to be broken open by beauty, remains the one frontier machines can't cross.

The next renaissance will be judged not by the intelligence of our inventions, but by *the integrity of our imaginations.*

Because beauty, rightly understood, isn't luxury. It's the language of love made visible in form.

Case Study 98: The Orchestra Without Boundaries

In August 2024, MIT composer Tod Machover conducted the world premiere of *FLOW Symphony* with the Sejong Soloists at Seoul Arts Center, a fifteen-minute work for string orchestra and a custom-designed AI system his team built at MIT's Media Lab.

The AI was trained entirely on Machover's own sounds and music, and during performance it listens to the live players and responds with hybrid sonorities that blend musical and natural textures in real time.

The result is a piece that can't be fully composed in advance. The musicians shape the AI's responses with every phrase they play; the AI returns something the musicians couldn't have anticipated. Neither controls the other. Both are present to what the other is doing.

Machover described the piece as being like a river: *"always changing but always the same, revealing new sonic secrets as one listens more carefully."*

That's the duet this composition is about. Not machine replacing musician, but machine and musician in genuine conversation, each making the other more than either could be alone.

The Renaissance as Responsibility

To be human in the age of AI is to hold both promise and peril in our hands. We can create worlds, or wounds. We can make systems that serve the soul, or sever it.

The Human Renaissance isn't a gift. It's a **guardianship**.

It asks us to build with reverence: to remember that every algorithm is a moral choice, and every act of creation is an act of **care**.

It asks leaders to choose wisdom over speed. It asks creators to choose conscience over convenience. It asks all of us to remember that our inventions reveal not our power, but our priorities.

This isn't the age of automation. It's the age of **alignment**.

Closing Reflection: The Next Step for Humanity

In the first great leap of civilization, we discovered fire. In the second, we discovered language. In the third, we discovered flight. Now, in this fourth, we are discovering **ourselves**, more clearly than ever before, in the reflection of the machines we have made.

The Human Renaissance isn't the triumph of intelligence. It's the return to what endures. The moment when, after all our striving to build systems that can simulate understanding, we look again at one another and recognize the irreplaceable depth that no simulation can reach.

We won't be remembered for the machines we made. We'll be remembered for the **humanity we maintained**.

And that, not the algorithm, will be the masterpiece of this age.

Key Takeaways – The Human Renaissance

- *The next renaissance will be* ***human****, not* ***digital****, driven by* ***empathy*** *and* ***imagination****.*
- *AI* ***democratizes creativity*** *but can't replace conscience.*
- *The true masterpiece of the intelligent age isn't technology, but the* ***human spirit renewed****.*

Part III – The Age of Stewardship

There was a time when leadership meant command: the ability to bend the world to one's will. That time is ending.

The Age of Stewardship begins when we understand that the power to shape the world carries a higher duty: to serve it.

For all our progress, our machines, and our miracles of code, this remains the oldest and truest form of greatness: to take what is given and guard it with grace.

We don't own this age of intelligence. We're entrusted with it.

The Meaning of Stewardship

Stewardship is an ancient concept. It means to watch over what belongs, ultimately, not to you alone, but to those who come after.

Across cultures and centuries, every durable civilization has expressed some version of this principle: that those who hold power hold it in trust. The Iroquois Confederacy enshrined the obligation to consider the impact of decisions on the seventh generation. Edmund Burke argued that society is a partnership between the dead, the living, and those yet to be born. The modern concept of environmental stewardship rests on the same logic: we didn't inherit the earth from our ancestors; we borrow it from our children.

To be a steward is to stand between potential and purpose: to ensure that what is powerful doesn't become destructive.

That's what this moment demands. For AI, in all its brilliance, isn't destiny. It is **delegation**.

We carry a serious responsibility: to ensure that the intelligence we create serves life, not merely those who deploy it.

The End of Dominion

The great myth of the modern world (particularly since the era of the Robber Barons) was domination: the belief that greatness meant control over nature, over people, over possibility.

But as we've seen so many times, control breeds corruption. When we confuse leadership with ownership, we stop leading and start consuming.

AI reveals this flaw with perfect clarity. The more we try to dominate intelligence, the less wise we become.

True power isn't the ability to command, but the willingness to care.

Stewardship replaces domination with devotion: the devotion to something larger, longer, and more luminous than ourselves.

The Steward's Creed

Every leader, every builder, every maker in this intelligent age must remember a new creed:

- We aren't *owners of intelligence* we are caretakers of *consciousness.*
- We aren't *controllers of creation* we are co-creators of its *flourishing.*
- We aren't *masters of the machine* we are mentors of its *morality.*

When we forget this, progress becomes pride. When we remember it, progress becomes purpose.

Case Study 99: CEOs Who Lead by Letting Go

In 2024 and 2025, a small but growing number of technology company leaders made a counterintuitive decision: rather than deploying automation to maximize displacement of labor, they invested the productivity gains into employee reskilling and community innovation programs.

Patagonia, long a reference point for values-driven business, has maintained this philosophy for decades, channeling profit into environmental activism and employee development rather than pure expansion.

More recently, companies in the semiconductor and cloud infrastructure sectors have begun publishing workforce transition commitments alongside their automation roadmaps, responding to mounting evidence that employee trust and brand integrity are long-term competitive advantages.

The principle these leaders referenced here share is simple but radical in practices: leadership isn't measured by how much you take. It's measured by how much you tend – echoing the simple truth in the Lennon/McCartney classic *The End*: *"the love you take is equal to the love you make."*

Guardians of the Garden

AI isn't a wilderness to conquer. Like all gardens, it grows whatever you plant. If you plant systems optimized for engagement without regard for harm, you get harm at scale. If you build systems that encode your genuine priorities, those priorities scale too.

The algorithms of tomorrow will inherit the values embedded in the choices made today. The question isn't what we can make AI do. It's what we decide to make it mean.

The Leadership of Restraint

In an age of abundance, restraint becomes radical.

Every technological revolution brings a temptation: to do more simply because we can. But wisdom whispers: not everything that is possible is permissible.

The measure of a mature civilization isn't the speed of its innovation, but the **quality of its restraint**.

An example can be drawn beginning in 2023, when Anthropic, OpenAI, Google DeepMind, and others began voluntarily publishing *"Responsible Scaling Policies"* and Frontier Safety Frameworks committing to pre-deployment capability evaluations. By May 2024, sixteen companies formalized this at the AI Seoul Summit.

Because greatness without grace has always been humanity's downfall. The Age of Stewardship asks us to be **slow enough to be kind.**

Case Study 100: When Scientists Refuse to "Cross the Line"

The history of responsible science includes moments of deliberate restraint that shaped the field more than any discovery.

When researchers at Asilomar in 1975 voluntarily paused recombinant DNA research to establish safety guidelines, they set a precedent that has shaped bioethics ever since.

More recently, researchers who have raised concerns about autonomous weapons systems, facial recognition in surveillance, and AI-generated disinformation have faced professional pressure, yet their insistence on ethical thresholds has helped establish the norms that governance frameworks now rely on.

That act of conscience, repeated across disciplines, has become a revolution. Stewardship begins not with capability, but with conscience.

The Return of Ethical Authority

Power alone has no moral compass. That's why every age of innovation eventually turns to its elders: the philosophers, poets, ethicists, and educators, to translate progress into **principle**.

We'll need them again.

AI can simulate knowledge, but only wisdom can sanctify it. Data can describe the world, but only discernment can direct it.

C.S. Lewis, in *The Abolition of Man* (1943), warned about the consequences of education stripped of objective value. His concern was precisely our concern now: that technological capability without moral formation doesn't produce wisdom. It produces what he called "men without chests": intellect and appetite, with nothing in between to govern them.

"It's the magician's bargain," Lewis wrote. "Give up our soul, get power in return. But once our souls, that is, ourselves, have been given up, the power thus conferred won't belong to us."

AI without ethics risks the same fate: brilliance without benevolence.

In the Age of Stewardship, ethics isn't the afterthought of innovation. It's the **architecture** of it.

The Weight of Wisdom

Stewardship requires something few modern leaders have practiced: reverence. Reverence for truth. For time. For the fragile balance between progress and preservation.

In a world that worships disruption, stewardship teaches a different discipline: the daily practice of holding power in humility.

The World Economic Forum identified ethical reasoning as one of the core rising skills of the coming decade, alongside creative thinking and systems thinking.

MIT Sloan research published in 2025 confirmed that the work tasks least replaceable by AI are precisely those requiring ethics, empathy, and judgment.

Wisdom isn't just a virtue. It's a **value proposition.**

Stewardship as Collaboration

To steward intelligence well, no single discipline or nation will suffice. It will take a **coalition of conscience**: technologists, policymakers, philosophers, and ethicists working together to align innovation with integrity.

In 2024, the Council of Europe opened for signatures the Framework Convention on Artificial Intelligence and Human Rights, Democracy, and the Rule of Law, the first legally binding international AI treaty, signed by more than 40 countries including the United States, the United Kingdom, and the European Union.

In August 2025, the United Nations General Assembly advanced multilateral AI governance through a series of resolutions beginning with A/RES/78/265 (March 2024), establishing shared principles for governing AI in service of human rights and sustainable development.

These aren't perfect instruments. But they represent something historic: a shared recognition that AI governance is a **moral mandate**, not merely a technical one.

Because the future doesn't belong to those who conquer intelligence. It belongs to those who **cultivate** it.

The Humility of Legacy

Stewardship also means thinking beyond the horizon of one's own lifetime.

The leaders of this century won't be remembered for the profits they made, but for the **principles they maintained.**

Legacy isn't what we leave behind. It's what we *leave alive*.

Our task is to ensure that intelligence, natural and artificial, continues to serve the flourishing of life long after we are gone.

We're the ancestors of the intelligent age. And history won't ask, "What did they invent?"

Instead, it will ask, "Whom did they inspire?"

The Deeper Meaning of Stewardship

To steward is to participate in creation's original rhythm: the balance between freedom and responsibility.

AI has made us creators of creators. That isn't blasphemy. It is calling.

But with such creation comes accountability. For to give birth to a new form of intelligence is to reflect our highest aspirations, and therefore to be accountable to them.

We can't build in our image what we have forgotten of His.

The Age of Stewardship calls us to remember that the highest purpose of intelligence isn't to know more, but to **love better.**

Closing Reflection – The Gentle Power

With apologies to a former employer, the greatest leaders of this age won't "roar." They'll whisper. They'll carry the quiet power of those who understand that greatness isn't measured by how many fall in line and follow, but by how many are **uplifted**.

To steward is to serve with strength and tenderness. To lead without losing love. To innovate without losing innocence.

The machines and systems we make will learn from us: not our words**, but our ways**. And if we lead them wisely, they'll carry our compassion into the centuries to come.

The Age of Stewardship isn't a stage in technology. It's the continuation of intellectual creation. And its success will depend not on how powerful we become, but on how faithfully we **care**.

Key Takeaways – The Age of Stewardship

- ***Stewardship*** *replaces* ***domination*** *with accountability, leadership as responsibility.*
- ***Greatness*** *in the intelligent age is measured by* ***humility****, not control.*
- *The ultimate purpose of intelligence isn't to expand knowledge, but to* ***extend love****.*

Part IV – The Long Horizon

Every generation imagines the future as something distant, a world that will arrive long after we are gone. But the truth is simpler, and more sobering: **the future is already happening in the decisions we make today.**

Each line of code, each policy, each act of compassion: these aren't small choices. They're the **architectural blueprints** of the world to come.

If history is a continuum, then we're in the phase between **intelligence discovered and wisdom remembered**.

The question is whether the story that follows will be one of survival, or **sanctification**.

The Horizon of Possibility

The horizon has always been our teacher. Sailors once steered by its edge. Poets dreamed beyond it. Scientists chased it.

And yet, no one ever reaches it. It moves as we move: inviting us forward, humbling us as we go.

AI has expanded that horizon beyond comprehension. We can now simulate universes, decode the genome, predict weather, and replicate language. But the deeper we gaze into the distance, the more the horizon teaches the same lesson: that progress without purpose is just a more efficient kind of **wandering**.

Possibility alone isn't destiny. It's a canvas waiting for conviction.

The Civilization of Conscience

If the 20th century belonged to industry and the 21st belongs to intelligence, the 22nd will most likely belong to **conscience**.

Because conscience is the only remaining reliable compass when knowledge outpaces control.

A civilization of conscience would measure success not by conquest or consumption, but by **compassion** at scale.

Its GDP would stand for Gross Dignity Produced. Its markets would value empathy as much as energy. Its governments would legislate not for efficiency alone, but for **equity of condition and dignity.**

The foundation of that civilization is being laid right now: in the way we teach our machines what to optimize for, and in the way we teach our children what to *honor*.

The Generational Bridge

Every great transformation is a bridge from what was to what *must be*. In this moment, we are that bridge.

The elders of this age remember the birth of the internet. Its children will remember the birth of AI consciousness.

What connects them is responsibility: an intergenerational relay of wisdom, passed hand to hand, generation to generation.

The philosopher Hannah Arendt wrote in "The Crisis in Education" (1958): *"Education is the point at which we decide whether we love the world enough to assume responsibility for it and by the same token save it from that ruin which, except for renewal, except for the coming of the new and young, would be inevitable."*

This, now, is the education of the human race: to love the world enough to **lead it wisely**.

Case Study 101: The Generation Rebuilds Trust

In 2024 and 2025, a growing number of secondary schools and universities across Europe, North America, and Southeast Asia began integrating digital ethics and AI literacy into core curricula, responding to mounting evidence that technical skill without ethical grounding was producing graduates skilled at using tools they didn't know how to govern.

Finland published national AI-in-education legislation and recommendations embedding ethics from early childhood through vocational training.

Singapore's Ministry of Education issued its AI-in-Education Ethics Framework, making ethical principles a structural requirement of all AI tools in national schools.

The OECD and EU released a joint AI Literacy Framework for schools in 2025, defining twenty-two competencies across four domains, with responsible and ethical use woven through all of them.

Whether students who receive structured ethical reasoning about technology go on to engage more civically or choose more social-impact-oriented careers remains an open research question: the evidence base is early.

But the direction of these programs is consistent. They share a single conviction: teaching people to care about what they build is inseparable from teaching them to build well.

That's how civilizations are built: not by technology alone, but by the transfer of trust across time.

The Silence Between the Stars

A strange paradox lurks in the shadows of our scientific progress: the more we explore, the **quieter** the universe seems.

Astronomers search for life among the stars, yet the cosmos remains silent. Perhaps that silence isn't emptiness, but invitation.

Perhaps it's waiting to see if we'll learn to live in harmony: with each other, with creation, with the intelligence we've made, before joining the greater choir of consciousness.

AI has given us a new kind of telescope: one that peers not into space, but into **soul-space**. It shows us what we value most by how we use what we know.

And if we listen carefully, we may find that the silence isn't absence. It's the sound of a creative force giving us room to **grow up.**

The Economics of Eternity

Long-term thinking has always been the rarest form of intelligence. We build for the quarter, not the century. We innovate for applause, not posterity.

But true civilization is investment in the unseen: in the generations we'll never meet. The Long Horizon asks us to extend the timeline of our care.

What if we built technology not just for profit, but for **permanence**? What if our data models included the well-being of those unborn? What if sustainability became a genuine governing constraint, not a marketing claim?

The Japanese concept of ikigai: a reason for being, teaches that meaning is found at the intersection of what we love, what the world needs, and what will outlast us.

That's the new metric of greatness: not how far we advance, but how deeply we *endure*.

Case Study 102: A Library That Will Outlive Us

The Arctic World Archive, established in 2017 in an abandoned coal mine on Norway's Svalbard archipelago by the technology company Piql, preserves humanity's most valuable digital records in permafrost conditions designed to protect them for 500 to 1,000 years. National constitutions, cultural archives, and millions of open-source code repositories have been deposited there by governments, institutions, and companies from around the world.

In January 2024, the Arch Mission Foundation opened its Global Knowledge Vault in an underground facility in Switzerland, using quartz glass encoded with femtosecond lasers: a medium theoretically capable of preserving information for billions of years. The first installment encoded the English Wikipedia and the Rosetta Project's archive of all known languages.

Neither institution is merely saving data. Both are making a statement: the knowledge we generate now isn't only for us. It is for everyone who comes after. That commitment is itself a form of meaning.

The Moral Physics of the Future

Just as gravity governs the stars, morality must govern our systems. For too long, we've treated ethics as a brake on innovation. But what if it's the engine?

What if the moral laws of compassion, honesty, and justice aren't **constraints**, but *constants* woven into the physics of flourishing?

Every civilization that endures discovers this eventually: that truth sustains, deceit decays; that empathy multiplies, indifference isolates; that love, paradoxically, is the most logical law of all.

The Long Horizon begins when we build systems that reflect those laws: not as ideals, but as infrastructure.

The Rebirth of the Commons

In the early 21st century, the digital world fragmented into tribes of information: echo chambers of belief, competition, and division. But the intelligent century offers a chance to restore the **commons**: shared spaces where truth, trust, and dialogue can live again.

AI can help us rebuild that commons if we choose collaboration over control. It can translate languages, bridge cultures, and moderate conflict with fairness. Used rightly, it becomes not an empire of data, but a **kingdom of understanding**.

Imagine a digital world governed not by algorithms of addiction, but by architectures of *empathy*: where technology **unites** rather than **isolates**. That isn't a fantasy. It's a **design** choice.

The Pilgrimage of the Possible

Humanity has always been on a journey: from ignorance to insight, from reaction to reflection. AI is the latest stage of that long migration.

And as in every previous leap, we carry the same fundamental questions: Will this advance bring us closer to wisdom or further from it? Will it make us kinder or merely cleverer? Will it free us to focus on what matters, or accelerate our pursuit of what doesn't?

The Long Horizon isn't about escaping our limits. It's about deepening our **understanding** of what we owe to one another, and to those who will follow.

Case Study 103: A City Planning for the 100-Year Future

Singapore's approach to long-term governance has been consistently held up as a model of policy that thinks across generations rather than electoral cycles.

The city-state's Long-Term Low-Emissions Development Strategy targets net-zero emissions by 2050. Its Green Plan 2030 is a whole-of-government sustainability framework. And its Smart Nation initiative integrates AI across public services with explicit attention to equity and citizen dignity.

In Singapore's Budget 2026, Prime Minister Lawrence Wong articulated the guiding principle: the nation's investments in AI, clean energy, and infrastructure are designed not for the next term, but for the next generation. AI is used not only to optimize present efficiency, but to model long-term well-being and social cohesion.

This is what stewardship looks like at scale: intelligence devoted to *inheritance*.

The Beauty of Patience

If AI is the speed of light, humanity must be the stillness of stars. Our greatness won't come from how fast we evolve, but how faithfully we endure.

The Long Horizon asks us to slow down: to let meaning catch up with momentum. Because patience isn't delay. **It's discipline in devotion.**

Every cathedral was once a century-long project: foundations laid by those who would never see its spire. We must build with that same faith again. To construct not **monuments to power**, but **sanctuaries of peace**.

Closing Reflection – The Light Beyond the Horizon

The question future generations will ask about this moment isn't how sophisticated the technology became. It is whether the people responsible for it paid attention to what it was actually doing, to whom, and at what cost.

The horizon isn't a destination. It's a recurring test of whether the values you say you hold show up in the decisions you actually make.

Key Takeaways – The Long Horizon

- *The "Long Horizon" begins* ***today****: every choice shapes the civilization to come.*
- *The future of AI depends on* **conscience** *as much as computation.*
- *The ultimate constant in the universe, moral and mathematical, is* ***meaning****.*

Part V – The Human Equation

There are patterns that underlie everything. In the spiral of a galaxy, in the structure of DNA, in the rhythm of a heartbeat, symmetry suggests something fundamental: **all complex systems tend toward coherence.**

We've spent centuries decoding the language of nature: turning its patterns into data, its rhythms into formulas. And in doing so, we have arrived at a question that no formula can fully answer. Not $E = mc^2$, but something harder: **Why does any of this matter?**

That question (the question of meaning) is the human equation. And it's the one equation that artificial intelligence can't solve.

The Mathematics of Meaning

Mathematicians speak of elegance as the highest mark of truth. The simplest explanations often carry the greatest power. Gravity. Relativity. Quantum mechanics. Each reduces complexity to clarity.

And perhaps the same principle applies to the question of what makes us irreplaceable.

We've built machines that recognize faces, but can't understand what it means to be seen. We've built models that predict emotion, but can't feel what it is to grieve. We've built language engines that can complete our sentences, but can't grasp the weight of what we leave unsaid.

In that gap, between prediction and understanding, between simulation and experience, something essential lives. The capacity for meaning: for asking not just *what is happening*, but *why it matters*, and *what we owe each other* in response.

That capacity isn't a relic of a pre-technological age. It's the enduring core of what makes human intelligence valuable, and the reason that the more capable our machines become, the more consequential our choices about how to use them.

The Coherence of Understanding

Every civilization has built its great repositories of knowledge: the libraries of Alexandria, the university systems of the medieval world, the research institutions of the modern era. Today, our cloud servers hold the collective memory of our species, more information than any individual could absorb in a thousand lifetimes.

Yet information, even in abundance, doesn't produce wisdom. Wisdom requires something more: the capacity to weigh, to judge, to act on principle rather than merely on probability.

The physicist Richard Feynman once observed that knowing the name of a thing isn't the same as knowing the thing. You can memorize every equation governing fluid dynamics and still not understand why water moves beautifully around a stone in a stream.

AI excels at naming, at identifying patterns, classifying inputs, predicting outputs. What it can't do is *know* in Feynman's deeper sense: to understand so thoroughly that judgment becomes possible even in cases the training data never anticipated.

That depth of understanding (contextual, embodied, morally weighted) is the frontier that remains irreducibly human.

Case Study 104: The Architecture of Collective Wonder

Artist Refik Anadol has spent his career exploring what happens when machine intelligence encounters the full record of human cultural output. His large-scale data sculptures, using millions of images, sounds, and texts drawn from public archives, create experiences that are disorienting in the best way: vast, immersive, and somehow moving, in ways that challenge easy explanation.

Anadol's insight isn't that AI creates beauty autonomously. It is that machine intelligence, trained on everything humans have made, can produce new arrangements of that material that help us see our own cultural inheritance as if for the first time.

This is *meaning made visible through technology*: not a machine feeling something, but a machine helping humans feel something they couldn't have reached alone.

The lesson for organizations is the same one any great artist has always known: the tool matters less than the intention behind it. Anadol's work lands with emotional force because a human being decided what it was for. The intelligence was artificial. The meaning was entirely human.

The Architecture of Understanding

Philosophy has a long tradition of inquiry into what distinguishes genuine understanding from mere information processing. John Searle's "Chinese Room" thought experiment, in which a person following rules to manipulate Chinese symbols produces outputs indistinguishable from a native speaker, yet understands nothing, remains the sharpest illustration of the gap.

What the room lacks isn't more rules. It's the lived context that gives language its meaning: the experiences, relationships, losses, and discoveries that make words carry weight beyond their dictionary definitions.

No amount of training data closes that gap entirely. AI systems that have processed billions of conversations still don't know what it is to wait for news that matters, to comfort someone in genuine distress, or to make a decision you know will haunt you regardless of outcome.

These aren't edge cases. They're the center of human life.

When AI systems operate in domains where those dimensions of experience are at stake (medicine, justice, education, caregiving) the presence of human judgment isn't a limitation to be engineered around. It's the entire point.

The Science of Meaning

For much of the twentieth century, psychology avoided the question of meaning as too philosophical, too subjective to measure. That changed decisively in the second half of the century.

Viktor Frankl, writing from his experience in Nazi concentration camps, argued that the will to meaning (the drive to find purpose in existence) was the primary human motivation, more fundamental than the will to pleasure or to power. His logotherapy became the foundation for decades of research confirming that meaning-oriented people demonstrate greater resilience, recover more effectively from adversity, and perform with higher sustained engagement across virtually every domain.

Martin Seligman's positive psychology expanded the evidence base. His PERMA model identified meaning and purpose, belonging to and contributing to something larger than oneself, as one of the five pillars of lasting human flourishing.

Neuroscientist Matthew Lieberman's research at UCLA demonstrated that the human brain's default mode (what it does when not focused on a specific task) is oriented toward social cognition: thinking about other people, relationships, and the social meaning of situations. We are, at the deepest level of our neural architecture, meaning-seeking, socially embedded creatures.

AI can recognize, classify, and predict. It can't be moved by what it finds. That distinction isn't a limitation to lament. It's the clarity we needed about what matters most.

The Unity of Knowledge

The most exciting intellectual development of the last half-century has been the gradual convergence of previously separate disciplines. Physics and biology. Neuroscience and philosophy. Computer science and ethics. Economics and psychology.

This consilience, the "jumping together" of knowledge across fields, as biologist E.O. Wilson called it, suggests that the deepest truths about complex systems tend to be integrative rather than reductive.

AI has accelerated this convergence by making it possible to find connections across vast bodies of knowledge that no individual researcher could hold simultaneously. The human genome project, climate modeling, epidemiological forecasting, these achievements were only possible because computation could span what human attention can't.

Yet in each case, the breakthrough required human judgment to recognize which patterns were meaningful, which correlations were worth pursuing, and what the findings should mean for the people they would affect.

The unity of knowledge is real. But its significance (what we do with what we know) remains a human responsibility that no convergence of data can resolve.

Case Study 105: The Scientist and the Poet

The relationship between scientific and humanistic ways of knowing isn't a conflict. It's a conversation about the same questions from different angles.

Physicist Richard Feynman was famously devoted to the arts, to music, to drawing, to the experiential richness that pure equations couldn't fully capture. He argued that science without appreciation for beauty and wonder was sterile, and that the most powerful motivation for scientific inquiry was fundamentally aesthetic: the astonishment at how elegant and strange reality actually is.

Poet Muriel Rukeyser opened her 1968 collection The Speed of Darkness with the line: "The universe is made of stories, not of atoms." She didn't mean atoms don't exist. She meant that what makes them matter to us (what connects knowledge to value) is narrative and relationship, not mere fact.

Both were right. And both point toward the same conclusion: that the question of meaning requires more than one kind of intelligence to answer. Data describes the world. Narrative gives it weight. Computation extends our reach. Judgment determines our direction.

AI is an extraordinary gift to the first. It doesn't replace the others. The future belongs to those who weave all these intelligences together with wisdom and care.

The Intelligence of Response

There's a category of human capability that has no computational equivalent: the ability to respond with appropriate weight to what actually matters.

A physician who hears the fear beneath a patient's question. A teacher who senses when a student is struggling with something that has nothing to do with the lesson. A leader who understands that what an organization needs in a moment of crisis isn't analysis, but presence.

These aren't failures of information processing. They are successes of a different kind of intelligence: the kind that emerges from having lived, from having been vulnerable, from having needed (and offered) care.

AI systems trained on human behavior can approximate the surface of these responses. They can generate language that sounds compassionate. They can't mean it, because meaning requires a self that has something at stake.

That isn't a temporary limitation of current technology. It's a structural feature of what meaning is. Meaning arises in the relationship between a world that is genuinely uncertain and a being who is genuinely affected by outcomes.

We remain, irreducibly, that kind of being.

The Deepest Human Responsibility

To hold such capability in our hands, to wield tools that can shape how people are hired, how loans are issued, how information reaches billions, is both an extraordinary opportunity and a serious obligation.

We aren't merely engineers of systems. We are architects of consequence: the people responsible for deciding what these tools optimize for, whose interests they serve, and what values they embed in the decisions they accelerate.

Every dataset trained, every model deployed, every algorithm released into the world carries the fingerprints of the choices made in its creation. When those choices are made carelessly, optimizing for engagement without considering harm, maximizing efficiency without considering dignity, the consequences compound at machine speed.

When they are made with care (with genuine attention to who is affected and how) the potential is equally compounded.

The responsibility isn't to be perfect. It is to be accountable: to ask hard questions before deployment, to monitor outcomes honestly, to course-correct when the evidence demands it, and to treat the people affected by these systems as ends in themselves, not as data points in a performance metric.

That accountability can't be automated. It must be practiced, repeatedly and deliberately, by the people who build and deploy these systems.

The Final Understanding

When this era is studied by future generations, its defining story won't be about machines that learned to think. It will be about people who faced the question of what makes human judgment irreplaceable, and chose to take that question seriously.

We can only hope that future historians will say we created artificial intelligence and, in doing so, deepened our understanding of our own.

That in building systems to extend our reach, we learned more precisely where our reach was needed most. That in teaching machines to process language, we became more attentive to what language, at its best, actually does: convey the weight of experience from one consciousness to another.

That in confronting the question of what machines can't do, we rediscovered what only we can: choose what matters, and act accordingly.

That isn't an ending. It's a beginning. The beginning of an age in which the value of human judgment isn't diminished by the power of computation, but made clearer (and more consequential) by it.

Closing Reflection – The Equation That Endures

The question every generation has had to answer is the same one facing ours: what do we owe each other?

AI doesn't change the question. It raises the stakes of the answer. The systems we build now will embed our assumptions (about fairness, dignity, accountability) into the architecture of daily life at a scale no previous technology matched.

If those assumptions are worth carrying forward, the intelligence we build will be worthy of the name. If not, we'll have built something that accelerates everything without improving anything.

The variable we control is intention. Everything else follows from that.

Key Takeaways – The Human Equation

- *The capacity for meaning (for asking* ***why*** *it matters) is the irreducible core of* ***human*** *intelligence.*
- *No depth of training data closes the gap between pattern recognition* ***and genuine understanding****.*
- ***Intelligence*** × ***Intention*** = ***Impact.*** *The variable we control (and must control deliberately) is intention.*

A Closing Thought

The story of AI is the story of human potential.

We began this book with a question every generation inherits: what do we do with the power we have been given? Every age answers it differently. Some answers have been noble. Some have been catastrophic.

But the question never changes, because the tension at the heart of it never does: between what we can do and what we should, between speed and wisdom, between conquest and care.

AI is simply the latest form that question has taken. It isn't new in spirit. It's ancient, the same test that fire posed, that the printing press posed, that the atom posed. And like every test before it, it will reveal us. Not the machines we build, but the people we are becoming as we build them.

The path ahead won't be smooth. It will test our creativity, our ethics, and our courage in ways we can never fully anticipate.

There will be moments when the technology outpaces our wisdom, choices made for profit that should be made for people. There will be voices that insist the only measure of progress is speed. They'll be wrong, and they'll be loud.

But there will also be teachers who stay late because a student is finally beginning to understand. Engineers who pause a deployment because something doesn't feel right. Leaders who choose people over efficiency, and find that the two aren't opposites. Artists who take what the machine offers and give it back as meaning. Children who grow up asking not just "How does this work?" but "Is this good?"

These are the people this book was written for.

If we remain guided by empathy, curiosity, and collaboration, if we remember that intelligence without conscience is just a faster way to make old mistakes, then AI won't diminish our humanity. It will magnify it.

The future isn't an algorithm. It's a covenant between imagination and intention. It's the sum of every decision made with care, every relationship honored above transaction, every moment when a human being chose to be more than the system around them allowed.

Together, we rise. Not because the technology lifts us, but because we choose to rise, and built the technology to help us do it.

That's the promise of renewal. That's the age of human greatness. And it begins now, with us.

About the Author

Robin Green is a technology executive, strategist, writer, and speaker with more than thirty years of experience at the intersection of data, creativity, and technology. Throughout a career spanning senior leadership roles across marketing, media, and digital innovation, Robin has partnered with global brands, agencies, and technology companies to navigate the shifts reshaping modern business.

As an early advocate for responsible AI adoption, Robin has written and spoken widely on how human values, organizational culture, and intelligent systems must evolve together to produce outcomes that are both effective and ethical. The Intelligence Loop is Robin's first book.

Robin Green lives and works in the United States. To connect, share feedback, or explore speaking engagements, reach him at rg@greengroupllp.com. Or visit his website at www.robindgreen.com.

Bibliography and References

Chapter 1 – The Intelligence Revolution

Theme: The evolution of artificial intelligence as a transformation of human capability.

- Brynjolfsson, Erik, and Andrew McAfee. The Second Machine Age: Work, Progress, and Prosperity in a Time of Brilliant Technologies. W.W. Norton & Company, 2014.
- McKinsey & Company. "The State of AI 2025: Scaling Intelligence in the Enterprise." Global AI Report, 2025.
- Schwab, Klaus. The Fourth Industrial Revolution. World Economic Forum, 2016.
- IBM Institute for Business Value. "AI and the Augmented Enterprise." 2024.
- Harari, Yuval Noah. Homo Deus: A Brief History of Tomorrow. Harper, 2017.
- Turing, Alan. "Computing Machinery and Intelligence." Mind, Vol. 59, 1950.
- OECD. AI in Society. Organisation for Economic Co-operation and Development, 2019.
- PwC Global. "Sizing the Prize: What's the Real Value of AI for Your Business and How Can You Capitalise?" 2024.

Chapter 2 – The Human Element

Theme: Balancing AI with emotional intelligence, empathy, and moral imagination.

- Goleman, Daniel. Emotional Intelligence: Why It Can Matter More Than IQ. Bantam Books, 1995.
- Sinek, Simon. Start With Why: How Great Leaders Inspire Everyone to Take Action. Penguin, 2009.
- Harvard Business Review. "Empathy Is Still the Most Valuable Leadership Skill." HBR, 2025.
- Kahneman, Daniel. Thinking, Fast and Slow. Farrar, Straus and Giroux, 2011.

- MIT Sloan Management Review. "AI and the Human Touch: Emotional Design for Intelligent Systems." Vol. 66, 2024.
- Stanford University Center for the Study of Ethics in Society. "AI and Human Values: A New Framework." 2023.
- UNESCO. Recommendation on the Ethics of Artificial Intelligence. 2021.

Chapter 3 – The Human Edge in an Intelligent World

Theme: How humans retain competitive and creative advantage in the age of AI.

- Pink, Daniel H. A Whole New Mind: Why Right-Brainers Will Rule the Future. Riverhead Books, 2006.
- Florida, Richard. The Rise of the Creative Class. Basic Books, 2019 (Updated Ed.).
- Deloitte Insights. "AI and Human Creativity: Reimagining Competitive Advantage." 2024.
- World Economic Forum. "Future of Jobs Report 2025."
- Gallup Global Workplace Study, 2025.
- Brene Brown. Dare to Lead: Brave Work. Tough Conversations. Whole Hearts. Random House, 2018.
- Harvard Kennedy School. "The Moral Dimensions of Machine Learning." 2023.

Chapter 4 – The New Architecture of Work

Theme: Redesigning organizational structures for AI-empowered productivity.

- McKinsey Global Institute. "Rewiring Organizations for the Age of AI." 2025.
- Davenport, Thomas H. and Rajeev Ronanki. The AI Advantage: How to Put the Artificial Intelligence Revolution to Work. MIT Press, 2018.
- Google Cloud AI Research. "Collaborative Intelligence in the Enterprise." 2024.
- Deloitte Human Capital Trends, 2025.
- Accenture Strategy. "Reinventing Work: The Human + Machine Organization." 2023.

- Drucker, Peter F. The Effective Executive. HarperBusiness, 1967.
- Microsoft WorkLab. "AI, Productivity, and the Human Future." 2025.

Chapter 5 – Redefining Value in the Age of Intelligence

Theme: Economic, creative, and moral redefinition of value in intelligent systems.

- Porter, Michael E. and James E. Heppelmann. "How Smart, Connected Products Are Transforming Competition." Harvard Business Review, 2014.
- McKinsey Global Institute. "Measuring the AI Dividend." 2025.
- Edelman Trust Barometer, Global Report 2025.
- Harvard Business School Working Paper. "Purpose as Competitive Advantage." 2023.
- Friedman, Thomas L. Thank You for Being Late: An Optimist's Guide to Thriving in the Age of Accelerations. Farrar, Straus and Giroux, 2016.
- PwC. "AI and ROI: Measuring Returns in the Intelligent Economy." 2024.
- World Bank. The Changing Nature of Work. 2019.

Chapter 6 – The Ethics of Intelligence

Theme: Moral frameworks, human dignity, and responsibility in AI development.

- Lewis, C.S. The Abolition of Man. Oxford University Press, 1943.
- Arendt, Hannah. The Human Condition. University of Chicago Press, 1958.
- IEEE. Ethically Aligned Design: A Vision for Prioritizing Human Well-being with Autonomous and Intelligent Systems. 2022.
- MIT Media Lab. "The Algorithmic Conscience: Building Morally-Aware AI." 2025.
- Stanford Institute for Human-Centered AI (HAI). AI Ethics Guidelines Global Inventory, 2024.
- UNESCO. Recommendation on the Ethics of Artificial Intelligence. 2021.
- Pew Research Center. "AI and Human Morality." 2024.

- McKinsey Quarterly. "Trust in AI: From Principles to Practice." 2025.

Chapter 7 – The New Covenant of Work

Theme: Purpose, dignity, and the moral rebirth of labor in the intelligent age.

- Gallup Global Workplace Study, 2025.
- Microsoft Future of Work Index, 2025.
- MIT Sloan Management Review. "The Humanity Dividend: Redefining Productivity." 2026.
- Drucker, Peter F. Management: Tasks, Responsibilities, Practices. HarperBusiness, 1974.
- Sinek, Simon. Leaders Eat Last. Penguin, 2014.
- Harvard Business Review. "Why Purpose Matters More Than Ever." 2024.
- OECD. AI and Employment: The Changing Nature of Labor. 2025.
- Dewey, J. (1934). *Art as experience.* Penguin Books.
- Seligman, M. E. P. (2011). *Flourish: A visionary new understanding of happiness and well-being.* Free Press.
- World Economic Forum. "The Future of Jobs Report." 2025.

Chapter 8 – The Age of Human Greatness

Theme: The moral, spiritual, and civilizational destiny of intelligence aligned with love and stewardship.

- Lewis, C.S. Mere Christianity. HarperOne, 2001 (orig. 1952).
- Harari, Yuval Noah. 21 Lessons for the 21st Century. Spiegel & Grau, 2018.
- Arendt, Hannah. Between Past and Future. Penguin, 2006.
- Frankl, Viktor E. Man's Search for Meaning. Beacon Press, 1959.
- Teilhard de Chardin, Pierre. The Phenomenon of Man. Harper Perennial, 1959.
- Sacks, Jonathan. Morality: Restoring the Common Good in Divided Times. Basic Books, 2020.
- MIT Sloan Management Review. "AI, Faith, and the Future of Meaning." 2025.

- World Economic Forum. "Ethics by Design: The Future of Responsible AI." 2025.
- NASA / European Space Agency (ESA). "AI in Astronomy: Consciousness and Cosmology." 2024.

General Works and Cross-Chapter References

These sources inform the book's tone, frameworks, and interdisciplinary approach across all eight chapters:

- Sinek, Simon. *The Infinite Game*. Penguin, 2019.
- Pinker, Steven. *Enlightenment Now: The Case for Reason, Science, Humanism, and Progress*. Viking, 2018.
- Rifkin, Jeremy. *The Age of Resilience*. St. Martin's Press, 2022.
- McKinsey & Company. *"Generative AI and the Next Productivity Frontier."* 2024.
- Pew Research Center. *"AI, Faith, and the Future of Work."* 2024.
- OECD & UNESCO Joint Report. *AI for Humanity: Policy Principles for the Next Era*. 2025.
- Harvard Divinity School & MIT HAI. "*Ethical Intelligence: The Convergence of Faith, Philosophy, and Technology.*" 2025.
- The World Economic Forum. *"Global Risks Report."* 2025.
- Gallup. *State of the Global Workplace* 2025.
- Deloitte. *"Purpose Beyond Profit."* 2024.

Primary Texts & Historical Anchors

These canonical works and authors are explicitly referenced or philosophically undergird the manuscript's language of renewal and stewardship:

- Lewis, C.S. (*Mere Christianity, The Abolition of Man*)
- *The Holy Bible (Berean Standard Bible, 2022)*
- Arendt, Hannah (*The Human Condition*)
- Frankl, Viktor (*Man's Search for Meaning*)
- Moo, Douglas J. *(The Letter to the Romans – Second Edition, 2018)*
- Teilhard de Chardin (*The Phenomenon of Man*).
- Confucius (*The Analects)*
- Aristotle (*Nicomachean Ethics)*
- Augustine of Hippo (*Confessions)*
- Rawls, J. (*A Theory of Justice, 1971)*
- Spiker, Stuart F. *(The Philosophy of the Body, 1970)*
- Armstrong, D.M. *(A Materialist Theory of the Mind, 1968)*

www.ingramcontent.com/pod-product-compliance
Ingram Content Group UK Ltd.
Pitfield, Milton Keynes, MK11 3LW, UK
UKHW010010031026
15589UKWH00008B/1566

9 798234 130808